The Rural Gothic in American Popular Culture

Also by Bernice M. Murphy

THE SUBURBAN GOTHIC IN AMERICAN POPULAR CULTURE

SHIRLEY JACKSON: Essays On The Literary Legacy (*editor*)

IT CAME FROM THE 1950s!: Popular Culture, Popular Anxieties
(*co-edited with Elizabeth McCarthy and Darryl Jones*)

The Rural Gothic in American Popular Culture

Backwoods Horror and Terror in the Wilderness

Bernice M. Murphy
Trinity College Dublin, Ireland

palgrave
macmillan

Softcover reprint of the hardcover 1st edition 2013 978-1-137-35371-9

First published 2013 by
PALGRAVE MACMILLAN

Palgrave Macmillan in the UK is an imprint of Macmillan Publishers Limited, registered in England, company number 785998, of Houndmills, Basingstoke, Hampshire RG21 6XS.

Palgrave Macmillan in the US is a division of St Martin's Press LLC, 175 Fifth Avenue, New York, NY 10010.

Palgrave Macmillan is the global academic imprint of the above companies and has companies and representatives throughout the world.

Palgrave® and Macmillan® are registered trademarks in the United States, the United Kingdom, Europe and other countries.

ISBN 978-1-349-46972-7 ISBN 978-1-137-35372-6 (eBook)
DOI 10.1057/9781137353726

This book is printed on paper suitable for recycling and made from fully managed and sustained forest sources. Logging, pulping and manufacturing processes are expected to conform to the environmental regulations of the country of origin.

A catalogue record for this book is available from the British Library.

A catalog record for this book is available from the Library of Congress.

Contents

Acknowledgements

To begin, I would like to acknowledge the support my family provided during the writing of this book. Many thanks therefore to John and Majella Murphy, my brother Eoin, my sister-in-law Emma, and my nephew Ieuan. Thankfully, they only *very* occasionally resemble the close-knit cannibal clans considered in Chapter 4, even though we do come from an area that epitomises a very Irish variety of 'Rural Gothic'. The encouragement of my cousins Sinead Murphy and Dr Sheila McCartan, and of the wider family circle, is also very much appreciated.

Stephen Matterson once again provided insightful advice throughout this project. Dara Downey's assistance was also invaluable, particularly whilst formulating the Introduction. Elizabeth McCarthy's notes on Chapter 4 were extremely useful, and Sorcha Ni Fhlaínn also provided helpful feedback on several chapters.

During the course of writing and researching *Rural Gothic*, I was fortunate enough to be able to use the classroom as a laboratory for many of the ideas that have found their way into this book (and some that justifiably haven't...). The enthusiasm and interest shown by students on my 'Rural Gothic' and 'Landscapes of Fear' modules was heartening, and our discussions definitely influenced this book for the better.

General thanks and appreciation are also due to those who have recommended books and films, or otherwise provided encouragement and advice. They include Erwan Atcheson, Sarah Cleary, Brian Cliff, Helen Conrad O'Brian, Caroline Egan, John Exshaw, Moira Fowley-Doyle, Edwina Keown, Hilde Langkjær Losnegård, Jarlath Killeen, Darryl Jones, Jenny McDonnell, Brian J. Showers, Brendan O'Connell, Elizabeth Parker, Maria 'Fight the Power' Parsons, and Pádraic Whyte. Thanks are also owed to Felicity Plester and Chris Penfold at Palgrave Macmillan.

The TCD Arts and Social Sciences Benefaction Fund made a generous contribution towards the research costs of this book. Its assistance was of immense help. Support from the fund also enabled me to present some of my work at the 2012 Popular Culture Association Conference in Boston. On that topic, I am profoundly grateful to my colleagues Dara Downey and Miles Link for not abandoning me in small-town

Massachusetts when it became horribly clear that my Ahab-like quest to see Plymouth Rock would involve an eight-mile round trip, on foot, in decidedly inclement weather.

Finally, this book is dedicated to the memory of my cousin James McCartan, who loved horror films. His loss is keenly felt.

Introduction: We're Not Out of the Woods Yet

The premise of the recent low-budget indie horror film *YellowBrickRoad* (2010) is simple. In 1940, the entire population of a small town named Friar, New Hampshire, suddenly decided to walk into the wilderness. Most of the townsfolk froze to death or were torn apart by unknown perpetrators. In the present day, a group of researchers decides to follow the same trail, in the hope of turning legend into 'recorded history'. However, within a few days, they find that despite all of their equipment and expertise, they are being changed by their time on the trail, and not for the better. As the tag line puts it, 'They were searching for an evil in the forest... But the forest found the evil in them.'

If this all sounds a little familiar, well, perhaps that is no surprise, given that the film's premise appears to resemble that of *The Blair Witch Project* (1999). Although *YellowBrickRoad* differs in some important respects from its better-known predecessor, the horror in both films pivots on the desperate fear of losing oneself in the wilderness. The further the characters stray from 'civilisation' and towards the intangible *something* that lurks at the heart of the American forest, the further they stray from their daylight, or rational *'original'* selves. *The Blair Witch Project* has protagonists who genuinely believe that 'It's very hard to get lost in America these days, and it's really hard to stay lost.' As it gradually becomes clear to them that this is a dangerously misguided assumption, they begin to experience fears that replicate those frequently expressed in what I have characterised as the 'Rural Gothic'.

One of the first intimations of trouble is a strange arrangement of rocks, of which they remark, 'It looks like an Indian burial ground' – an indication of their fear of the nation's 'buried' racial past. Then, their fears turn to terror of a hostile *human* presence: 'Have you ever seen *Deliverance*?' This sense of escalating unease gradually evolves into a more nebulous feeling that 'We're obviously not wanted here' and that the forest itself is actively malevolent. When one of the trio, Josh, is kidnapped by someone (or something) unseen, and indications that something of an occult nature is afoot pile up, team-leader Heather's prediction that 'We're all gonna die out here' becomes a self-fulfilling prophecy.

Like the researchers in *YellowBrickRoad*, Heather and her friends have gone looking for trouble in the forest, and been horrified to find it. The same could be said of the title character in Nathaniel Hawthorne's 'Young Goodman Brown' (1835), one of the most influential American horror stories ever written.[1] Hawthorne's young Puritan insists upon entering the forest that encircles Salem Village at night despite his wife's grave concerns. Like the characters in the films just mentioned, Brown's journey is no random foray into the wilderness: he has an appointment to keep. In observing this rendezvous, he will forever taint his relationship with his wife, the community, and, finally, himself. Goodman Brown's most horrific discovery of all is the realisation that he is himself 'the chief horror of the scene'.[2] It is a realisation that we find repeated again and again in the Rural Gothic.

As this book shall illustrate, American horror and Gothic narratives frequently return to the forests that confronted European settlers and explorers in the early colonial period. It is a tendency that can perhaps be most aptly explained by comparison with experiments conducted in the 1950s which proved that human travellers have a constant veering tendency. 'The result of uncorrected veering is that, on an uncorrected journey, the traveller may follow a spiral path, eventually returning to the vicinity of the origin.'[3] In other words, the traveller making his or her way in a territory without easily recognisable landmarks tends to end up back where they started. As we shall see, it is no coincidence that when American authors and film-makers fantasise about the end of civilisation as they know it, they so often produce narratives which unconsciously evoke the beginnings of European settlement. In their imaginings of an American end, like the disorientated forest traveller, they return to where it all began.

The US in the twenty-first century may be a predominately urban (and suburban) nation, but something keeps drawing writers and film-makers back to this point of initial contact, and to the cultural constructions that have sprung up around it. Perhaps this is at least partially because, as William Cronon has suggested, 'In the wilderness, the boundaries between human and nonhuman, between natural and supernatural, have always seemed less certain than elsewhere.'[4] It is that uncertainty, combined with the powerful historical and cultural legacy that sprang from the first encounters between European settlers, the North American landscape, and its original inhabitants, that has helped to give rise to the Rural Gothic tradition as outlined here.

The Rural Gothic in American Popular Culture: Backwoods Horror and Terror in the Wilderness (*The Rural Gothic*) explores the reasons why this is the case, and argues that the complex and often negative initial responses which early settlers expressed towards the North American wilderness continue to influence American horror. William Carlos Williams (1925) once observed, 'In America, the legend of horror before the war-whoops of the Indians gives some inkling of the great dread the colonists experienced – but there is rarely a countering legend of joy.'[5] This book, focusing as it does upon 'the legend of horror', undertakes a detailed analysis of literary and filmic texts situated within consideration of specific historical, cultural, political, and ecological contexts. It does so with the aim of bringing to light illuminating and often unexpected connections between popular and canonical texts, and of bringing a fresh perspective to bear on the origins and evolution of the American Gothic.

Before I delve into the Rural Gothic itself in more detail, I would like to briefly outline what I mean by 'Gothic', and how the Rural Gothic relates to the American Gothic more generally. The long and often contradictory history of the term 'Gothic' is an indication of the characteristic blurring of literary categories associated with the genre. Historically, the Goths were a fierce Germanic tribe – a band of bloodthirsty warriors regarded as uncivilised and barbaric. At the close of the Dark Ages, as Devendra Varma has noted, 'the word "gothic" had degenerated into a term of unmitigated contempt' – an insult to be hurled at one's enemies.[6] During the eighteenth century, there was 'a shift in the meanings and connotations of the term "Gothic" ', and it broadened out to become descriptive of anything preceding the mid-seventeenth century.[7] There are several specific reasons offered by critics to account for the emergence of the Gothic as a literary *form*. Perhaps the most common of these is the thesis which says that its emergence represented a 'rebellion of imagination' against that the Augustan tyrannies of all-encompassing reason. As David Punter said, 'the Classical was well ordered; the Gothic was ornate and convoluted; the classics afforded a set of cultural models to be followed; the Gothic represented excess and exaggeration, the product of the wild and uncivilised'.[8] The emergence of the Gothic represented an important precursor to Romanticism, which also embraced emotion over rationality, and looked to nature, to an idealised past, and to the primal power of the emotions for inspiration.

Only ten years would pass between the publication of the novels of Anne Radcliffe and M.G. Lewis (two of the most notable European Gothic authors), and the appearance of the first American Gothic romances.[9] Yet, the differences between the American Gothic and the European Gothic were substantial. The most notable conventions of the European Gothic form were clearly ill-suited to the moral, intellectual, and emotional landscape of the US. The American landscape lacked the most convenient relics of Gothic fiction as it had previously existed – the physical reminders of a feudal past, the legends and myths that proved so useful to European authors, the grand aristocracies and centuries of religious intolerance and conspiratorial intrigue that had proved such irresistible crowd-pleasers within the European context. Richard Davenport Hines argues that 'Gothic' means pessimistic, reactionary, (occasionally) ironic, and class-ridden, whilst American culture, on the other hand, is puritanical, progressive, optimistic, earnest, and ostensibly egalitarian.[10] Theresa Goddu highlights similar antagonisms when she claims that the very idea of the Gothic unsettles that of the US, and 'the modifier American destabilises understandings of Gothic'.[11] What both critics have seized upon is the inherent contradiction between everything that the US as a nation believed itself to be – a rational, secular, utopian society – and the characteristics embodied in the Gothic, which embraces irrationality, disorder, and chaos.

In order to overcome the inevitable shortcomings of the European formula, the American Gothic had to look to its own landscape for inspiration. The imaginative exploitation of four indigenous features would prove vital to the establishment of the local strain. Allan Lloyd Smith has persuasively suggested that these are the frontier, the Puritan legacy, race, and the consequences of political utopianism.[12] All four of these elements also feature prominently in my definition of 'Rural Gothic', which I consider to be a distinct sub-genre existing within (and closely related to) the wider American Gothic tradition. As such, this book is also part of the current trend in Gothic studies towards exploring specific categories within the wider scope of the genre, an approach which has resulted in the identification and classification of sub-genres such as 'Organisational Gothic', 'Medical Gothic', 'Eco Gothic', 'Suburban Gothic', and 'Urban Gothic'.

As in the American Gothic more generally, racial contexts are extremely important within the Rural Gothic. My first three chapters roughly trace the history of white–Indian relations up until the mid-nineteenth century. It is important to highlight, however, that this study is mainly concerned with discussing *white* perceptions of Native Americans, and as such, by necessity provides a notably one-sided take on the settler/first people paradigm. The legacy of slavery will be a key component of my fourth chapter, as are current academic approaches to the study of 'whiteness'.

The experiences of 'wilderness' discussed here are also very often male ones. With the exceptions of Mary Rowlandson and Charles Brockden Brown's Clara Wieland, Stephen King's Wendy Torrance, Alfred Hitchcock's Melanie Daniels, and Charlotte Gainsbourg's significantly unnamed character in *Antichrist* (2009), female characters are often in the minority, save in the backwoods horror film, where they frequently emerge as embattled 'Final Girl' figures. The wilderness/backwoods setting is often depicted as a space inhabited or journeyed through by men, a trend that becomes most notable in the concluding section of Chapter 5, which discusses American imaginings of the post-apocalyptic landscape from which women are often almost entirely absent (though this is not the case in the most recent narratives of this kind). The connection between masculinity and the wilderness will also be considered in detail in Chapter 3, in which the closely related figures of the 'Wildman' and the 'Indian Killer' are discussed.

Though it is intended to function as a stand-alone piece of work, *The Rural Gothic* is a companion piece to my previous monograph, *The Suburban Gothic in American Popular Culture* (*The Suburban Gothic*) (2009). Whilst the Suburban Gothic is rooted in a particular post–World War II historical and cultural context, that sub-genre nevertheless replicates a paradigm that has existed since the earliest days of European settlement in North America – namely, the tendency to gravitate towards either utopian idealism or apocalyptically inspired pessimism that has so often been a hallmark of American culture. As we shall see, Puritan conceptions of the wilderness as both a heaven and a hell would have a major influence upon the theological, literary, and psychological development of the 'New World'. We also see another familiar trope of national history played out in both the Rural Gothic and the Suburban Gothic: that of the optimistic white settler who leaves the corrupt, diseased, hierarchical 'Old' World behind in order to settle in a promising 'New' one, which, inevitably, has drawbacks of its own.

There are, however, some significant differences between the Suburban Gothic and the Rural Gothic. The Suburban Gothic arose out of a specific set of historical and cultural circumstances (*The Suburban Gothic* only discussed texts published or released between 1948 and 2008) but that kind of limited historical focus does not apply here: the texts discussed range from early colonial captivity narratives to recent television shows. My use of the term 'Rural Gothic' is also more diffuse than my use of the term 'Suburban Gothic'. I will be discussing narratives relating to three distinct but closely related kinds of environments: the 'wilderness', the 'backwoods', and the 'rural' setting. As such it is, therefore, important to briefly outline the ways in which I shall be using these terms – the first, and most important, being the question of what, exactly, constitutes 'wilderness'.

As the considerable scholarship on this topic indicates, the very concept of 'wilderness' carries with it considerable theological, ideological, and theoretical baggage. It is, as Michael Lewis (2007) states, 'simultaneously a real thing and a human construction', or, as William Cronon (1996) has called it, 'quite profoundly a human creation'.[13] As such, the way in which the term has been employed within an American context has evolved. For instance, many more recent conceptions of the term owe much to the terms of the 1964 Wilderness Act, which stated that 'wilderness, in contrast with those areas where man and his works dominate the landscape, is hereby recognised as an area where the earth and its community of life are untrammelled by man, where man himself is a visitor who does not remain'.[14] 'Wilderness' is, therefore, according to this definition, a place defined by the fact that humans are absent or present only on a transitory basis. It is a classification which owes much to the sea change in attitudes towards the natural landscape which took place in the late nineteenth century, when figures such as John Muir and Henry David Thoreau encouraged Americans to see the 'wilderness' in a very different light from earlier conceptions of the space: as a restorative and regenerative space that provided a refuge from the pressures and materialism of so-called 'civilisation'. As Cronon asserts, 'Wilderness had once been the antithesis of all that was orderly and good [...] and yet now it was frequently likened to Eden itself.'[15] This was, as Steven Stoll notes, a very different way of viewing the 'wilderness' from that experienced by settlers during the early colonial period:

> Though settlers entered regions that we would call wilderness, they almost never used that term, and their use of it carried none of the associations we give it – of places valued for the relative absence of human presence, places worthy of legal protection from human activity. Until the twentieth century, wilderness served as a relative, not an absolute category. It defined times and places when

> humans did not yet control their environment, or where they had lost control.[16]

When the term *was* used, as we shall see in Chapter 1, it was often loaded with biblical associations, 'for it was used over and over again in the King James Version to refer to places on the margins of civilization where it was all too easy to lose oneself in moral confusion and despair'.[17] As a result:

> As late as the eighteenth century, the most common usage of the word 'wilderness' in the English language referred to landscapes that generally carried adjectives far different from the ones they attract today. To be a wilderness then was to be 'deserted,' 'savage,' 'desolate,' 'barren' [...] Its connotations were anything but positive, and the emotion one was most likely to feel in its presence was 'bewilderment' or terror.[18]

Then there is the fact that, as Roderick Nash observes in *Wilderness and the American Mind* (1967), 'only for the white man was nature a wilderness'.[19] The long-lasting ramifications of this difference between the way in which the settlers and the Indian tribes viewed the natural world forms a key strand of this study. Michael Lewis notes that:

> [...] to a seventeenth-century Iroquois, a mid-Atlantic forest might look quite different than it would to a European explorer. The Iroquois might see the forest as a mosaic of habitats: some wilder wilderness sections, some periodically burned and managed for easy hunting of deer and turkey, and some former village or farming sites, now regenerating young shrubs and trees. The European explorer might see all of the forest as pure wilderness, a dark and mysterious landscape illustrating God's original paradise, a fearsome haunt of the devil, or even a collection of marketable commodities.[20]

Because of its focus on horror and Gothic, this study will concentrate on constructions of the wilderness which depict it in a negative rather than a positive light: my interest here is on 'dark and mysterious landscapes' rather than 'God's original paradise'. As such, I will pay particular attention to texts in which the wilderness is depicted as a hostile and even actively malevolent space that poses a threat to the safety of the white settler and his/her descendants.

As we shall see, conceptions of the 'wilderness' and the 'backwoods' are, geographically and psychologically, very closely related. My conception of 'Backwoods Horror' is most relevant in Chapter 4, which discusses horror films in which the rural poor are depicted as degenerate and violent aggressors. Stephen Stoll characterises the backwoods as '[...] a settlement culture that possessed such a startling capacity to create openings that nothing but the geographical contours of the continent stopped them'. Backwoods pioneers 'in their own view, lived "beyond the settlements" and clearly distinguished themselves from the inhabitants of longer-populated districts'.[21] They were also associated with log cabins (that will frequently feature in this study), the keeping of pigs, small close-knit kinship groups, and genetic and cultural mixing with the Indians.[22] As Terry Jordan and Matti Kaups have observed, they were also often unfavourably contrasted with the permanent settlers who replaced them.[23] Chapter 4 will argue that backwoods horror films belong to this long-standing tradition in which backwoods inhabitants are depicted in a negative light. It is also my contention that, in recent decades, the long-standing historical sense that those who dwell in backwoods are prone to savagery and degeneration has gradually begun to affect the way in which rural areas more generally are depicted in the American horror film.

This trend also reflects the fact that, during the past century, the US has become increasingly disconnected from its rural origins. As recently as 1900,

> [...] more than 60% of Americans lived in rural areas, defined as small towns (population less than 2,500), the open countryside, or farms (U.S. Census Bureau 2010a). Today, more than 80% of Americans live in urban areas: the largest 10 metropolitan areas alone account for more than 25% of the U.S. Population.
>
> (U.S. Census Bureau, 2010a)[24]

What was, until very recently, a predominately rural nation is now largely urban and suburban. Some idea of the sense of crisis that many commentators identify in the rural US can be gleaned from the titles of some recent books on the topic: *Hollowing Out the Middle: The Rural Brain Drain and What It Means for America*; *Survival of Rural America*; *Forgotten Places*; *Broken Heartland*; *Challenges for Rural America*; and *Those Who Work, Those Who Don't: Poverty, Morality and Family in Rural America*.[25]

Yet, surveys conducted since the 1970s have repeatedly discovered amongst Americans 'a strong public preference for rural areas and small towns' as places to live. This 'positive rurality' comprised 'statements about the quality of family and community relationships, neighbourliness and closeness to nature', and was associated with a correspondingly negative view of the urban setting, which was felt to be lacking in these positive attributes.[26] It is a disparity between positive practical attributes and negative fictional depictions that is also found in relation to American attitudes towards suburbia (but in reverse). Most Americans live in suburbs and have positive experiences of the milieu, and yet it is frequently depicted in popular culture as a repressive, soulless, and dehumanising hellscape (sometimes literally). By way of contrast, rural areas are generally perceived in practical terms in a positive light, yet most Americans do not live there. In the backwoods horror movie subgenre, as in the 'Rural Gothic' more generally, this 'positive rurality' is transformed into something very negative indeed.

Negative depictions of the countryside and its inhabitants are, of course, by no means unique to American literature and popular culture. However, I would suggest that no other nation has so *consistently* produced horror narratives of this kind. In one of those odd contradictions which so often arises in popular culture, it seems that whilst Americans in real life have a high opinion of rural areas and their inhabitants, they have a fondness for watching horror films in which rural and wilderness locales are depicted in a deeply negative light. Part of this undoubtedly relates to the fact that the 'city versus country' paradigm taps into ways of seeing the world that long predate the European settlement of North America. As Clover points out:

> An enormous proportion of horror takes as its starting point the visit or move of (sub) urban people to the country [...]. The situation, of course, rests squarely on what may be a universal archetype. Going from city to country in the horror film is in any case like going from village to the deep, dark forest in traditional fairy tales. Consider Little Red Riding Hood, who strikes off into the wilderness only to be captured and eaten by a wolf (whom she foolishly trusts), though she is saved by a passing woodsman. Multiply and humanize the wolf, read 'rape' for 'eat', skip the woodsman (let Red save herself), and you have *I Spit on Your Grave*. [...] The point is that rural Connecticut (or wherever), like the deep forests of Central Europe, is a place where the rules of civilisation do not obtain.[27]

The origins of this 'universal archetype', and the ways in which it was reconfigured to reflect a specifically North American context, will be considered in Chapter 1. Clover's observation that the rural or wilderness setting is a place where the 'rules of civilisation' do not normally apply is one that will be expanded upon throughout this study.

One of my principal contentions is that the Rural Gothic is characterised by negative encounters between individuals who have permanently settled in one place, and those who are defined by their mobility and lack of permanent relationship with the landscape. As I will outline in Chapter 1, one of the things that helped to distinguish early colonial-period settlers from the Indians was the fact the Indians simply did not think of themselves as 'owning' the land in the same way that the colonists did. They had adapted to the seasonal diversity of their environment by moving their settlements in accordance with the changing of the seasons.[28] The English, however, built permanent settlements. This was partially in order to stake a claim to the territory but it was also because this was the way things were done back home. 'English fixity sought to replace Indian mobility; here was the central conflict in the way Indians and colonists interacted with their environments.'[29] It is also, I would argue, the central conflict in the Rural Gothic. Those who stay in one place are threatened by those that don't, and vice versa.

There are, therefore, two main kinds of closely related Rural Gothic narratives. The first is that in which those who reside in settled, apparently secure, communities are menaced by outsiders characterised by their freedom of movement and dangerous unpredictability. This configuration obviously replicates the unease and paranoia experienced by the colonists (most particularly those of the Puritan persuasion) as they set about establishing and consolidating permanent settlements. Mary Rowlandson's Indian captivity narrative (1676) – a real-life Puritan horror story – provides an early example of this paradigm. Her village is razed to the ground by ruthless 'hell hounds' who stream out of the forest. After watching many of her friends, neighbours, and family members being murdered, Rowlandson is forced to accompany her captors on a lengthy journey that opens her eyes to the existence of a parallel, *Indian* world, in which the only traces of English settlement are the occasional sight of cattle tracks in the mud. She becomes increasingly estranged from both her previous life, and from her original self. Yet, in order to survive her ordeal, she must, in essence, become more 'Indian' herself.

A settled community is also violently disrupted by the arrival of a rootless, 'foreign' other in Charles Brockden Brown's *Wieland: Or, An American Tale* (1798), and the trope is one that persists in American literature and popular culture up until and including the present day. For instance, part of the reason why Truman Capote's *In Cold Blood* (1965) has achieved such cultural prominence, I would suggest, is because the murder of the Cutter family adheres to this classic formula: decent, settled, prosperous people are attacked by ruthless strangers who appear to have no true ties to anything or anyone. The fact that one of the murderers, Perry Smith, was half-Indian, only adds to the historical resonances of the crime.

A common variation upon this first variety of Rural Gothic text can be found in narratives in which bad things happen to individuals or groups of individuals who decide to leave the community behind and venture into the wilderness, of their own free will. *YellowBrickRoad* and *The Blair Witch Project* fit into this category, as does Charles Brockden Brown's *Edgar Huntly* (1799), and, of course, 'Young Goodman Brown'. The fate of the Donner party and the Torrance family in *The Shining* (1977/1980) also replicates this trope. The implications are clear: when you leave 'civilisation', you will inevitably become less civilised, often as a result of a process of adaptation and transformation that turns you into something partially or wholly monstrous. It is a fear that has its roots in the anxieties of the Puritan settlers in particular, who constantly questioned whether '[...] living in a savage environment release the inner wilderness that all men and women restrained only through constant struggle'.[30] It is particularly telling that these tropes, and those of the second variety of Rural Gothic narrative, have persisted in the American cultural imagination so many centuries past the time when they had any real-life foundation. As we shall see throughout this study, their persistence demonstrates that the way in which the US perceives itself is still strongly influenced by early European impressions and experiences of the North American landscape.

The second kind of 'Rural Gothic' narrative is essentially a reversal of the first type. Here, people whose stay in the locality is meant to be only temporary are subject to the dangerous attentions of locals characterised by their fixity. The villains in this case are people who have settled in one place, whilst we are expected to empathise this time with characters who are defined by their freedom of movement and sense of adventure. Too much time in the backwoods, it is suggested, renders a people resentful, savage, and degenerate. As we shall see, horror narratives of this kind often bestow a highly suggestive racial and cultural 'otherness' upon their antagonists.

My methodology is fairly straightforward. Each chapter will situate the texts under discussion within a historical framework that considers both the broad progression of national history in general as well as certain key events which I believe have had a particular influence upon the origins and development of American horror. Amongst them are the disappearance of the colony at Roanoke (1587–88); the 'Starving Times' at Jamestown (1609–10); the Puritan migration to the 'New World' (1620); the Indian Wars (1622–1890), the Salem Witch Trials (1692); and the establishment of an independent US (considered mainly in Chapter 2). Other key historical factors include the mid-nineteenth-century movement West and the fate of the Donner party (1846–47). Adherence to the belief in a national 'Manifest Destiny', as well as ramifications of the US's emergence as an imperial power in its own right will also be considered. Chapter 4 discusses the perception that the South is the aberrant 'Other' to the rest of the US and considers the machinations of the Eugenics Records Office (1910–44). Finally, the impact made by the publication of Rachel Carson's *The Silent Spring* (1962) and the growing awareness that the natural environment was being irrevocably damaged by humanity is considered in Chapter 5. My methodology, therefore, involves treating certain historical events as 'texts', and setting them alongside fictional narratives which they have influenced or directly inspired.

Before discussing the content of specific chapters in more detail, it is important to note that there are some significant existing publications which touch upon some of the topics I will explore here. Amongst them are Theresa Goddu's *Gothic America: Narrative, History and Nation* (Columbia, 1997), which argues that the American Gothic has long been actively engaged with the historical and political concerns of the nation (and, in particular, slavery and its legacy).[31] Both *American Gothic: New Interventions in a National Narrative* (edited by Robert K. Martin and Eric Savoy) and Allan Lloyd-Smith's *American Gothic Fiction: An Introduction* (2005) further Savoy's contention that the enduring appeal of the Gothic reflects '[...] an America haunted by the dark recesses of its own history'.[32] Charles L. Crow's 2009 book *American Gothic* provides a similarly historicising overview of the genre and its recent critical contexts. *Frontier Gothic: Terror and Wonder at the Frontier in American Literature* (edited by David Mogen, Scott P. Sanders, and Joanne Karpinski, 1993) stresses, as I do here, the immense significance of the initial Puritan reaction to the wilderness in shaping American literature generally and the Gothic mode in particular. More recently, W. Scott Poole's *Monsters in America: Our Historical Obsession with the Hideous and the Haunting* (Baylor, 2011) considers configurations of monstrosity and 'Otherness' in the national cultural psyche, and like this study, also discusses 'classic' literary texts alongside more recent popular narratives. My approach to the material differs considerably, however, in that it is specifically focused on the human relationship with the American landscape.

It is, therefore, the case that as well as engaging with existing works on American literature and history, *The Rural Gothic* draws upon that of scholars working in the fields of human geography, environmental history, and ecology. My first chapter discusses the work of Yi-Fu Tuan, author of the landmark text *Landscapes of Fear* (1979). My first and final chapters also draw upon the scholarship of authors working on environmental and ecological issues, such as Frederick Buell (*From Apocalypse to Way of Life*), Roderick Nash, and environmental historians William Cronon (*Changes in the Land: Indians, Colonists and the Ecology of New England*, 1983) and Alfred W. Crosby (*The Columbian Exchange: Biological and Cultural Consequences of 1492*, 1972). My interest in the environmental consequences of colonisation and their impact upon cultural constructions of the American landscape helps to further distinguish this book from previous studies of the American Gothic. It is, certainly, my intention to provide a fresh perspective to bear on well-known and often-considered texts and authors, and I shall also consider narratives which have been critically neglected or overlooked entirely.

The basic outline of the book is as follows. The opening chapter begins with a brief discussion of Drew Goddard's 2011 film *The Cabin in the Woods*, and then discusses Lars von Trier's film *Antichrist*. It also provides a historical and cultural context for the rest of the study by discussing the way in which North America was initially perceived by the earliest European settlers. Two influential Puritan narratives will be discussed: William Bradford's *Of Plymouth Plantation* (1630–47), and Mary Rowlandson's *The Sovereignty and Goodness of God* (1676), to establish the importance of Puritan perceptions of the 'howling wilderness' to later cultural constructions of the North American landscape, as well as the centrality of the conflict between the perceived 'chaos' of wilderness and the 'order' of settlement.

Chapter 2 discusses two closely linked fears that have haunted the North American psyche since the earliest days of European settlement: the spectre of the colony that fails, and that of the community that uses ritual and tradition to help create the bonds necessary to survive in the 'New' World. The primary texts discussed are Charles Brockden Brown's *Wieland* (1798) and selected short stories by Nathaniel Hawthorne. I also discuss Shirley Jackson's 'The Lottery' (1948), Stephen King's 'The Children of the Corn' (1977), Thomas Tryon's *Harvest Home* (1973), T.E.D. Klein's *The Ceremonies* (1984), and M. Night Shyamalan's *The Village* (2004).

Chapter 3 considers what happens to those who leave the settlement behind in order to seek opportunities elsewhere. The pioneer who ventures into uncharted landscapes has to undertake considerable adaptations and compromises – not all of them pleasant – to survive. The chapter discusses the long association between cannibalism and the Americas, particularly the ways in which Europeans used it to help to differentiate between themselves and the 'Savages'. Texts discussed here include *Edgar Huntly* (1798), *The Shining* (1977/1980), Cormac McCarthy's *The Road* (2006), and the 1998 film *Ravenous*. The doctrine of 'Manifest Destiny' will be discussed alongside Native American Windigo legends. I will argue that the hunger for human flesh is often explicitly related to the national hunger for land in American fiction and film.

Chapter 4 opens with a discussion of the 1964 film *Two Thousand Maniacs!*, which helped to establish the backwoods horror movie subgenre. It argues that with the success of *Deliverance* (1972) and *The Texas Chain Saw Massacre* (1974), the poor white Southerner was established as the perfect villain for numerous narratives in which naive middle-class urban or suburban travellers encounter resentful locals. The chapter concludes with a detailed analysis of the main themes, settings, and plot tropes of the backwoods horror movie.

Finally, in Chapter 5, I conclude by discussing the revolt of nature seen in modern eco-horror films, as well as the significance of the post-apocalyptic American landscape in recent popular culture. Texts discussed include *The Birds* (1963), *The Silent Spring* (1962), *The Happening* (Dir: M. Night Shyamalan, 2008), *The Last Winter* (Dir: Larry Fessenden, 2006), *Take Shelter* (Dir: Jeff Nichols, 2011), 'The Scarlet Plague' (1912), *Earth Abides* (1949), *The Hunger Games* (2012), and *Revolution* (ABC 2013–).

In a book which covers such a wide historical and geographical span as this, there are inevitably some texts and topics which may seem like they should merit a mention but which are overlooked or considered only in passing. It is my hope, nevertheless, that *The Rural Gothic* will encourage other scholars to look at topics and texts which have been neglected here, and that the reader will forgive my necessary omissions and accidental oversights.

1
The Cabin in the Woods: Order versus Chaos in the 'New World'

'Five friends go to a remote cabin in the woods. Bad things happen. If you think you know the story, think again.' The tag line for post-modern horror comedy *The Cabin in the Woods* (2011) emphasises the fact that the basic premise of the film is one that has been replicated time and time again. In fact, the very predictability of the scenario is what allows the film to undermine our expectations. The audience doesn't need to have it explained to them that the isolated cabin in the midst of the deep, dark forest is a locale in which horrific events will take place: they've seen it all before. The film, therefore, works as a deconstruction of the horror genre precisely because the setting has long since become the stuff of cliché. The fact that we think we 'know' the story is what allows the film's disorientating opening sequence and the reality-warping revelations that follow to so effectively wrong-foot us.

It begs the question: why choose *this* particular locale as the starting point for a narrative in which the concept of horror-as-entertainment is slyly interrogated? Why not call the film 'The Old Dark House' or 'The Indian Burial Ground' instead? Why does it *have* to be 'The Cabin in the Woods'? Well, perhaps because this is the true starting point of American horror. The premise brings us back to the beginnings of the European relationship with the North American landscape. The titular structure is, after all, a vulnerable shelter constructed in the midst of a wilderness whose extent and inhabitants remain unknown, a refuge which is, itself, constructed from materials hewn from that same landscape. The cabin in the woods is to the American Gothic what the haunted castle is to the European – the seed from which everything else ultimately grows. A significant difference, however, between the European and American Gothic lies in the fact that whilst the 'Old World' castle as a setting has mostly faded into irrelevancy – displaced by the new fears which accompanied mass industrialisation – for American horror and Gothic narratives, the image of the cabin in the woods has never lost its potency. The cliché retains its power precisely because the nation is still, more than 400 years after the first faltering attempts at European settlement, grappling with the legacy of colonisation, expansion, and consolidation.

'There is something in the proximity of the woods which is very singular', wrote Crévecœur in *Letters from an American Famer* (1782). That suspicion persists, even if the 'woods' are not what they were in his time. So does his belief that proximity to the wilderness has significant effects not just on animals and plants, but also on men too: 'They are entirely different from those that live in the plains. [...] By living in or near the woods, their actions are regulated by the wildness of the neighbourhood.'[1] This feeling that the wilderness has a profound, and not always *positive* effect, upon those who resides there is one informed not only by long-standing perceptions of wilderness *itself*, but also of the individuals and the communities that exist within it or just outside its boundaries. These suspicions would also have a lasting influence upon how the rural US was perceived. The small town or village outside of the suburb or the city is still, in horror and Gothic narratives, a place where bad things related to the wilderness happen – just at one remove. The 'singular' nature of the wilderness is frequently perceived as extending beyond the boundaries of wilderness itself.

As we shall see, a key component of this perception lies in the belief that the forest beyond the settlement is the place where the representatives of 'civilisation' are pitched against forces that embody 'savagery', and order – moral, psychological, and geographical – is opposed to 'chaos'. It is a dynamic that we shall see replicated again and again in this study. Later in this chapter, I will discuss this idea with specific reference to the Puritan captivity narrative, but I will first consider one of the most recent (and most interesting) expressions of this paradigm: that found in another film in which the archetypal American 'Cabin in the Woods' has a key role: Lars von Trier's *Antichrist* (2009).[2]

Critical discussions of *Antichrist* have thus far tended to ignore the American setting, perhaps because the film contains so many interpretative possibilities that the question of national setting may seem somewhat less important than the complex theological, psychological, and theoretical possibilities the film so knowingly encompasses.[3] This is an understandable, but serious oversight. The America-as-fallen Eden paradigm is one that has existed since the earliest days of European interaction with the 'New World', and *Antichrist* is one of its most interesting modern manifestations. von Trier has set this story in the US (the forests of Washington State, to be exact) for a reason.

Though set in a specifically *American* wilderness, the film was shot in Germany, and directed by a Dane who objects 'to this idea that you can't make a film about a country where you haven't been. That's exactly what Hollywood has done for very many years and they don't give a shit'.[4] In other words, like von Trier's other American-set films, *Dancer in the Dark* (2002), *Dogville* (2003), and *Manderlay* (2005), *Antichrist* depicts a America constructed from European preconceptions – a *created* America. As A.O. Scott noted of *Dancer in the Dark*: 'the movie presents a curious blend of the alien and the familiar: it is a fantasy of America, but not an American fantasy'.[5] With this in mind then, it is telling that one of the most interesting things about *Antichrist* is the way in which the natural landscape is depicted.

There are only two characters in the film – 'She' (Charlotte Gainsbourg) and 'He' (Willem Dafoe): a married couple whose young son plummets out of an upper-story window during the self-consciously operatic (and pornographic) opening scene. Their grief at the child's death is compounded, especially for his mother, by the fact that he toddled to his doom whilst they were too busy making love to notice that he had climbed out of his cot (the the level of culpability which can be attributed to Gainsbourg's character regarding the child's death will, crucially, be revisited later in the narrative). In an ill-advised bid to jolt his wife out of the near-catatonic depression which afflicts her following the tragedy, 'He' decides to treat her himself, brushing aside the counselling profession's strict admonitions against having one's own family members as patients by arrogantly (and wrongly) telling her 'No therapist can know as much about you as I do'. The moment he says this, there is an ominous close-up of the flowers which sit in a vase full of suggestively murky water in his wife's hospital room: an early indication of the association between unruly femininity and the hidden depths of the wilderness made explicit later ('Women do not control their own bodies. Nature does', 'She' declares at one point, in a sign of things to come).

Gainsbourg's character fears the forest above all else – for her, 'Eden', as they have called their cabin in the woods, is the place where, whilst working on her doctoral dissertation on 'gynocide' (the mass killing of women), she first felt her grip on sanity begin to slip. There's something about the wilderness, the film suggests, that brings primal and destructive impulses oozing to the surface. 'She', as later events imply, may well have had serious problems even before her time in the forest, but in von Trier's American forest 'Chaos reigns', and people are subject to urges which they are unable to control, much less understand. 'Let fear come if it likes. What the mind can conceive and believe, it can achieve', the husband glibly states, but therapeutic jargon is no match for the primal power of nature, or madness. Soon the woman's guilt and self-loathing/internalised misogyny begins to aggressively manifest itself in her dealings with her husband – first, through desperate demands for sexual intimacy, and then through wince-inducing acts of torture and self-mutilation (significantly, much of this violence is directed at genitalia, both her own and his), and finally imprisonment and attempted murder.

Of course, if Dafoe's character had any familiarity at all with the American Gothic, he would have known that an isolated cabin in the middle of a teeming forest populated by sinister wildlife (such as the talking fox who gets the film's signature line: 'Chaos reigns') is the last place in the world anyone should go for a spot of psychological recuperation. Whilst there is, in American culture more generally, a long-standing feeling that 'returning to nature' can act as a powerful physical and mental restorative (for naturalist John Muir, for instance, 'Wild country [...] had a mystical ability to inspire and refresh'), that is definitely not the case here.[6,7] As in the Rural Gothic more generally, positive impressions of the natural landscape are reversed. The forest intensifies rather than soothes mental torment and spiritual malaise.

The woman's belief that the very landscape is infected with innate evil, and her assertion that during the previous summer, she '[...] understood that everything that used to be beautiful about Eden was perhaps hideous' can be seen as either reflections of her growing madness or a reaction to the terrifying true nature of reality.[8] Whatever the truth of the matter – and *Antichrist* is a film which offers a multitude of interpretative possibilities – her resoundingly negative view of the wilderness is actually one that the Puritans would have agreed wholeheartedly with. For them, nature – and particularly nature as they came across it in the simultaneously seductive and terrifying 'New World' – really was, as Gainsbourg's character puts it, 'Satan's Church', the living corollary to the darkness that lurked in every human heart. Faye Ringel observes in *New England's Gothic Literature* (1995), 'Psychologically, the less learned settler was prepared to find devils in the forest; all the reassurances to the contrary could hardly prevail against such primal fears.'[9]

In *Antichrist*, as so often in the Rural Gothic, these 'primal fears' continue to resonate, and we are presented with a scenario in which individual madness and a much older, more elemental kind of malevolence collide. The relationship between sex, violence, and death which is made explicit in the opening sequence of von Trier's film comes to a Grand Guignol climax, with the cabin in the woods as its inevitable stage. *Antichrist*, therefore, owes as much to 'Young Goodman Brown' as it does to the European art-house tradition.[10] The horrors of *Antichrist*'s finale, far from rendering it a self-indulgent art-house oddity, in fact place it squarely in a century's-long tradition in which the natural world itself becomes a threatening and otherworldly place. Lars von Trier is by no means the first European to find something sinister in the American forest. For the remainder of this chapter, therefore, I shall discuss how and why this deeply negative perception of the wilderness would take such a prominent place in American Gothic and horror narratives, beginning with a consideration of the historical context for this tendency. I also argue here that the non-fiction writing of Puritan chronicler William Bradford, and colonist-turned-captive Mary Rowlandson helped establish some of the principal tropes of the American horror film, which so often pivots on the relationship between a naive white person and the territory which they perceive to be 'wilderness'. In particular, these early, theologically influenced responses to the North American landscape and its native inhabitants helped establish the conflict between settled community and mobile outsider, which is a major distinguishing feature of the Rural Gothic.

Malcolm Bradbury and Richard Ruland have suggested (1991) that the originating tradition of American literature 'came from the meeting between the land with its elusive and despised "Indians" and the settlers who left the developed, literate cultures of Renaissance Europe, first to explore and conquer, then to populate, what they generally considered a virgin continent – a "New World" promised them in their own mythology'.[11] For the settlers, the Americas were a kind of metaphorical and literal tabula rasa upon which they could project their deepest fears, longings, and anxieties; a space filled with both promise and terror. For the Puritans, it was simultaneously a space in which one could fulfil God's plans for his chosen people and the natural site for the Devil to inhabit so that he could snare the unworthy.

Like the settlers who crossed the Atlantic for more obviously utilitarian (and often, commercial) reasons, the Puritans would irrevocably change the American landscape. What they did not take into consideration at first were the ways in which the land would change *them*. Adaptation is, after all, a two-way street, and if there is one basic tenet of the early European experience of the 'New World', it is this: you may possess the land, but you should never forget that it also possesses *you*.[12]

It is at least partially for this reason that the wilderness and its inhabitants have for so long functioned as the perennially mysterious, and at times, overtly threatening 'Other' to North America's urban, and later, *sub*urban self.

To really come to terms with the reasons why this relationship has come to play such an important role in shaping the American sense of self, we first need to consider just what it was that the wilderness and the landscape represented to the first Europeans to arrive in the 'New World'. As Roderick Nash notes (1967, 1982), 'the wilderness was the basic ingredient of American civilisation. From the raw materials of the physical wilderness Americans built a civilisation; with the idea or symbol of wilderness they sought to give that civilisation identity and meaning.'[13] Nash also makes clear that the wilderness had long been perceived as a physical analogue to the essentially uncontrollable and unknowable aspects of the *self*: 'the wilderness was the unknown, the disordered, the uncontrolled'.[14] Even the very etymology of the term is telling: the Norse/Teutonic root of the 'wilderness' is 'will', which has a descriptive meaning of self-willed, wilful, or uncontrollable.[15] From 'villed' came 'wild', which was used to convey the idea of being lost, unruly, and confused. Once the word 'deor' or 'animal' is added to 'willed' you end up with 'wild-deor-ness' – i.e., the place of wild beasts.[16]

Wilderness is, thus, the region of wild animals over which human beings have no control. Wild beasts in Northern Europe lived in forests. As a scene or environment, 'wilderness' is a forest, and indeed the word 'wild' may have another root – 'weald' or 'W*oe*ld', the Old English word for forests. Cultivated fields are the familiar and harmonised world. By contrast, the forest surrounding it seems alien, a place of possibly dangerous strangers.[17]

From the earliest times, therefore, the wilderness was perceived as a place where a person was likely to get into a disordered, confused, or 'wild' condition. In fact, the word 'bewilder' is derived from the term 'wilderness'.[18] To return to von Trier's talking fox for a moment, the feeling that the untamed land beyond 'civilisation' is where 'Chaos reigns' is one that significantly pre-dates European settlement. As Yi-Fu Tuan makes clear, the Europeans in the 'Old World' had, in practical terms, quite a lot to fear from the unmapped and unregulated terrain that surrounded their first cities and towns. The wilderness was where the unwary and underprepared traveller could lose his or her way, or be assailed by wild animals and wild men. It is no coincidence that so many European folk tales begin with the protagonist wandering alone in the forest, having somehow strayed from the beaten track. The phrase

'Landscapes of Fear', Tuan suggests in his study of the same name, refers to both psychological states and tangible environments. Small wonder then that whilst there certainly exist positive descriptions of the American landscape from this period, many of the first European arrivals in the 'New World' often viewed with fretful ambivalence (or outright negativity) the new vistas which greeted them upon landfall.

It is important to highlight just how much those first European reactions to the American landscape were informed by their own long-held and preconceived notions about the wilderness and what it represented (and as we shall see, it represented many different things).[19] 'The intellectual legacy of the old world not only helped determine initial responses but left a lasting imprint on American thought.'[20] As Walter B. Mignolo (2003) emphasises, the very act of describing and mapping the North American continent was weighted from the outset with ideological perspectives and aspirations.[21] He notes that even the phrase 'New World' is deeply problematic – 'That lands and peoples unknown to a European observer should be called "New World" simply because the observer had no prior knowledge of them brings to the foreground the large issue of the arrogance and ethnocentrism of observers for whom what is unknown does not exist.'[22] Part of this misunderstanding also arose from the fact that 'America' existed in Europe as a concept even before the continent was 'discovered' – in the form of the speculative writings of the Classical, Medieval and Renaissance mind, in which the tempting prototype of a vast and fertile new land in the West was frequently discussed.[23]

It was between the late fifteenth century and the early sixteenth century that Europeans developed the maritime technology and imperial ambitions which allowed them to conquer the oceans.[24] In the 50 years before 1500, voyages to the Americas, around Africa, and across the Indian Ocean brought a dizzying array of commercial products back home to Europe – precious metals, sugar, tobacco, maize, potatoes, and of course, slaves.[25] The first voyages to the Americas were also undertaken for nakedly commercial reasons therefore, as much as in order to fulfil imperial, military, and theological imperatives. The earliest maps of North America drawn by Europeans were difficult to read and frequently inaccurate, at least partially due to the fact that they mixed real and imaginary features.[26] The East Coast of mainland North America was explored and mapped by 1600, but it took until 1700 for the maps of the region to become acceptably clear and accurate,[27] and it took even longer than that for the West Coast to be fully charted.[28]

The first step towards gaining full control over one's surroundings – towards quelling the anxiety which arises from being in strange and uncharted territory – is to become familiar with its extent. After all, 'the process of familiarisation with and adaptation to unfamiliar landscapes had been an integral part of colonisation and settlement throughout hominid history'.[29] By the end of the sixteenth century, the area the English named 'Virginia' had been charted by John White and Thomas Hariot.[30] As Quinn observes, whilst the map made by White and Hariot was exceptionally accurate for the time, it was by no means free from ideological influence. Whilst the surveyors included many Indian settlements, tellingly, they were depicted as being very much smaller than the English ships which encircled the coastline. 'One has the impression, looking at the map, that a conquering people is coming to take over an almost empty country, and this fantasy later in fact becomes the European justification for the invasion of America.'[31]

It could be said, therefore, that 'putting the Americas on the map from the European perspective was not necessarily a task devoted to finding the shape of the earth; it was also related to controlling territories, diminishing non-European conceptualisation of space, and spreading European cartographic literacy'.[32] Crucially, the territory on which the Europeans settled was 'neither new, nor Virgin, nor unsettled'.[33] The land that Puritan settler William Bradford would later characterise as a 'hideous and desolate' wilderness had, in fact, long been populated and cultivated by numerous Indian tribes.[34] The popular misconception that the Americas were virtually empty and just waiting to be settled could not be further from the truth. As Francis Jennings argued in 1975, in *The Invasion of America* (in which he recounts the history of the colonial period from the Indian, rather than the European, perspective):

> *European Explorers and invaders discovered an inhabited land.* Had it been pristine wilderness then, it would possibly be so still today, for neither the technology nor the social organisation of Europe in the sixteenth and seventeenth centuries had the capacity to maintain, of its own resources, outpost colonies thousands of miles from home. Incapable of conquering true wilderness, the Europeans were highly competent in the skill of conquering other people, and that is what they did. They did not settle a virgin land. They invaded and displaced a resident population.[35]
>
> [italics in original]

In fact, current estimates suggest that at the time of initial contact between Europeans and Indians, there were around fifty million native peoples on the two American continents – five million of whom inhabited land north of Mexico.[36] It *suited* European explorers and settlers to characterise North America as a virtually uninhabited, untamed land not only because this perception neatly fitted in to their pre-existing ideas about a tempting *terra incognita* ripe for the taking, but also because categorising the 'New World' in this way provided a convenient justification for their aggressive commercial, imperial, and later, theological ambitions. 'The New World was also wilderness at the time of discovery because Europeans *considered* it such.'[37] The forest beyond the settlement had long been an important part of European folklore, and its 'dark, mysterious qualities made it a setting in which the pre-scientific imagination could place a swarm of demons and spirits'.[38] To a considerable extent, this pre-existing paradigm was superimposed onto early impressions of the 'New World' and its native inhabitants.

The 'wilderness' had long served as the sinister 'other' to the supposed safety of 'civilisation': in this context, controlling and cultivating such territory – and of course, subjugating or exterminating the 'wild' people who lived there – was not only to be desired but was necessary in order to ensure one's own safety and security. Thus, as Nash observes, Europeans re-experienced in the US their old, insecure relationships to wilderness.[39] It was a re-enactment of the often fraught relationship between humanity and the natural environment which had already existed for thousands of years. As Jennings suggests, '*Civilisation* necessarily implies not only technical but moral superiority over the stages assumed to be lower on the evolutionary scale.' Considered as what he terms an 'absolute quality', it is also 'omnipresent in American history and literature':

> Roy Harvey Pearce [author of *The Savages of America: A Study of the Indian and the Idea of Civilisation* (1953)] has shown how our writers have developed a myth of social structure in which civilisation and savagery stood as reciprocals, each defined as the other was not, and both independent of any necessary correlation with empirical reality.[40]

This complex and ideologically loaded relationship between 'civilisation' and 'savagery' is one that will frequently surface in this study.

The first European explorers were amazed by the difference between the 'New World' and their homelands. There existed a wealth of distinctive flora, fauna, and human cultures in the Americas.[41] For several years, visitors only experienced land within easy reach of the East Coast, and it was for this reason that, for the whole of the sixteenth century, maps of New England 'consisted of a single line separating ocean from land': the interior remained blank.[42] The vessels dispatched to survey New England had been sent as moneymaking enterprises: they were essentially speculators. They thus looked over the land with a keen eye for the valuable commodities it offered, placing an invisible price tag on everything they came across.[43] By the time Europeans began to visit North America regularly, explorers such as Richard Hakluyt had already complied a ready list of valuable commodities just waiting to be shipped back home.[44] Chief amongst these was wood. Significant levels of deforestation in England meant that wood for fuel and building was becoming ever more costly.[45] The earliest settlers thus sent back to the imperial centre lists of the various types of trees they had seen, for they constituted a hugely important and increasingly scarce natural resource.[46]

The deforestation of New England was beneficial to the settlers and merchants for two reasons: it raised money and helped fulfil a valuable need back home, but it also had the equally useful effect of helping to advance efforts to replicate the European way of life on new soil. They sought to recreate the old patterns and modes of existence in their new environment. Therefore, 'reducing the forest was an essential first step toward reproducing the Old World mosaic in an American environment. For the New England landscape, and for the Indians, what followed was a new ecological order: for the colonists, on the other hand, it was an old and familiar way of life.'[47]

That is not so say that the Indians had never cultivated the land or cut down trees. In fact, many tribes had for centuries implemented a careful and ecologically sound system of land management.

> It would be a mistake to think of the American forest in the seventeenth-century as a nearly impenetrable tangle of trees and underbrush. On the contrary, the newly arrived settlers found extensive areas of open land and even the remains of planting fields that had once been cleared by the Indians for agriculture.[48]

Although many Europeans were shocked by what they considered to be the poverty of those who lived 'in the midst of a landscape endowed so astonishingly with abundance'[49] – and attributed this to laziness, particularly in relation to the males of the tribe (a belief that further justified their own eagerness to make 'proper' use of the land) – what was largely overlooked was the fact that the Indians had learned to live in relative harmony with their environment, and did not see it, as the newcomers did, as a resource waiting to be exploited.

Many English settlers were wrong-footed from the start by the fact that the descriptions of the land and its characteristics they had read before crossing the Atlantic were written by spring and summer visitors who made their observations at the time when fish, fruit, and fowl were at their most plentiful and accessible.[50] It didn't take them long to realise that the New England coast in July differs greatly from the same place in January. The Indians had learned to capitalise upon the seasonal diversity of their environment by moving their communities according to the vagaries of the seasons.[51] By moving from habitat to habitat and gathering the maximum amount of food with the minimum outlay of effort, the Indians reduced their impact upon the land significantly.[52] Conversely, the English were preoccupied with building permanent settlements.[53] This 'struggle over two ways of living', would, as discussed in the Introduction, help create the major recurring conflict found in the Rural Gothic: the problematic relationship between those who have permanently settled in one place, and are defined by their fixity, and those who remain mobile, rootless, and unsettled. We see the first major literary expression of this conflict in the Indian captivity narrative.

From the moment that the first European settlers began to establish themselves, they changed the landscape in ways both intentional and unintentional. Cronon argues, 'American colonisation wrought an environmental revolution unprecedented in pace, scale and impact in the history of humanity.'[54] Less than 100 years after colonisation began, the landscape of New England had been so physically transformed that the traditional Indians' ways of interacting with their own territory had become impossible.[55] Indeed, 'colonisation literally alienated the land from its native inhabitants'.[56]

One of the ways in which this was accomplished was by erecting boundaries: 'in the hands of the colonists, New England became a land of fields and fences'.[57] Before the settlers arrived, there were no horses, sheep, pigs, or cattle in the Americas; the Indians had no concept of animal husbandry.[58] They were primarily hunters and gatherers, though they did also cultivate some of their own crops. There were no rats until they came over on European ships, and whilst the Indians kept dogs (their only domesticated animal), they had no cats. These animals all arrived after 1620, with the first major wave of European settlement.[59] Livestock means fences: crops and animals must be kept separate.[60] To the colonists, the fence therefore 'represented perhaps the most visible symbol of an "improved" landscape': when John Winthrop denied that the Indians possessed anything more than a "natural" right to property in New England, he supported his argument by arguing that they "enclose no land" and "had no tame cattle to improve the land by" '.[61,62]

The European takeover of the US was also greatly hastened by the fact that the sailors, explorers, merchants, and settlers who had travelled from the 'Old World' brought with them diseases which the Indians had no immunity against. Every contact between native and newcomer spread pathogens between the two societies. The toll which this took upon the native tribes was simply staggering: the arrival of Europeans brought death on an unimaginable scale.[63] Though the settlers feared the Indians, the Indians actually had much more to fear from them. Colonisation was a horror story for the native inhabitants of the Americas, as it had been for the Irish before them. But at least in Ireland, the native inhabitants had long been used to foreign visitors, and had had the chance to build up their immunological defence mechanisms. Things were very different in America. 'Everywhere the first European explorers and colonists reported horrifying and unprecedented epidemics among the native peoples.'[64] The Indians had no prior experience of common European diseases such as chickenpox and measles, or more lethal organisms such as the bubonic plague, malaria, and yellow fever.[65] They therefore had no acquired immunity – '[...] as a result, European diseases struck Indian villages with horrible ferocity'.[66] Mortality rates in the initial outbreaks were rarely less than 80 or 90 per cent – entire villages were wiped out in a matter of weeks.[67]

The first recorded epidemic amongst the Indians (most likely shingles) occurred in 1616, and lasted for three years. Smallpox, dysentery, TB, typhus, and measles spread like wildfire through the Indian communities, and wave after wave of fresh epidemics appeared as new, non-immune generations came of age.[68] The effects were noted by the Europeans themselves:

> Thomas Morton told of villages in which only a single inhabitant was left alive. So many died that no one remained to bury the corpses, and crows and wolves feasted on them where they lay. When colonists arrived a few years after the epidemic had spread itself, they found such quantities of bleached bones and skulls that as Morton said, 'It seemed a new found Golgotha.'[69]

For the Indians, therefore, the arrival of Europeans heralded the beginning of what Alan Taylor has described as a 'demographic catastrophe' that would unfold for generations to come.[70] Within a decade of first contact, almost half of them had died from new diseases.[71] In the first 75 years of the seventeenth century, the total number of Indians in New England fell from well over 70,000 to fewer than 12,000, and in some places the decline was even steeper.[72]

Whilst absolutely devastating for the Indians, their rapid decline was a boon for the new arrivals. The epidemics which raged in New England during this period were almost entirely one-sided – American diseases did not kill the colonisers in anything like the proportions that European diseases claimed the lives of the Indians.[73] In fact, it has been suggested that the only major disease to be transmitted from the US to Europe was syphilis.[74] Not only did the epidemics severely deplete the Indians making them much less able to resist European encroachment, but also the empty villages and cleared land that they left behind made highly convenient settlement sites for the colonists. It was common for the settlers to set themselves up on sites that had recently been occupied by dying Indians. More than 50 of the earliest European settlements in New England were established in such locations.[75] By dying in such large numbers, the Indians were seen to have surrendered the right to their own crops and villages.[76] It is no wonder then that the trope of the Indian burial ground should resurface so frequently in American horror. Many of the first major European settlements were actually established on Indian burial grounds, and the colonists were gifted rich new lands by dint of the diseases they had unwittingly brought with them from the 'Old World'. Even the Plymouth colonists had their pick of abandoned Indian villages with conveniently cleared land.[77] The 1616 epidemic had wiped out the original inhabitants.[78] Outwardly, at least, the Puritans had no qualms about establishing their 'City upon a hill' – a mass grave of recent vintage – because to them, '[...] the epidemics were manifestly a sign of God's providence – "in sweeping away great multitudes of the nations [...] that he might make room for us there"'. John Winthrop saw this 'making room' as a direct conveyance of property rights: '"God," he said, "hath hereby cleared our title to this place."'[79] It seemed only fitting to the Puritans then that their path to permanent settlement should be so conveniently smoothed over by divine providence, and that the land's troublesome sitting tenants were quickly and dramatically diminished by 'heaven-sent' malady.

Even with the rapid decline in Indian populations caused by the rampant spread of European diseases, it is important to remember that that *nowhere* did the colonisers find the *truly* empty land promised them in their own mythology.[80] Although the population collapse suffered by the Indians made it easier for the newcomers to establish themselves as the dominant power, this process still took nearly four centuries to complete.[81] Many generations would pass before those of European descent would finally gain control over the *entire* North American continent. In the meantime, two very different civilisations were forced to exist side by side. It is in the attitudes of the early Puritan settlers, in particular, that we can see dramatised the deeply hostile feelings they had towards the original inhabitants of the land they saw as theirs by divine right. As Ruland and Bradbury make clear, the Puritans were first and foremost *pilgrims*, not explorers, merchants, or planters, and therefore took a different approach towards chronicling the American experience than many who had preceded them.[82] Their response to the new land was irrevocably influenced by their theological and spiritual imperatives, and this inevitably filtered into their writing. In the next section I shall briefly discuss early English responses to the landscape and peoples of the 'New World', before concluding with a consideration of the captivity narrative of Mary Rowlandson as the unintended foundation of a specifically *American* Gothic tradition.

Devils in flesh

The earliest 'American' writings were narratives of travel and exploration, letters home, and detailed descriptive reports for masters back home.[83] Many of these accounts were really just descriptions of the new landscapes that were being encountered and detailed 'shopping lists' of exploitable natural resources. John Smith's *A Description of New England* (1616) reads, at times, like a glowing estate agent's report on a desirable new property:

> So freely hath God & his Majesty bestowed those blessings on thee that will attempt to obtaine them, as here euery man may be master and owner of his owne labour and land; or the greatest part in a small time. If hee haue nothing but his hands, he may set vp this trade; and by industrie quickly grow rich; spending but halfe that time wel, wch in *England* we abuse in idlenes, worse or as ill. Here is ground also as good as any lyeth in the height of forty one, forty two, forty three, &c. which is as temperate and as fruitfull as any other paralell in the world [sic].[84]

As noted earlier, many of the first accounts of the North American landscape were, like Smith's, overwhelmingly positive. Melanie Perreault notes that 'there was no single view of the American wilderness during the early colonial period' and lists details the various ways in which the Europeans variously depicted the American wilderness during this period: '[...] as virtual paradise, a commodity producing warehouse, a frightening malevolent entity, or a blank slate waiting to be brought to its full potential'.[85] For the Puritans, whose impressions would leave the most lasting mark upon the American Gothic tradition, the wilderness that presented as much threat as it did opportunity. It epitomised chaos, whilst *they* were the bringers of order:

> Instead of viewing the pre-colonial landscape as beautiful, the leading Puritans perceived, in William Bradford's phrase, 'a hideous and desolate wilderness full of wild beasts and wild men'. The New English saw the Indians as their opposite – as pagan peoples who had surrendered to their worst instincts to live within the wild, instead of labouring hard to conquer and transcend nature.[86]

As John Gatta notes, 'probably the most frequently cited illustration of Puritan hostility towards the New World environment' is William Bradford's description of the Pilgrim landing at Provincetown in *Of Plymouth Plantation*.[87] Bradford began his account in 1630, and completed it in 1657.[88] In it, he discussed the reasons why he and his fellow Puritans left Holland, where they had safely resided for 12 years, and travelled to the dangerously uncharted 'New World'. According to Bradford, part of their mission as Puritans was to go about 'propagating and advancing the gospel of the Kingdom of Christ in those remote parts of the world'.[89] It seemed an obvious choice then to venture to the remote new land in the West. Little thought was given to the peoples who were already living there, on the grounds that their numbers are thought to be few and their manners so uncivilised that they were hardly more than animals anyway:

> The place they had thoughts on was some of those vast and unpeopled countries of America, which are fruitful and fit for habitation, *being devoid of all civil inhabitants, where there are only savage and brutal men which range up and down, little otherwise than the wild beasts of the same.*[90]
>
> [my italics]

Bradford succinctly lays out the bare bones of Puritan feeling towards the Indians and their land; the 'New World', for a start, is significantly described as 'unpeopled'. Bradford characterises himself as being very aware of the many potential dangers which awaited his people – the change of diet, increased susceptibility to disease caused confinement for many weeks on a ship, and so on. From the very outset, however, he makes clear that it was the Indians which concerned him most. They are described in explicitly monstrous terms:

> And also those who should escape or overcome these difficulties should yet be in continual danger of the savage people, who are cruel, barbarous, and most treacherous, being most furious in their rage and merciless when they overcome, not being content only to kill and take away life, but delight to torment men in the most bloody manner that may be; flaying some alive with the shells of fishes, cutting off the members and joints of others piecemeal and broiling on the coals, eat the collops of flesh in their sight [...][91]

As Gatta notes, 'the profound distrust Bradford experiences towards the American environment must be understood [...] within the context of his history's peculiar genre, purpose, occasion, and audience'.[92] By conflating 'wild beasts and wild men' and ignoring the many existing Indian settlements so that they can describe the place as a kind of elemental wilderness,[93] Bradford both neatly envelopes his real-life narrative into the framework of the pre-existing Puritan mindset. Adding extra impetus to this process was the fact that, for the Puritans, the outer 'wilderness' represented more than just land that needed to be tamed: it also functioned as a powerful metaphor for the wilderness *within*. This feeling had its roots in the long-standing prejudice against the wilderness that had existed in Europe for centuries.[94] The dichotomies between good and evil, wilderness and civilisation, and order and chaos had long persisted in Western thought, and 'negative images of the forest are old and enduring. In time, they migrated from Europe to the New World, 'where as late as 1707 Cotton Mather could write about "dragons" and "droves of devils" in New England's primeval forest'.[95]

Bradford's fear was inspired by practical concerns as well. The Puritans were far from home, in a land that they knew little about. As Bradford's description of the New England coast makes clear, they were all too aware that the vast expanse of the Atlantic Ocean separated them from all that they had once known. If, as Tuan has suggested, anxiety is at its most powerful when an animal is placed within a strange and disorientating milieu, one can hardly conjure a scenario more anxiety-spawning than that which confronted Bradford and his fellow pilgrims in 1620.[96]

That the process of settling the New World would not be an easy one had already been highlighted by the fate of the first permanent English colony on American soil, which was established on Roanoke Island, Virginia, in July 1587. Unlike later Puritan arrivals, these settlers were motivated not by religious beliefs, but by commercial and imperial ones – dispatched by Sir Walter Raleigh in order to help secure the English claim to American soil. Their uncertain fate is one that would help reinforce the perception that the forests of the 'New World' contained forces at best unwelcoming and at worst actively malevolent.

The colonists had planned to establish their settlement on the much more hospitable land around Chesapeake Bay, but were obliged to settle on Roanoke when the ship's navigator refused to take them any further (it has been suggested that he had been paid off by the Spanish). Amongst the settlers was John White, their governor, who had taken part in Richard Grenville's exploration of North Carolina several years earlier. It was soon clear that the colonists were going to find it difficult to survive in their new surroundings, especially during the winter. The 15 soldiers left behind to safeguard the site, after the *first* failed attempt at settlement on Roanoke less than two years previously, had vanished. That their fort had been destroyed by the local Indians and reclaimed by nature also boded ill.[97]

After only six weeks, faced with dwindling resources and increasingly inhospitable local Indian tribes – who were soon angered by the aggressive way in which they were being treated by the newcomers – White decided to leave his people behind (the colonists included his own daughter and newborn granddaughter) in order to seek supplies and reinforcements from home. He had expected to be gone, at most, for a couple of months, but war with Spain mean that it took him three years to secure passage back to Virginia.

When he finally did make it back to the settlement, White and his companions found a scene that inspired the founding myths of the American Gothic tradition: the disappearing colony. The 117 settlers were nowhere to be seen. The footprints of Indians were everywhere, and the compound had been dismantled and plundered. Barely any traces of the colonists remained. It had been agreed before White's departure that in case of distress or other circumstances that necessitated the abandonment of the colony, certain marks would be made on doorframes. However, 'There are no carvings on the door posts, because there are no doors anymore. No doors, no houses, no sheds, no buildings, not a lock, not a board, not a nail. A bare clearing, devoid of life. As though the colonists had never been there.'[98] White later recalled:

> [...] and having well considered of this, we passed toward the place where they were left in sundry houses, but we found the houses taken downe, and the place very strongly enclosed with a high palisado of great trees, with cortynes and flankers very Fortlike, and one of the chiefe trees or postes at the right side of the entrance had the barke taken off, and 5 foote from the ground in fayre Capitall letters was graven CROATOAN without any crosse or signe of distresse.[99] [sic]

Imagining the scene that greeted White when he sorted through the personal possessions he had carefully stowed away before his departure three years previously, one commentator frames the moment in distinctly Gothic terms, describing him as looking 'ruefully over his maps and charts spotted by rain and mildew, his pictures torn from their frames, his once bright and serviceable armour eaten through with rust. Here truly the horrid hand of the wilderness had reached out and grasped them to himself.'[100]

Though many theories – some more unlikely, and more uncanny, than others – were mooted, the simplest, then, as now, seemed the most likely. The colonists were dropped off in the wrong location. They had quickly alienated the local Indians, who might otherwise have provided the knowledge necessary to help them survive in the unexpectedly harsh new landscape (as would later happen in Plymouth). The expedition had been ill-supplied, and White was not a particularly effective leader. Those he had left behind had most likely fled into the wilderness, and been killed by the Indians, or by the Spanish, who were eager to prevent the English from gaining a valuable foothold.

It would be some time before the English tried to establish a colony in North America again. 'By that time the Lost Colony was well on its way to becoming one of those strange white legends that lit the American landscape with a strange and awesome glow, pointing out to the settling whites the ways they must go and the perils that crouched along those ways.'[101] The spectre of Roanoke haunted the European imagination, serving as a permanent reminder of the fact that things could, and indeed *would* go very wrong for those who were ill-adapted to their new surroundings and their new way of life. What better symbol of the tenuousness of settlement than the mysterious fate of Virginia Dare, the first English child born on American soil, who seemed to have vanished into thin air? As W. Scott Poole notes, 'The lost colony of Roanoke has produced fantasy and romance as well as mystery. Numerous fictional narratives about the fate of the colony have clustered around Virginia Dare [...] Speculation about her fate has created folk legends, historical romances, science fiction and even comic book narratives.'[102]

In 1607, the first lasting English settlement was established at Chesapeake Bay. The colonists named their new community 'Jamestown', but apart from the accomplishment of having survived the arduous sea journey, there was little to be proud of. They died in their dozens from disease and hunger. In December 1609, there were 220 colonists: by the following spring, all but 60 were dead.[103] Jamestown was built next to putrid swampland, and the inhabitants were quickly felled by malaria, dysentery, and typhoid.[104] An English critic belatedly remarked, 'instead of a plantacion [sic], Virginia will shortly get the name of a slaughterhouse'.[105] Many of the colonists arrived with the expectation that they wouldn't have to plant any crops or till the land themselves, and believed that the Indians would provide for them. They soon became tired of arrogant Europeans demanding to be fed from their limited and carefully rationed supplies, and were not averse to making their point felt with violence.

When John Smith, who commanded the colony during 1608–09, made his fellow settlers work in the fields, his attempts to make the colony self-sufficient were ill-received, and he was forcibly ejected.[106] Jamestown starved in the winter following his departure, and there were even tales of desperate men resorting to cannibalism (an oddly overlooked chapter in early colonial history that will be discussed in much greater detail in Chapter 3). Their fate, in part, illustrates Douglas Leach's 1963 contention that adaptation is the key to survival:

> The greatest secret of successful living on the frontier was to have the will and ability to modify habitual practices in the light of new conditions. People of rigid habits often failed to make a successful transition from civilisation to frontier, for they were unable to alter their urges to meet the peculiar demands of the wilderness environment. This did not mean that Europeans had to become Indians to survive, but they did have to be able to draw upon the resources of common sense and the experience of others, including the Indians, to solve problems that were rather different from anything they had previously known.[107]

In the end, it was the cultivation of tobacco in accordance with farming methods learned from the Indians which saved the colony. European demand for the crop meant that new immigrants and new money came flowing from the Old World, and the colony's position was finally secured. (As we shall see in Chapter 4, the dependence on slave labour, which underpinned Virginia's economic success, would have immensely damaging consequences.)

Although New England was a less obviously temperate locale than Virginia, the later settlement of that region was rather less fraught, at least partially due to the fact that it attracted a different type of colonist.[108] Most Chesapeake settlers were poor and unhealthy indentured servants (or aristocrats unused to hard work and deprivation), but New England attracted those who could pay their own way, and who had Protestant beliefs that stressed the importance of hard work and self-reliance.[109] Still, during that first harsh winter, the Puritans, as Bradford puts it (in something of an understatement), experienced 'hard and difficult beginnings'. Within three months of landfall, half of their company of 102 had died from hunger and disease. January and February of 1621 were particularly brutal. It was a bitter winter, and they lacked proper houses as well as most other comforts. The Puritans had also been weakened by scurvy and other conditions contracted during their voyage. By the end of winter, 'scarce 50 remained'.[110] At one point, there were only six or seven colonists healthy enough to care for the rest. Even the sailors who remained on-board ship were dying in droves. It was only when the weather finally turned, and hospitable Indians showed the newcomers how to sow corn and other crops 'Indian style', that the tide began to turn. Of course, these initially cordial relations were not to last.

One reason for this is because, for the Puritans, the business of transforming the 'wilderness' into 'civilisation' (which to them meant as close to an approximation of their English homeland as possible) was their spiritual duty. After all, 'transforming the wild into the rural had spiritual precedents which the New England pioneers knew well':[111]

> While the Puritans and their predecessors in perfection often fled to the wilderness from a corrupt civilisation, they never regarded the wilderness itself as their goal. The driving impulse was always to carve a garden from the wilds; to make an island of spiritual light in the surrounding darkness... *paradoxically, their sanctuary and their enemy were one and the same.*[112]
>
> [my italics]

One of the principal tropes of the Judeo-Christian tradition is the conflation of the wilderness with evil. The Israelites spent 40 years wandering the desert, which was 'the testing ground where chosen people were purged, humbled, and made ready for the land of progress'.[113] The Puritan tendency to refer to the North American landscape as a 'howling wilderness' comes from the passage in 'Deuteronomy' (32:10) in which Jacob is found in the 'waste and howling wilderness'.[114] Their use of the term in an American context highlights the fact that they saw their situation and that of the Israelites as analogous, and provides a further indication of the fact that the landscape they describe in their writings is perhaps even more indebted to their own theologically inclined preconceptions than the physical reality of their surroundings. Paul Johnston (1997) points out that William Bradford 'tells us without apparent sense of contradiction that the Pilgrims chose for their settlement in the wilderness the cleared fields of the native inhabitants', and notes that accounts of the New England landscape provided by non-Puritan settlers such as Roger Morton emphasised the fact that significant swathes of ground had been cleared for agricultural purposes by the local tribes.[115] In other words, whilst Puritan writing emphasised the 'barren' and 'howling' nature of wilderness, the landscape they described was informed by their imaginations as much as by environmental reality.

As Abrams states, 'this tendency to polarize wilderness into the dark Other of civilized order lies rooted in the religion and cultural history of Northern and Western Europe, where well into the seventeenth century, as historian John R. Stilgoe observes, "wilderness" is felt to shadow humanly organised space as its alien antithesis'.[116] For the Puritans, New England was the physical embodiment of a spiritual ideal: a wilderness waiting to be transformed into paradise. This belief would have profound implications for the ways in which they perceived the Indians. If the wilderness was the natural home of the Devil (who would do all that he could to frustrate the building of heaven on earth), and the wilderness was where the Indians lived, then it seemed logical (as well as convenient) to conclude that that they were servants of Satan. 'The Puritans, believing themselves God's chosen people on a mission to establish the New Zion on this continent, equated Native Americans with the devil, creatures for them to be exterminated from the land in a righteous cause.'[117] By this rationale, if one's enemies are nothing more than godless animals, any kind of behaviour towards them is justified; hence, we get the likes of Cotton Mather in *Marginalia Christi Americana* (1702) introducing his history of the Indian wars with the observation, 'Nations of wretches whose whole religion was the most explicit sort of devil-worship would naturally form the shock troops of their satanic master.'[118] In a similar vein, William Bradford gloats over John Mason's destruction of the Pequot. The indiscriminate mass slaughter of 'Total War' is explicitly valorised and described as a 'sweet sacrifice', and 'Satan's supposed alliance with the Indians provided legitimacy for the worst atrocities'.[119,120] As Poole notes,

> The Puritan understanding of the Indians made the threat they posed more than human, transforming it into a threat from the satanic and the monstrous. An entire discourse among early American theologians concerned itself with why the natives had never heard the Christian message. Most concluded that it was because the devil had thoroughly enslaved them and held them in his power.[121]

However, whilst the Puritans feared the Indians, there was one thing that they were even more afraid of – and that was *becoming* like them: '[...] suspecting also that the wilderness was seductive as well as evil, Puritan leaders also feared that their own people would degenerate into Indians from prolonged contact with native ways and the native land'.[122] As Taylor suggests, the further one got from the 'civilised' regions of the colony, the more in danger one was of losing sight of one's original, Puritan self. 'Would living in such a savage environment release the inner wilderness that all men and women restrained only through constant struggle?'[123] Nowhere is their fear of becoming 'wild' more vividly expressed than in the Indian captivity narrative. The most famous of all is that written by Mary Rowlandson, who was taken prisoner by Narragansett Indians in 1676. She was one of approximately 700 English settlers taken captive in New England between 1675 and 1713, the period which included more than 20 years of war between the English colonists, the French, and various Indian factions.[124]

The return of the native

In the captivity narrative, we see dramatised in vivid and visceral detail the conflict between Puritan and Indian, and Puritan and landscape, in a manner that, characteristically, had a rich symbolic and theological significance. These accounts tended to conform to the same basic formula:

> The Captivity stories tell of being taken by the Indians, suffering dreadful hardships, witnessing horrors, facing the cruelty of captors towards their prisoners, then of a rescue or escape which restores

> the narrator and permits him or her to recount their adventures to seek out their providential meaning. Captivity narratives were stories of trial and persecution endured in the Satanic world of darkness that lay just beyond the conventional settlement. In the prose of a devout believer, the entire adventure could be shaped into a lived allegory of salvation, not just for the individual, but for an entire people.[125]

The captivity narrative helped establish the blueprint for an independent American literary culture. As Kathryn Zabelle Derounian-Stodola observes, 'Some critics believe that the Indian captivity narrative functions as the archetype of American culture, or its foundation text, in which initial contact between Europeans and Native Americans inevitably evolved into conflict and finally colonial conquest.'[126] Susan Faludi (2007) argues, 'The captivity narrative, the only genre indigenous to American literature, wasn't merely a recording of that ordeal. It was the medium through which these haunting memories would be contained, reconstructed, and effectively repressed in the centuries to come.'[127] Violence and bloodshed permeate Rowlandson's vivid account, and the attitudes she expresses towards the wilderness and those who have taken her prisoner would leave a permanent impression. The melodramatic and sensationalist elements found in many captivity narratives helped 'make them factually exaggerated horror fictions'.[128] The fact that captivity narratives unintentionally helped inspire (and sate) public demand for a distinctly American brand of sensation fiction is also discussed by David Reynolds in *Beneath the American Renaissance* (1989, 2011): he classifies them as a precursor to what he terms the 'Dark Adventure' mode, in which, as in Rowlandson, blood drinking and cannibalism are two of the most common motifs, and the two most common settings are, respectively, the frontier 'with its wild landscape and often savage inhabitants' and the slums.[129]

Paying particular attention to Rowlandson's relationship with both her captors and the American landscape, therefore, I will conclude this chapter by suggesting that her account provides us with the most significant early example of a trope which constitutes the principal paradigm of the Rural Gothic: that of the violent encounter between the settler and the nomad, between a community that is firmly anchored in one place, and individual defined by their rootlessness and territorial mobility.

Born Mary White in Somerset around 1636, Rowlandson's family settled in the frontier village of Lancaster, 30 miles west of Boston, when she was an infant. In 1656, she married local clergyman Joseph Rowlandson, with whom she had three children.[130] He happened to be away when the village was attacked by local Indians in February 1676. As Ringel notes, Indian attempts to win back their lands during the Pequot wars and King Philip's war were invariably seen by the Puritans as 'campaigns by the devil against the Kingdom of God'.[131] For them, the Indians were not just godless heathens; they were active disciples of Satan who had been given a very specific mission.[132] As a result, when Rowlandson '[...] calls the Indians "hell hounds" and their dancing a "resemblance of hell", she means what she says; the Indians are servants of Satan, their celebrations an emblem of spiritual death'.[133] For Michael Wigglesworth in 'God's Controversy with New England', 'the dark and dismal western woods' were 'the devil's den', whilst Cotton Mather (whose father Increase had a great deal of influence upon the editing, publication, and presentation of Rowlandson's narrative)[134] believed that Satan had seduced the first Indian inhabitants of the land in order to establish a powerful stronghold on earth.[135]

This belief in the 'satanic' nature of the Indians was bolstered by the fact that they displayed such an obvious knowledge of, and affinity with, their natural environment. As Crévecœur once wrote, in a particularly evocative remark, '[...] the wilderness [...] is a harbour where it is impossible to find [the Indians] [...] a door through which they can enter our country whenever they please'.[136] For Rowlandson and her neighbours, the attack upon the 'civilised' community they had constructed out of the 'desolate' wilderness encountered by Bradford and his cohort two generations before was an assault by the forces of Satan himself. Accounts such as Rowlandson's dramatised with grim fidelity the worst fears of the settler communities – and also, crucially, furthered the belief that their presence on North American soil was all part of a larger battle between the forces of good (and order) and the forces of evil (and chaos). Partially for these reasons, captivity narratives were amongst the most widely read literary forms in America from 1682 (the year that Rowlandson's account was published), until around 1720. They would remain widely read for 150 years afterwards,[137] and Rowlandson's book was one of only seven that sold more than 1,000 copies during any decade between 1660 and 1690.[138] The landscape played a crucial role in these narratives – indeed, 'their claims became much more empirically valid in the setting of American wilderness'[139] – because the forest beyond the settlement had long been perceived as a place where the boundaries between reality and fantasy, order and chaos – were weak, or even non-existent.

In another indication of the extent to which elements contained within the early American Gothic continues to resonate, it could be argued that Rowlandson-the-survivor is in some senses reminiscent of the 'Final Girl' figure in the modern horror film. She is the spiritual ancestor of the many other female 'sole survivors' who would turn up time and again, from Charles Brockden Brown's Clara Wieland to the likes of Lila Crane (*Psycho*, 1960), Laurie Strode (*Halloween*, 1978), and Dana in *The Cabin in the Woods*. Whilst, for obvious reasons of historical and cultural accuracy, it wouldn't be advisable to posit too unproblematic or, indeed, too *direct* a link between the slasher-film formula and Rowlandson's account, Carol J. Clover's oft-cited description of the 'Final Girl' figure does bear repeating here:

> The image of the distressed female most likely to linger is the image of the one who did not die: the survivor, or Final Girl. She is the one who encounters the mutilated bodies of her friends and perceives the full extent of the preceding horror and of her own peril; who is chased, cornered, wounded; whom we see scream, stagger, fall, rise and scream again. She is abject terror personified. If her friends knew they were about to die only seconds before the event, the Final Girl lives with the knowledge for long minutes or hours. She alone looks death in the face, but she alone also finds the strength to stay the killer long enough to be rescued (ending A) or to kill him herself (ending B).[140]

Like Clover's paradigmatic female survivor, Rowlandson sees friends and family butchered, suffers terrible hardship and loss, and lives with the knowledge that she is unlikely to survive the experience. If fellow captivity-narrative author Hannah Dunstan (who, according to Cotton Mather, apparently took up a tomahawk herself and led a revolt which killed her captors in a spectacularly gruesome fashion)[141] epitomises 'ending B', then Rowlandson, who, through her faith in God manages to survive long enough to be delivered from her nightmare experience, surely confirms to 'ending A'. Like the 'Final Girl' during the final moments of a slasher film, Rowlandson is separated from those whom she loves and forced to battle for survival against all the odds. Her status as sole survivor is also important. As Bauer notes, whilst she mentions early on that 24 settlers (including herself) had been taken captive, 'her authority depends on an erasure of 23 other potential narratives. Therefore, she declares, Job-like, "I only am escaped alone to tell the news" '[142] – an assertion that her own narrative explicitly contradicts, but one which emphasises the singular nature of her experience, just as in the typical stalk-and-slash horror film, the killer might murder even dozens of poor saps, but the focus sooner or later always comes back to the Final Girl (or occasionally, a Final Boy).

This aside, apart from the fact that the 1980s slasher film and the seventeenth-century captivity narrative obviously belong to very different genres, mediums, and, it goes without saying, eras (and the captivity narrative is explicitly an account of *true* events), the slasher film also lacks any theology or propaganda element. Nevertheless, they do also share an intense focus upon individual anguish and the violence that can be done to the human body. One of the things that is most striking about 'The Sovereignty and Goodness of God', is the graphic nature of the horrors Rowlandson describes. Heads are caved in by Indian hatchets, pregnant women are burnt alive, throats are slit, and settlers are disembowelled as their tormenters dance in manic glee. It remains an (often literally) incredibly visceral document.

The horror begins with Rowlandson's account of the initial attack. Sweeping in from the forest (of course) at sunrise on 10 February 1676, the Indians (allied with the rebellious Metacomet, who was dubbed 'King Philip') proceeded to massacre many of the colonists and raze the settlement. According to her, they showed their victims scant mercy. When one of her neighbours begged for his life, '[...] they would not hearken to him but knocked him in the head and stripped him naked, and split open his bowels'. Thus, 'those murderous wretches went on burning and destroying all before them'.[143] For Rowlandson, it was, in her memorable phrase, 'the dolefulest day that ever mine eyes saw'. Yet, she captures with an almost novelistic attention to detail the sights and sounds she observed. For instance, we are told that 'bullets rattled against the house, as if one had taken a handful of stones and threw them'.[144] Her description of the terrified settlers huddled inside their homes is similarly evocative: 'some in our house were fighting for their lives, others wallowing in their blood, the house in fire over our heads, and the bloody heathens ready to knock us on the head if we stirred out'.[145] Their disbelief is captured with the lines, 'Thus were we butchered by those merciless heathen, standing amazed with blood running down our heels.'[146]

The catalogue of brutal acts which occurred during this initial assault is, even years after the fact, described with melancholic exactitude:

> Oh, the little that we think of such dreadful sights, and to see our dear friends and relations, lie bleeding out their heart-blood upon

> the ground. There was one who was chopped in the head with a hatchet and stripped naked, and yet was crawling up and down. It is a solemn sight to see so many Christians lying there in their blood, some here and some there, like a company of sheep torn by wolves, all of them stripped naked by a company of hell-hounds, roaring, singing, ranting and insulting, as if they would have torn our very hearts out.[147]

Rowlandson makes it very clear that being taken captive by these 'hell-hounds' represented her worst nightmare come to pass. There is a definite 'it could happen to *you*' feel to the account, and she makes it clear that until such a thing happens, no one really knows how they will react.

> I had often before this said that if the Indians should come, I should choose rather to be killed by them than taken alive, but when it came to the trial, my mind changed. Their glittering weapons so daunted my spirit that I chose to go along with those (as I may say) ravenous Beasts, than at any moment end my day.[148]

As Bauer suggests, 'Her narrative is intended to input upon the reader the awe and horror felt when God's truth is suddenly revealed to the passive Protestant human subject at the moment of Apocalyptic rupture',[149] but whilst the theological implications of her account are obviously significant, so too is the evocative account of individual suffering and despair which Rowlandson provides.

She notes of her first morning as a prisoner that her captors forced her to 'turn back upon the Town, and travel with them into the vast and desolate wilderness, I knew not whither'.[150] It is that reluctant trek into the unknown – the unknown being both a physical and psychological state – that terrifies her most of all, and with good reason. 'The Puritans who established the Massachusetts Bay colony were particularly concerned about the possibility of becoming wild in the American wilderness. Only a thin veneer separated humans from beasts, they believed, and one most remain ever vigilant to avoid letting the inner beast take over.'[151] To experience enforced and prolonged exposure to the 'howling wilderness' of the Puritan imagination was to also risk losing one's soul. Even the most 'civilised' individual could degenerate, given the right (or rather, the *wrong*) circumstances. As we shall see, fear of exactly this kind of 'degeneration' recurs time and again in Rural Gothic narratives.

Rowlandson was kept moving from place to place by her captors, who were trying to avoid English soldiers. They refused to give their prisoners food and water for several days. Her torment was intensified by the fact that she was carrying an extremely sick child (her own) – she describes sitting 'with the picture of death on [her] lap'. The account becomes even more tragic when the child dies, ten days later. Already, Rowlandson has been irrevocably changed by her ordeal: before being taken prisoner, she could not bear to be near a corpse, but now 'the case is changed; I must and could lie down by my dead babe, side by side all the night after'.[152] This is much more, then, than merely a literal journey into unfamiliar geographical territory. As Richard Vanderbeets states, it is 'the interior journey that holds our attention, the symbolic landscape more than the literal one, and the darkness of the forest that represents that of the soul when God turns his face away'.[153]

We see from this point on a certain reluctant surrender to the inevitable and acceptance of the practicalities of the situation, and of God's presumed will. Rowlandson also charts a gradual surrender to the landscape itself, and to the changes that it will enact upon her. Consider her comments on the devastating moment when she is forced to leave behind the body of her dead infant: 'There I left that child in the wilderness, and must commit it and myself also in this *wilderness-condition* to him who is above all.'[154] Yet, Rowlandson also finds the occasional glimmer of spiritual comfort. One of these arises when she is given a Bible by one of the Indians. She sees this as precious evidence of the good Lord's providential ways, but glosses over the fact that the good book was passed on to her by one of her captors, presumably because to dwell for too long upon this act would significantly complicate her characterisation of them as devilish savages.

Nevertheless, there are further interludes of unadulterated horror here, such as Rowlandson's account of the fate of the 'Goodwife Joslin', a fellow captive, who is pregnant and accompanied by her young child. According to Rowlandson, after the Indians had grown tired of the woman's pleas for release, they stripped her naked, sang and danced around her in a brutal and humiliating ceremony, and then threw the woman and her infant into the fire. It's a horrific scene that wouldn't be out of place in a particularly sadistic torture-porn film, but not one that Rowlandson witnessed in person. The story was related to her by someone else, and inserted into her own account, thereby blurring the line between personal experience and possible hearsay.[155] Those around Rowlandson are often violently dispatched even when she is absent, further highlighting her 'special' status. She is the one who makes it to the end of the story: the survivor.

Apart from the ever-present threat of physical harm, what worries Rowlandson most is that as her captors travel ever further, she is spirited deeper into the wilderness. As she writes of the 'Sixth Remove', 'I went along that day mourning and lamenting, leaving further my own country, and travelling into the vast and howling wilderness.'[156] Her sense of geographical estrangement increases when she is taken to an Indian town and finds herself completely surrounded by 'heathens'. Here, the alignment of her captives with the natural world is explicitly stated: 'The Indians were as thick as the trees. If one looked before one, there was nothing but Indians, and behind one, nothing but Indians, and so on either hand I found myself in the midst and no Christian soul near me.'[157] Even the sight of grass trampled by English cattle gives her some comfort, for here is tangible evidence that her own people, and her own world, still exist. Throughout her account, Rowlandson is haunted by physical traces of her 'other' life, as in the scene where the Indians scavenge for corn in a deserted field planted by English settlers. We repeatedly get the sense of two civilisations uncomfortably superimposed, one on top of the other.

Most terrifying of all for Rowlandson is her realisation that for all the 'civilised' settlements that the English have built, there still persists a 'howling' wilderness populated by resourceful and resentful 'savages'. Safety and security are really just a comforting illusion, a façade pasted over an inherently unstable surface. Traces of each world bleed into the other, so that the Indians will inevitably come across signs of colonisation, and the colonists will never quite be able to avoid visible reminders of the Indians. Rowlandson is genuinely amazed by the sheer number of 'pagans' living in the forest, just as she is baffled by their erratic treatment of her – 'sometimes I met with favour, and sometimes with nothing but frowns'.[158] And yet, ultimately, she survives because she is able to adapt to her new circumstances. Her will to go on is reawakened when she is given some of their food to eat: an indication of the fact that she is in danger of becoming as 'wild' as her captors comes with her observation that she ends up with 'blood about my mouth'.[159] (Scenes in which white protagonists in perilous wilderness settings end up with blood smeared on their faces recur frequently in the Rural Gothic, as we shall see in later chapters, and the motif is always a signifier of degradation, deprivation, and occasionally, downright savagery.)

One of most important strands of Rowlandson's narrative with regards to the characteristics of the Rural Gothic in general comes with her realisation that, in order to survive, she must become more like her captors – there can be no room for squeamishness or self-pity. The sheer will to endure, along with her faith, becomes Rowlandson's best friend, and helps her to stay alive in conditions that her earlier, more sheltered self would have found simply unthinkable. For instance, when she finds herself eating bear meat given to her by a friendly Indian woman, Rowlandson realises that her European mores have been jettisoned in order that she may make best use of what the world has provided: 'Now that was savoury to me that would once have been enough to turn the stomach of a brute creature.'[160] Mind you, she immediately follows up this observation with a Bible quotation, 'To the hungry soul every bitter thing is sweet',[161] lest we fear that she's become too immersed in the 'Wilderness Condition'. Nevertheless, she has, albeit reluctantly, embraced the Indian attitude that one must make use of everything that nature provides. Another example of appetite conquering social niceties comes when she tells us she ate the flesh of a young deer killed in utero, and, 'thought it was very good'.[162] Yet, one inviolable barrier remains: the Indians drink the animal's blood, but Rowlandson cannot bring herself to join in because she finds the idea sickening, but also perhaps because such a Catholic-seeming ritual offends her Protestant sensibilities.

Rowlandson's reluctant consumption of Indian food also taps into classical mythology (she is a Puritan Persephone, trapped in the underworld of the American wilderness) and European fairy tale: Irish legends, for instance, have always held that those who can be persuaded to eat food provided by the fairies will find themselves trapped in their otherworldly realm.[163] The focus on food in her narrative also brings to mind the frequency with which American horror narratives depict cannibalism within the wilderness setting.

As we shall see in Chapter 3, amongst the principal requirements of 'civilisation' is the taboo against consuming human flesh: we're not supposed to eat other people. However, as Rowlandson now knows, hunger can drive a person to do things that would otherwise seem decidedly unpalatable and, indeed, 'unchristian'. In her case, this includes devouring the flesh of wild beasts from the forest, and even, as she rather remarkably admits, snatching a horse's hoof from a young child (and an English one at that) who is making heavy work of eating it. By partaking of the raw flesh of wild animals, Rowlandson was, almost against her own will, becoming one with her natural surroundings in the same way that her captors were. Almost as unsettling is the fact that, despite the harshness of their surroundings, her captors still manage to survive in surroundings she finds deeply hostile. 'Strangely did the lord provide for them.'[164] The unspoken question hanging over this observation is, of course, why the good Lord spares these savages in the first place.

Along with the many instances in which she grudgingly describes Indian acts of kindness, it's a facet of Rowlandson's narrative that complicates her initial portrait of them as servants of Satan. Rowlandson's captors certainly do terrible things, but they are also recognisably human, with families, rituals, social hierarchies, and foibles just like her own. They even have a sense of humour, although it is often cruelly expressed towards their captives. And whilst Rowlandson reports her own response to the death of her mistresses' child as being gratitude that there is now more room in the tepee, she nevertheless describes the grief experienced by the community. Although, she admits, 'I could not much condole with them' – understandable given the fate of her own child – she has again furnished us with a decidedly three-dimensional portrait of her captors.

Yet, conversely, as a Puritan, Rowlandson's *psychic* survival depends upon her ability to frame the Indians as an alien Other. To see them as anything other than heathen savages – as 'hell-hounds' – is to admit that there is a profound flaw in the world view which she and her fellow Puritans have been conditioned to perceive as an absolute reality. Hence, her resistance towards assigning the rituals of the Indians with any significance, such as the moment when her description of Metacomet's ceremonial pipe-smoking descends into a disingenuous rant about the evils of tobacco. In order to try to protect her own sense of self-definition, Rowlandson must resist the urge to identify too closely with her captors. It is a form of psychological and spiritual self-defence which isn't altogether successful.

Rowlandson is finally redeemed – like an item in a pawn shop – for the price of 20 pounds and some guns. Freedom comes not through rescue by the forces of righteousness, but through trade, meaning that the Indians got exactly what they wanted when they took her prisoner – a valuable bargaining chip.[165] Rowlandson is finally restored to her husband, her two surviving children, and battle-scarred community. But crucially, we are left with the impression that she will never again be quite who or what she was before 'the dolefulest day'. She has experienced 'chaos' at first-hand and life will never again be what it once was. 'Although she does come home, Rowlandson returns as an ambivalent and alienated creature. She has been thoroughly unsettled by her captivity and in turn, she has become an unsettling presence within the society to which she returns.'[166] Consider the mixed feelings with which she concludes her narrative:

> I can consider the time, when I used to sleep quietly without workings in my thoughts, whole nights together, but now it is other ways with me. When all are fast about me, and no eyes open but his who ever waketh, my thoughts are upon things past, upon the awful dispensation of the Lord towards us; upon his wonderful power and might in carrying of us through so many difficulties, in returning us in safety, and suffering none to hurt us. I remember in the night season how the other day I was in the midst of thousands of enemies, and nothing but death before me. It is then hard work to persuade myself that I should ever be satisfied with bread again. But now we are fed with the finest of the Wheat, and, as I may say, with honey out of the rock...Oh! The wonderful power of God that mine eyes have seen, affording matter enough for my thoughts to run in, that when others are sleeping mine eyes are weeping [...][167]

On the one hand, she presents her deliverance from the wilderness as proof that those who bend themselves to God's will can be saved; her freedom is proof of his power. But on the other hand, her account remains an extremely disconcerting one, highlighting as it does the fact that, no matter how secure and safe one's community may seem, attack by Satan's 'shock troops' may come at any moment. Rowlandson's story, therefore, becomes an almost paradigmatic account of one individual versus the wilderness and the 'beasts' who dwell there. It is also a testament to the fact that, no matter how desperately you try to hold back the forces of chaos, they will always find a way through the chinks in your armour. Even if one is lucky enough to find their way back to 'civilisation', the wilderness will have left its mark. If the ultimate horror in the Suburban Gothic comes when individual identity is absorbed by the mass, the equivalent terror in the Rural Gothic, I will suggest, comes from losing sight of the rational, orderly self that enables one to function in conventional society. Yet, paradoxically, survival in the wild, as Rowlandson discovers first-hand, is only possible when one adapts to these new surroundings. As Richard Slotkin has noted of the Puritans:

> They wished to make the Indian and the wilderness their victim, the subject of their will and their vision, and they could impose that will only by gaining the ability to meet the Indian on terms imposed by the Indian's world. Fascinated by their opportunity for creating

> a world, the Puritans were also repelled by the nature of the means necessary to their conquest.[168]

Similarly, Rowlandson's presence as one who has experienced suffering in the wilderness and survived to tell her tale will, despite outward appearances, profoundly unsettle the community to which she has returned. She is living proof that European attempts to tame the land – and the people – of the New World have some way to go yet. Her story is an unwelcome reminder of the Puritan fear that the wilderness will always look for a chance to change you as much as you have changed it. Whilst we see in narratives such as Rowlandson's a very conscious attempt to frame the experience in terms which explicitly valorise and promote the Puritan cause, in Rowlandson's case, there exists a parallel story to the main account, one in which one's captors become disturbingly familiar, what was once inedible becomes savoury, and the self begins to change in accordance with brutal circumstance. They are reminders, in other words, that of the fear that 'Chaos reigns', and of the gnawing suspicion that the communal bonds that lay at the heart of the European foray onto American soil would not be strong enough to resist the seductive and terrifying power of the 'howling wilderness'.

2

'We Are But a Little Way in the Forest Yet': The Community in the Wilderness

On 17 November 1978, US Congressman Leo Ryan travelled to Guyana in order to investigate the jungle encampment led by controversial preacher Jim Jones. Less than 24 hours later, Ryan was dead, gunned down by followers of the man known as 'Dad' to his acolytes.[1] In the hours that followed, almost every man, woman, and child who lived in the Jonestown settlement perished, many of them willing participants in what Jones dubbed 'Revolutionary Suicide'.

The abject failure of Jim Jones' errand into the wilderness, and the magnitude of the death toll (more than 900 people died that day) helped make the 'Jonestown Massacre' one of the most notorious events in late twentieth-century American history. And yet, whilst Jones was very much a product of his specific time and place, the story of Jonestown also has striking parallels with the history of European settlement in North America. The spectre of the colony that fails is one of the most powerful anxieties in the American psyche, and manifests itself time and again in the Rural Gothic. Which makes it all the more ironic then that in the background of video footage of Ryan addressing the Jonestown faithful shortly before his death, one can see a neatly handwritten sign that paraphrases George Santayana's axiom: 'Those who do not remember history are condemned to repeat it'.[2]

Jonestown embodied a paradigm that has been replicated time and again in the history of European settlement in North America: the movement of a supposedly 'unique' special interest group to an alleged sanctuary in the 'New World'. Guyana had even '[...] been seriously considered by the Puritans as a potential promised land – enticed by Sir Walter Raleigh's description of a "countrie [...] rich, fruitful and blessed with perpetual spring"'.[3] Choosing to settle outside of one's home nation in order to escape conflict and establish your own society is not, of course 'a new phenomenon, and nor for marginal religious groups an unreasoned choice':[4]

> A general theory of religious migration suggests that a deviant and 'persecuted' religious group may attempt to solve the problem of its persistence through collective migration, an act that breaks any conflicting social ties and achieves a heightened sense of commitment among the faithful who embark upon the journey.[5]

Breaking with the old patterns of thought and of living further tightens the collective bond, and undertaking an arduous and time-consuming journey dramatises the hardship this decision has caused. Communal solidarity arises from a collective sense of persecution, and from the fact that everyone – sometimes literally – is in the same boat. Like the Puritans, who were by no means the first Europeans to settle in North America, but like many to come, certainly perceived themselves as the most important, the People's Temple members who trickled into the Guyanese jungle during the mid-late 1970s saw themselves as fulfilling a powerful destiny promised by God. The Puritan journey was, as Sacvan Bercovitch (1993) observes,

> a radical troping of Christian tradition to fit the fantasies of a particular sect [...] they used the Biblical myth of Exodus and conquest to justify imperialism before the fact. The Puritans might sometimes appear as isolationists, but basically they were as eager as any other group of emigrants for land and gain. The difference was that they managed more effectively to explain away their greed. Other peoples, they explained, had their land by 'common providence,' *they* had it by prophecy and promise.[6]

The Puritan intention was to create a New Jerusalem for a 'New World', the fabled 'City upon a hill' that would stand as both inspiration and a reproach to the rest of humankind. They perceived their fledgling settlements as part of what Anne Bradstreet called 'this great household upon the earth'.[7] John Winthrop established the central of the communal and family bond in his famous shipboard sermon 'A Model of Christian Charity' (1630). For Winthrop, and, indeed, for many of his flock, the familial bond would become 'the guiding analogy of American life'.[8] In reaction to this, 'a particularly intense degree of insecurity, compressed into a domestic setting, became the hallmark of Puritan experience and writing'.[9] It is partially for this reason that the isolated, close-knit community in the American wilderness so often becomes the setting for narratives in which the assumption that communal bonds will bring safety is violently undermined. By looking at texts from Charles Brockden Brown and Nathaniel Hawthorne, and from twentieth-century authors such as Shirley Jackson, Thomas Tryon, and Stephen King – as well as M. Night Shyamalan's film *The Village* (2004) – I will discuss the ways in which these anxieties continue to manifest themselves in American literature and popular culture.

Utopianism has long been a facet of the European relationship with the Americas. 'Utopianism is embedded in the American dream of the "land of opportunity", in concepts of the "New World Experiment" and in what Marxists criticise as "American Exceptionalism" '.[10] It is for this reason that:

> [. . .] it is in the United States that most of the world's communes have been established, even though men and women for thousands of years have made plans for utopias. An American continent filled with comparatively inexpensive and unspoiled land encourages such social experimentation [. . .] A basic belief in the establishment of all communal experiments is that it is possible to shape the future by deliberately laying foundations in the present.[11]

Even as the first influx of Puritan settlers landed at Plymouth in 1620, they would have been aware that the brief history of colonial New England and Virginia had seen some catastrophic failures. The most famous of these, of course, involved the murky fate of the 117 English colonists who arrived on Roanoke Island, Virginia, in July 1587. In addition to the dangers and the tensions that accompanied the fraught processes of initial settlement, the maturation of the first- and second-generation of colonists raised in North America, would, for Puritan New England in particular, bring about a sense of crisis that greatly affected how people perceived their own communities.

As Charles Berryman (1979) has noted, three forms of change helped fuel the disillusionment felt by many of their most notable second-generation thinkers: '[. . .] the increasing material wealth and opportunity in New England was enabling the settlers to be less dependent on providence; the separatist tendencies inherent in Puritanism were dividing congregations [. . .] and a decline in the experience of conversion was threatening the very survival of the community of Saints'.[12] The so-called Jeremiad – 'The literature of self-condemnation'[13] – became an increasingly common form of self-expression during the 1660s and 1670s. The lamentations of the second generation revealed 'a deep disquietude' with how things had turned out for the settlers, and commonly used analogies which emphasised the (often literal) parent–child relationship between the original settlers and their unsatisfactory offspring.[14]

The poster child for this sort of self-scourging was Cotton Mather (whose grandfathers and father had helped found New England). He railed against the corrupting effects of the new affluence, remarking that 'religion had brought forth prosperity, and the daughter destroyed the mother'.[15] *Magnalia Christi Americana* (1702) was 'full of lamentations over the declension of the children, who appear, page after page, in contrast to their mighty progenitors, about as profligate a lot as ever squandered a great inheritance'.[16] One approach to reinforcing the values upon which the community had been founded was to 'exaggerate the spectre of doom in order to awaken the people who were distracted by worldly concerns'[17] but this was proving increasingly ineffective, as 'Fear of the strange wilderness and the consequent dependence upon God were yielding to confidence and self-assertion'.[18]

For Berryman, the witch-hunts which convulsed Salem Village during the early 1690s were 'the last desperate inquisition staged by the dying theocracy of Massachusetts'.[19] The standard account of events has it that the outbreak originated with a group of impressionable young girls and their crude (and strictly forbidden) attempts at fortune telling and divination during the long, difficult winter of 1691–92. Explanations for their strange symptoms have been many and varied over the years, and most scholars now agree that some combination of sociological, theological, and psychological factors provides the most likely rationale for the behaviour of the 'afflicted'.

One of the most persuasive analyses can be found in Paul Boyer and Stephen Nissenbaum's *Salem Possessed: The Social Origins of Witchcraft* (1974) which suggested that the outbreak had its origins in underlying tensions within the geographically close but economically divided communities of Salem Village and Salem Town.[20] At the time of the trials, a new charter was being drawn up for the colony of Massachusetts, the previous government had been dissolved, and there was for some time no governor. This meant that there was a lack of clearly defined central authority in the colony, save the soon-to-be-curbed power of the Puritan church.[21] As the trials dragged on throughout the spring and summer of 1692, more and more members of the wider community, male and female, rich and poor, respectable and otherwise, were dragged into the proceedings (although most of those accused, and almost all of those executed, were female). The trials had an immensely disruptive effect on the community, and helped create a febrile atmosphere of terror, paranoia, and mistrust.[22] The outbreak may have peaked in less than a year, but the long-term consequences would take much longer to dissipate. New England would forever after be associated with the supernatural, and the region would, even centuries later, serve as the setting for many of the most notable American Gothic narratives.

Two key (and interconnected) tropes found in Rural Gothic texts that focus on community – that of the difficult parent–child relationship and that of the small town which hides a terrible secret – are particularly influenced by the Puritan legacy in general, and by the witch trials in particular. The disillusionment of third-generation colonists such as Cotton Mather, and that generation's fear that they had let their illustrious predecessors down was combined with the suspicion that through the scourge of 'witchcraft', God was punishing them for these failings. Though order was restored with the reinstatement of a governor, and most of those still imprisoned were released by the autumn of 1692, the trials had deeply unsettled New England. Perhaps the deepest disquiet of all came from the recognition that the community in the wilderness could turn against itself with frightening rapidity.

'Kill All Your Idols': *Wieland* (1798)

Just over a century after the witch trials, the first major American Gothic novel was published. Fittingly, we find dramatised in it many of the anxieties just mentioned. Charles Brockden Brown's *Wieland; Or, The Transformation* like so many of the American horror tales discussed in this study, was inspired by true events, in this instance, a case that occurred in upstate New York in 1796 when a farmer named James Yates, told by 'voices from God' to 'Kill all your idols', murdered his wife and four children.[23]

It is entirely fitting that a real-life act of family annihilation directly inspired the first major American novel. The trope of the family (either nuclear or extended) that violently turns against itself is one that recurs time and again in the nation's horror and Gothic texts. So too does the theme of conflict between the older generation and their successors. In *Wieland,* as in all of the texts considered in this chapter, the influence of the older generation is a harmful one. *Wieland* is in part about the impossibility of evading the obsessions that consumed those that came before you. Peter Kafer's useful biographical reading of the novel (2005) relates it to the psychological scars inflicted upon Brown by his father's imprisonment during the Revolutionary War: fittingly, his chapter on the novel is entitled 'Sins of the Fathers'.

The history of the Wieland family outlined in the opening chapter highlights the importance that both ancestral lineage and the experiences of one's formative years have upon the psychological development of the individual. Clara and Theodore may be American born, but the family still has one foot in Europe. 'Here is a novel with a German title, almost all the characters are Germans, (either natives or of German descent). They speak German, and reflect, almost unconsciously, Germanic tendencies of thought and of the homeland.'[24] Along with those fleeing religious persecution in England, settlers of German origin were one of the main groups that settled in Pennsylvania. William Penn had visited German Quaker groups, and had his promotional pamphlets for the fledgling colony distributed in the Rhineland, where they met with considerable success.[25] Wieland Senior's journey was one that had plenty of real-life antecedents, therefore.

Though of aristocratic origin, Wieland Sr, founder of the American branch of the clan, was raised in poverty and sent into indentured servitude at a young age, with the result that: 'His heart gradually contracted a habit of morose and gloomy reflection.'[26] The tedium of this hardscrabble existence was interrupted by his discovery of a tract 'written by one of the teachers of the Albigenses, or French Protestants'.[27] Given that his mind was '[...] in a state peculiarly fitted for the reception of devotional sentiments', the effect is profound. Wieland Sr undertakes an intense course of study, and soon formulates his own unique creed. In true proto-American fashion he is as liberated as he is constrained by his lack of formal education and indifference to authority. It is a mindset particularly conducive to the cultivation of religious fanaticism. 'His construction of the text was hasty, and formed on a narrow scale. Everything was viewed on a disconnected position.'[28]

Like many another religious innovator, Wieland Sr realises that if he wants to pursue his religious principles, he will have to leave Europe. Furthermore, 'He had imbibed an opinion that it was his duty to disseminate the truths of the gospel among the unbelieving natives'.[29] As Kafer notes, the elder Wieland's religious struggles evoke events that took place during the early years of Penn's colony, as religious dissenters from all over Europe arrived in pursuit of religious freedom.[30] For the first Wieland in the US, the 'New World' holds the promise of religious and intellectual liberty. In addition, the advantages of American life – in particular cheap, abundant land and the labour of African slaves 'gave him who was poor in Europe, all the advantages of wealth' – and after

14 years, Wieland Sr has established himself so comfortably that he can devote himself entirely to religious study. It is significant that Brown makes it clear that the US's 'free' land and slave labour have benefited Wieland so much, as it connects the Wieland family with the racial and territorial anxieties which often manifest themselves in the Rural Gothic. His religious freedom and prosperity are built on the suffering of others.

The Wieland family farm (whose name 'Mettingen' further evokes their European origins)[31] is located on the banks of the Schuylkill River. We are no longer in the midst of the 'untamed' wilderness that so unnerved the first generation of European settlers: this is territory that has already been transformed into a reassuringly pastoral landscape, even if traces of 'wildness' remain. Wieland's farm is 'within a few miles of the city', but still affords him enough space and seclusion to erect his own private temple:

> At the distance of three hundred yards from his house, on the top of a rock whose sides were steep, rugged, and encumbered with dwarf cedars and stony asperities, he built what to a common eye would have seemed a summer-house. The eastern verge of this precipice was sixty feet above the river which flowed at its foot. The view before it consisted of a transparent current, fluctuating and rippling in a rocky channel, and bounded by a rising scene of cornfields and orchards. The edifice was slight and airy. It was no more than a circular area, twelve feet in diameter, whose flooring was the rock, cleared of moss and shrubs, and exactly levelled, edged by twelve Tuscan columns, and covered by an undulating dome.[32]

It is in this edifice that Wieland meets his unlikely demise. A (literal) bolt from the blue strikes him down at worship, and his dying account of what has happened – related to his horrified next of kin as he lies dying of incurable burns and a 'crawling putrefaction' that anticipates Poe – describes his initial sense of wonderment: 'Within the columns he beheld what he could no better describe, than by saying that it represented a cloud impregnated with light. It had the brightness of flame, but was without its upward motion.'[33] If this is, in fact, a close encounter with the Divine, the almighty certainly has a strange way of behaving towards his followers (indeed, the God-as-unreliable-Patriarch motif echoes the fatherly failings of both Wieland Sr and his son Theodore). The question of what actually happened to him haunts his children. As Clara, our narrator, reflects,

> I was at this time a child of six years of age. The impressions that were then made upon me, can never be effaced. I was ill qualified to judge respecting what was then passing; but as I advanced in age, and became more fully acquainted with these facts, they oftener became the subject of my thoughts.[34]

Despite this, she and Theodore believe they have been able to move beyond the traumatic events of their childhood. For a while, all the omens seem like good ones:

> [...] Wieland's two children Clara and Theodore grow up with a kindly maiden aunt, and they seem destined for happiness and fulfilment. And why not? The time is that of the enlightened American mid-eighteenth century. The dark, twisted, 'European' mystical strain that had deranged their father would seem to have no claim on them. They were cultured and sociable Pennsylvanians.[35]

One of the greatest attractions that the 'New World' held for the more theologically minded colonist was that it presented the opportunity for those with non-mainstream beliefs to pursue their own values free from outside interference. However, with that freedom came danger. For Jane Tompkins, who asks, 'What happens in Wieland?' (1986), authority – or rather, the lack of it – is key to a proper understanding of the text.[36] She argues that a historicist reading provides the plot with a much more satisfying meaning than would otherwise be the case (an approach later built upon by Kafer). For both critics, the novel is very obviously about the problems and anxieties of the post-revolutionary US.

> [...] *Wieland* is worth attending to not because it manages to *escape* the limiting features of its particular historical situation, but because it presents a shocking and uncharacteristically negative view of what it meant to survive the War of Independence. If Thomas Paine and Thomas Jefferson wanted to convince the populace of the glories of independence, Brown wanted no less to warn people of its horrifying consequences [...].[37]

As seen in Chapter 1, the Puritans feared the consequences of surrendering to their baser impulses in the dangerously unregulated wilderness, and so set about imposing physical and psychological control over their new environment in order to help reinforce it in themselves. Allan Lloyd-Smith (2000) has noted that the dread that the democratic experiment would violently collapse in on itself (as happened during the French Revolution) haunted the nation's political consciousness in the aftermath of the revolutionary era:

> As Jean Baudrillard has remarked, America is 'a utopia which has behaved from the beginning as though it were already achieved'. The utopian visions of freedom and prosperity that brought the early settlers to North America gained new vigour from enlightenment arguments about the possibility of an ideal society and were enshrined in the founding constitutional principles of the US. But along with the utopian inspiration came profoundly pessimistic insights into the dangers of trusting a society to the undisciplined rule of the majority, fear of faction in democratic government, the rule of the mob and the danger of a collapse of the whole grand experiment.[38]

Seen in this light it becomes clear that the attempt by Clara and Theodore to establish their own happy little community on the site of the tragedy that robbed them of their father will be similarly problematic. As well as evoking the deliberate denial of history that so often characterises the official history of the US, their behaviour parallels the movement from religious fanaticism to 'enlightenment' supposedly undertaken by the nation itself.[39] The greatest mistake made by the Wieland children is to think they are able to move beyond the obsessional ideations of their father. This failure is, therefore, as much a reflection of national anxieties as it is of personal ones. A similar preoccupation with the impossibility of ever completely stepping outside of the shadows cast by familial and national history infuses the work of Hawthorne and the other writers discussed in this chapter.

For Clara and Theodore the 'temple' is still of great significance, even if its original function has ostensibly been abandoned. The temple has become a lively intellectual salon, adorned by a bust of Cicero, the archhumanist. The site of tragedy has seemingly been transformed into a place of joy and scholarly edification. The secular devotion the siblings feel towards one another is strengthened by the addition of Catherine Pleyel (Clara's best friend and Theodore's future wife) to their insular little world. 'Every day added strength to the triple bonds that united us. We gradually withdrew ourselves from the society of others, and found every moment irksome that was not devoted to each other.'[40] The fact that the two sets of siblings pair up with each other only adds to the incestuous undertones which recur throughout the novel.

Like his father before him, Theodore becomes a gentleman farmer, a profession which leaves him with plenty of time to devote to learned pursuits. The younger Wieland is similarly obsessed with books – except his usual subject is the works of Cicero, rather than the Bible.[41] The felicity that exists between the siblings is enhanced by the fairness with which their father's estate has been divided. Clara, though unmarried, is provided with land and a household of her own. Significantly, the family property belongs as much to her as it does to her brother, even if it is he who will carry on the family name (though in actuality he will be the one who terminates it). Clara insists that the slight distance that separates the two households only enhances their pleasure in each other's company. It is during these walks across the property – and those to and from the summerhouse – that many of the novel's most uncanny incidents occur.

Theodore's happy marriage seems to place even more distance between happy present and tragic past. As Clara relates in sorrowful retrospect, 'The felicity of that period was marred by no gloomy anticipations. The future, like the present, was serene. Time was supposed to have only delights in store.'[42] In comparison to his father, whose individualistic beliefs were strengthened by isolation, Theodore's enlightenment education and close personal and intellectual ties with the opinionated Henry, who rejects 'all guidance but that of his reason' seem like they will protect him from the kind of fate that awaited his father. Rationalism is mistakenly viewed as a kind of inoculation against fanaticism.

An early suggestion that their contentment is in fact a sign of dangerous insularity comes with Clara's admission that 'The sound of war had been heard, but it was at such a distance as to enhance our enjoyment of affording means of comparison. The Indians were repulsed on the one side, and Canada was conquered on the other.'[43] The quartet may spend their days in peaceful contemplation and lively debate, but chaos and disorder are never far away:

> The Wieland's utopia has implicit parallels with the newly constituted United States: it is rationalist, based on enlightenment principles, and significantly without recourse to external authority. The children have been 'saved from the corruption and tyranny of colleges and boarding schools' and left to their own guidance for religious education. The dreadful collapse of this happy and independent society could suggest a pessimism about the future of self-government, as Jane Tompkins points out: 'Brown's picture of

> the disintegration of the Wieland's miniature society is a more or less direct reflection of Federalist scepticism about the efficacy of religion and education in preparing citizens to govern themselves [...]'[44]

As we shall see repeatedly in this study, the isolated rural community – be it the cabin in the woods, lonely farmhouse, or a small town in the middle of nowhere – is seldom left in peace for long. Sooner or later, internal pressures will cause a violent implosion, or outside forces – supernatural or otherwise – interrupt the status quo. It is typical then that despite the fact that the young Wielands have isolated themselves, the outside world – in the form of a mysterious stranger, Caleb Carwin – comes to them, and that he sparks off events that bring their cosy existence to a chaotic and violent end.

As has already been noted, in the Rural Gothic, encounters between those who have settled in one spot, and those who have no fixed abode, or who are 'passing through' seldom end well. Such is the case in *Wieland*, which features the familiar trope of the disruptive stranger. Carwin is essentially an American version of the classic European Gothic villain, whose claim that his only crime is 'curiosity' could equally be placed in the mouths of any number of other arrogant, meddling anti-heroes. The fact that even *he* seems genuinely disturbed by the depths of Theodore's madness later in the novel shows us just how far from sanity Clara's brother has strayed.

A startlingly articulate wanderer whose origins (like those of the Wieland's themselves) are both European *and* American, Carwin disturbs Clara first of all simply because he so firmly resists categorisation.[45] Tellingly, Carwin's rootlessness and disdain for conventional mores are emphasised in Clara's first glimpse of him. She assumes that he is a beggar, an impression heightened by his shabby clothing and the fact that he is blithely tramping across her brother's neatly maintained lawn.[46] When he returns a little later to ask for something to drink, Clara is taken by his well-modulated voice (which moves her to tears) and physical form. His face, she tells us 'was of coarse grain, and sallow hue. Every feature was wide of beauty [...]'.[47] Yet, something about him mesmerises her.[48] In the aftermath of their meeting, Clara is left unsettled and intrigued. The encounter also prompts her to think about the tenuous nature of their pastoral idyll. Thoughts of her nieces and nephews, and her beloved brother, are swiftly followed by gloomy contemplations of mortality.[49] It is during this time that Carwin's biloquism first makes an appearance, as he conjures up visions of murderous cut-throats lying in wait for a vulnerable woman. Though this event is dismissed as a dream by the others, Clara is convinced of the fidelity of her experiences, and soon her cherished independence has been tainted by insecurity and anxiety.[50]

It is amongst the rocks that surround the riverside, that Carwin makes his most audacious move yet. Having fallen asleep in a picturesque edifice, Clara awakens, disorientated (*bewildered*), in pitch darkness, as a mysterious voice warns her to avoid this spot. The fate of her late father is invoked: 'Remember your father, and be faithful.'[51] All that she and her brother had done their best to forget rises up once more. Though Clara is able to return home safely, her thoughts are inexorably drawn towards her father. Her delicate composure is further shaken by the sight of the guest whom Henry Pleyel suddenly brings into the midst of their charmed circle: Carwin, who turns out to be an old acquaintance of his from Europe. And so the wandering intellectual who, in true American fashion, appears to contain multitudes, is invited into the community the Wieland and Pleyel siblings have created.[52]

However, it would be very misleading to say that Carwin is entirely responsible for the tragedies that follow. Certainly, his amoral meddling does much to undermine the delicate equilibrium of the Wieland siblings, and contributes to Theodore's rapid decline. He is, after all, a man said to 'wage a perpetual war against the happiness of mankind'.[53] Furthermore, Carwin's treatment of Clara is deeply disturbing: he breaks into her home, spies on her movements, and interferes with her growing relationship with Pleyel. Yet, as Lloyd-Smith notes,

> Carwin's very unacceptableness, which makes him so suggestive of taboo, renders him a potent object for Clara. Her version of what transpires with Carwin in her room is so preposterous that many readers accuse Brown of literary carelessness: it is almost impossible to account for her actions on the grounds that she herself gives. The best she can come up with is the idea that 'her actions and persuasions are at war' and that her actions were 'dictated by phrenzy'.[54]

Clara's reluctance to take on 'the office of betrayer' despite the obsessive behaviour of a man who regularly threatens her life suggests that she may be in subconscious sympathy with his disruptive influence. The years following the deaths of her parents have apparently been settled, happy ones, but something in Clara recognises that there are dark forces lurking just below the surface. Furthermore, she is neither as reliable nor, perhaps, as clear-minded as we might initially assume. She has a suggestive penchant for catastrophic thinking. Even before Theodore becomes a killer, he figures in her subconscious as a figure much more threatening than Carwin. When she falls asleep by the banks of the river, she dreams that her brother is beckoning her on towards a large pit: later, when she realises that someone is hidden in her closet in her room (Carwin, of course), she again expects it to be Theodore.[55] Carwin's interference also prompts Henry Pleyel to display his true colours. When he wrongly believes that Clara's virtue has been compromised (never mind the fact that he has himself been secretly engaged all along) he berates her in the most unpleasant terms.[56]

In summary, what Carwin does is widen cracks that were there in the first place. He is 'the living embodiment of a society in which there are no rules that define and fix the self'.[57] In more senses than one, he has no fixed abode. It is no wonder then that he is associated with the rugged countryside rather than with the indoors, nor that his voice most strikingly manifests itself outside. Carwin is dangerous because he does not belong anywhere. By way of contrast, it is fixity that will prove fatal to the Wieland siblings. They may have repurposed the temple, but the pathology that helped lead to their father's bizarre demise has lived on in them, and their devotion to rationality is much more tenuous than it first appears. Theirs is a new world that will not last.

Clara values the independence that comes with having her own household, but it is in this house that she has most to fear, both from Carwin and from her brother. There are several scenes in which she finds herself cowering in her bedroom: on one such occasion she is all too aware of her own vulnerability and of Carwin's strength.[58] Soon after her final (and rather baffling) audience with Carwin, she finds her bed occupied by her sister-in-law Catherine's mutilated corpse, a discovery that, characteristically, paralyses her on the spot. She stands frozen even when the clearly deranged Theodore advances towards her. Clara is only saved by the intervention of the wider community, as a group of neighbours rush into the house to help. Apart from Clara's disastrous trip to Philadelphia, this incident, along with Wieland's abortive trial, marks one of the few occasions when outside authority intervenes in events at Mettingen. Even then, the fact that Theodore breaks out of jail *twice* and returns to try and kill first Pleyel and then her suggests that the powers of law and order are of little use. Clara's life is only saved at the novel's climax by the fact that Theodore experiences a final horrified glimmer of self-recognition that prompts him to take his own life (realising that you yourself are the 'chief horror of the scene', as Hawthorne puts it, is a common development in the Rural Gothic narrative).

For Tompkins, the fact that the Wielands and their companions are beyond the reach of external authority is a key element in the tragedy:

> When something happens that troubles their relations with one another, the Wielands have no authorities of any kind to tell them what to do: no Kings or Princes, no officials of the court; no priests of the church, no professors from the university; no judges; no representatives of 'society', or of commerce; not even a neighbour to give some friendly advice. Because the social spaces of Wieland are empty, the space of authority is vacant in a double sense [...][59]

As Tompkins elaborates, this 'vacancy', means that family are without any effective means of checking the validity of their perceptions. Their isolation means that they have only their own impressions of the world to rely on – but as the success of Carwin's manipulations demonstrates, these impressions can easily be fooled. The second effect of this vacuum of authority lends itself more readily to political/national interpretation, in that the tempting freedoms of the New World are seen as leaving one vulnerable to the devastating effects of disorder and chaos. Yet again, this chaos ultimately comes from internal rather than external pressures:

> When institutional supports are absent, it is not so much a question of protecting the worthy against the licentious as of protecting citizens, worthy or otherwise, against themselves. It is not Carwin who murders his wife and children, but Wieland, the devout, well-educated farmer, the very epitome of the man on whom Jeffersonians staked their vision of republican order.[60]

Unlike his ancestors, Theodore Wieland has no oppressive external authority, no aristocratic tyrant or religious bigots to rebel against.[61] Like Clara, he is free to reject or accept the teachings of their father as he chooses, to work whenever he wants to, to marry anyone he likes, and to spend money in any way he sees fit. The siblings are beholden to no one but themselves. Yet, the end result is neither enlightenment nor contentment, but insanity and murder, and the termination of the family line in the US. Carwin's meddling bilolquism certainly had a harmful effect, but it was listening to the voices in his own head that made Theodore into a psychotic murderer. His suicide is the climactic act in the orgy of self-annihilation which earlier resulted in the deaths of his wife and children. As Clara's uncle says to her after the killings:

> Your brother's frenzy is, indeed, stupendous and frightful. The soul that formerly actuated his frame has disappeared. The same form remains; but the wise and benevolent Wieland is no more. A fury that is rapacious of blood, that lifts his strength almost above that of mortals, that bends all his energies to the destruction of whatever was once dear to him, possesses him wholly.[62]

The rational, educated landowner is no more, and in his place stands a man whose deranged sense of purpose serves as a horrible parody of the sense of mission that his father and other, earlier, theologically minded European colonists possessed. It is no wonder then that following Theodore's second escape, their uncle, the last (sane) representative of patriarchal authority, urges Clara to leave the US. 'You must flee the country [...] no precaution will ensure your safety, but that of placing the ocean between you.'[63]

By the end of the novel, the Wieland family no longer has a presence in the US. Though she had wished for death, Clara manages to survive Theodore's second assault on, and even carves out some vestige of happiness with Pleyel. In this, she is aided by the fact that her brother is dead. The destruction of the family home by fire also marks a watershed moment in her recovery:

> I was in some degree roused from the stupor which had seized my faculties. The monotonous and gloomy series of thoughts was broken. My habitation was levelled to the ground, and I was obliged to seek a new one. A new train of images, disconnected with the fate of my family, forced itself on my attention, and a belief insensibly sprang up, that tranquillity, if not happiness, was still within my reach.[64]

As she relates in the coda, she finds herself, unexpectedly, 'a thousand leagues from my native soil, in full possession of life and of health, and not destitute of happiness'.[65] Like Pearl at the end of *The Scarlet Letter*[66] (another second-generation immigrant who finds true happiness and freedom only when she 'returns' to Europe), Clara exchanges the New World for the Old. She knows only too well that her father's quest for personal and religious autonomy has had disastrous consequences, so perhaps it is to be expected that she would return to the strictly delineated hierarchies and authoritarian structures of Europe. Though Clara ends her account by sadly reflecting on how Carwin's schemes would have been repelled if only 'Wieland had framed juster notions of moral duty, and of the divine attributes; or if I had been gifted with ordinary equanimity or foresight', she now knows that theirs was an American dream doomed from the outset.[67] After all, as Tompkins states, 'The Wielands catastrophe does not stem from anything they have done or neglected to do, but from their history, which is to say from their position as orphans of civilisation in the New World.'[68]

'The chief horror of the scene . . .': Hawthorne's Gothic wilderness

In Nathaniel Hawthorne's 'Roger Malvin's Burial' (1831), as in *Wieland*, the sins of the father have tragic consequences for the younger generation. The story also illustrates that 'much of the writing of Nathaniel Hawthorne suggests the persistence into the nineteenth century of the Puritan conception of the wilderness. For him wild country was still "black" and "howling" as well as a powerful symbol of man's dark and untamed heart.'[69]

The story's action begins during a bloody interlude in the Indian wars, in the year 1725, as the gravely injured Roger Malvin and his future son-in-law Rueben Bourne are left by their retreating comrades. They come to rest in a clearing surrounded by a huge rock 'not unlike a gigantic gravestone'.[70] Rueben is persuaded to seek help despite the certainty that Malvin will die before aid can be summoned, but promises 'either to save him or to bury him'.[71] It is not a promise that he takes lightly:

> An almost superstitious regard, rising perhaps from the customs of the Indians, whose war was with the dead as well as the living, was paid by the frontier inhabitants to the rites of sepulture, and there are many instances of the sacrifice of life in the attempt to bury those who had fallen by the 'sword of the wilderness'. Rueben, therefore, felt the full importance of the promise which he most solemnly made to return and perform Roger Malvin's obsequies.[72]

Death here is personified in a way that makes it clear that it is equated with both the Indians and the natural landscape: '[. . .] stealing gradually towards him through the forest, and showing its ghastly and motionless features from behind a nearer and nearer tree'.[73]

On returning to the safety of the settlement, Rueben falls into a feverish state. When he returns to his full senses, he pretends to his devastated fiancée Dorcas that he has already buried her father. It isn't made clear whether he has done this in order to spare her delicate sensibilities or because he simply cannot bear the thought of going back. Though he knows that Malvin cannot possibly have survived, he is haunted by the thought that 'his father-in-law was yet sitting at the foot of the rock, on the withered forest leaves, alive and awaiting his pledged assistance'.[74] Indeed, 'an unburied corpse was calling to him out of the wilderness'.[75] It brings to mind Harry Levin's observation (1958): 'Hawthorne foresaw that, wherever there were closets, sooner or later a skeleton would be rattling.'[76] In this case, the 'closet' is, of course, the forest – and the skeleton Bourne's guilty conscience.

Like Goodman Brown – another young man forever sadly changed by a wilderness experience – Rueben becomes a haunted, bitter individual in the years that follow. He neglects the family farm (inherited from Malvin), instigates petty lawsuits, and shirks his responsibilities as a husband and father. His comeuppance comes when he embarks upon an expedition, many years later, with his still loyal wife and much-loved son Cyrus, to find land to clear for timber from and establish a new home upon. After an idyllic scene which anticipates the dreamy forest interlude in *The Scarlet Letter* (1850), Bourne unwittingly leads his family ever deeper into the landscape that furnishes his own guilty conscience.[77] He has not even realised that it is the anniversary of Malvin's death.

Realising, at last, that he has led his family back to the spot where he left Malvin to die, Bourne believes 'that a supernatural voice had called him onward and that a supernatural power had obstructed his retreat' (supernatural voices and troubled patriarchs are a very dangerous combination, as we shall see).[78] Expiation is on its way, he believes: once he buries Malvin's bones he will surely be able to experience peace. Upon hearing a rustling sound in the undergrowth, he lifts his gun, and fires. It is then that he sees the tree where he had tied the bloodstained handkerchief that marked the spot where Malvin was left. The topmost bough – the youngest part – is 'withered, sapless and utterly dead'.[79] Even as Dorcas innocently reflects that 'it was better to journey in the wilderness with two whom she loved than to be a lonely woman in a crowd that cared not for her', her faith in her husband is shattered. Rueben has killed their son. 'This broad rock is the gravestone of your near kindred, Dorcas... [...] your tears fall at once on your father and your son.'[80]

Though he was writing at considerable historical remove from the Puritan settlement of New England, Hawthorne was extremely conscious of the ways in which the past can seep into the present. He clearly found much to admire in his progenitors, but he was disturbed by their black-and-white perceptions of the world. He also recognised that his character and fiction owed a great deal to those who had come before him. In the 'Custom House' prologue to *The Scarlet Letter,* his authorial surrogate makes it clear that he feels more of a sense of connection with the Salem of the past than of the present.[81] As Robert Miller notes, whilst some writers are imaginable apart from their birthplace, Hawthorne is certainly not one of them.[82] He furthered his immersion in the past by reading documents and histories related to the Puritan period (just as Clara Wieland finds herself drawn to her father's papers, and Cotton Mather immersed himself in the history of the Massachusetts colony). Hawthorne's research, tellingly, centred on the time of the witch trials.[83]

As noted earlier, the Salem witch trials marked one of the most severe challenges faced by the Puritans. They took place against the backdrop of not only the lengthy and psychologically damaging Indian wars, but also at a time when the patterns of thought and existence established by the founding generation was starting to fall apart in the face of accelerating political and demographic change. They also marked one of the most notable early examples in American life of officially sanctioned scapegoats being singled out in order to atone for the perceived shortcomings of community at large. True horror, for Hawthorne, as for the Puritans, lay in the breaking down of boundaries, be they psychological, moral, sexual, or territorial. For him, the forest beyond the settlement is neither evil (nor good), but it is the location where '[...] a frightening gulf, both literal and figurative, existed between the civilisation and the wilderness'.[84] It is no wonder, therefore, that Hawthorne was also fascinated by the relationship between the individual (and their conscience) and their community.

Hawthorne had also played a small part in trying to establish a utopian settlement himself. Brook Farm, located in West Roxbury, Massachusetts, 'began as a product of the transcendentalist movement and a showplace of Christian socialism'.[85]

> Most of the inspiration for this movement came from Unitarian ministers, people like William Ellery Channing, who believed that the spirit had gone out of the churches and that religion needed a new vision [...] They defended the right of each individual to follow the

dictates of his or her own conscience rather than established religious authority.[86]

Brook Farm attracted many prominent intellectuals and writers. Hawthorne spent the summer of 1841 there. Although he left in a state of considerable chagrin, and satirised the community in *The Blithedale Romance* (1852), as a '[...] a counterfeit arcadia' he still characterised his stay as 'the most romantic episode of his life'.[87] By turns affectionate, mocking, and melancholy, *The Blithedale Romance* depicts misguided idealists whose misconceptions about the world (and each other) result in tragedy. As Hawthorne knew from both his historical research and first-hand experience, utopian visions of community life seldom survive the transition from the hypothetical to the actual. Along with other mid-nineteenth-century communal experiments – such as Bronson Alcott's Fruitlands (1843–45),[88] Hawthorne's sojourn at Brook Farm, like Thoreau's time on Walden Pond, provided a vivid example of the utopian impulse that flourished amongst a certain strain of New England-based mid-century intellectual.

In Hawthorne's vision of New England's rich but not always edifying past, the will of the community more often than not expresses itself in ways that seem contrary to basic human decency and compassion, and those who waver from the officially sanctioned 'path' are ruthlessly punished. The ill treatment meted out to the Quakers and their kind is vividly dramatised in 'The Gentle Boy' (1832). Having 'appeared in the province as if conveyed by supernatural power', Quaker missionaries who venture into Salem are brutally persecuted, a development that actually feeds even more strongly into their fanatical sense of purpose (behaviour which Hawthorne assures us that is in 'a singular contrast to the calm and staid deportment of their sectural successors in the present day').[89] Ibrahim, a small boy whose father has recently been indulged with 'the crown of martyrdom', is found by a kindly and conscience-stricken Puritan farmer, Tobias Pearson, whose own children have not survived the transition from European to American soil. The boy's mother, Catherine, has been cast into the wilderness to die. Tobias and Dorothy, his similarly good-hearted wife, cautiously welcome the child into their home. They are recent immigrants, whose home has displayed on one wall the tools necessary for carving out a new life in the wilderness. But although New England has meant new land and new opportunity for the Pearsons, insecurity, both physical and psychological, is a persistent feature of their lives in America, and their home remains barred to the outside.[90]

Though their only motives for taking in the boy – whose very name denotes exotic difference – are compassionate, the couple find themselves singled out for persecution by their fellow Puritans. Things come to a head when the Pearsons bring him to the meeting house. The revulsion felt by the rest of the congregation is described in terms that evoke their fear of moral infection. 'Even the mild-mannered maidens seemed to dread contamination, and many a stern old man arose, and turned his repulsive and unhealthy countenance upon the gentle boy, as if the sanctuary were polluted by his presence.'[91] Things only get worse when a mysterious woman suddenly rises from the back of the congregation and gives an unhinged but powerful sermon that reveals her to be as fanatical as they are. Even the woman's wild appearance challenges Puritan notions of propriety and emphasises her indifference to their social conventions.[92] The woman is Catherine, Ibrahim's mother.[93] Exile has simply made her even more certain of the rightness of her cause, and has further encouraged her to shirk her maternal responsibilities so that she engage in 'wild fanaticism'. Nevertheless, moved by the genuine goodness of the Pearsons, Catherine consents to him being raised in their religion, knowing that he will be better off. Even the usually unforgiving congregation are moved by this sad display and stand aside so that she may leave unharmed. However, although this scene concludes with a moment of compassionate forbearance, Ibrahim is subjected to horrific ill treatment shortly thereafter, set upon by a group of children whose behaviour is the epitome of intolerance:

> A hush came over their mirth the moment they beheld him, and they stood whispering to each other while he drew nigh; but, all at once, the devil of their fathers entered into the unbreeched fanatics, and sending up a fierce, shrill cry, they rushed upon the poor Quaker child. In an instant, he was the centre of a brood of baby-fiends, who lifted sticks against him, pelted him with stones, and displayed an instinct of destruction far more loathsome than the bloodthirstiness of manhood.[94]

Ibrahim is severely weakened by the beating, and psychologically devastated by the fact that the fanaticism of the older generation has been so maliciously replicated by their children. Having fallen mortally ill, Ibrahim is visited on his deathbed by his stricken mother. He dies in her arms, but Ibrahim's decency and humility have had a profound effect on those around him, even inspiring his adoptive father to become a Quaker himself. In a development that anticipates Hester's gradual acceptance by the community at the end of *The Scarlet Letter*, we are told that although Catherine's 'Fanaticism became wilder by the sundering of all human ties', in time, 'the rigid old Puritans eyed her rather in pity than in wrath'.[95] However, the fact remains that an innocent child has died because he was caught between two unyielding brands of adult fanaticism. 'The Gentle Boy' may have a slightly more hopeful ending than many of Hawthorne's tales, but as in *Wieland* and 'Roger Malvin's Burial', children die here because of parental misdeeds.

As Hawthorne recognised, the Puritans feared losing sight of what they valued most in themselves in the 'New World'. In 'The Maypole of Merry Mount' (1836), their terror of 'going native' is combined with abhorrence towards reverting to the sinful old ways epitomised by the revels and rituals of 'Merrie England'. Michael Zuckerman notes that although the 'tale of the Maypole at Merry Mount seems almost too trivial to take seriously [...] American poets, playwrights and novelists have always seen something immensely suggestive in the tawdry Contretemps'.[96] The story further illustrates that in Hawthorne, unease is often generated by the blurring or outright violation of Puritanism's psychologically and theologically crucial boundaries. The Midsummer Eve's festivities are initially described to us as in a largely benign fashion – we are told: 'Garden flowers and blossoms of the wilderness laughed gladly back and forth amid the verdure.'[97] The 'wild throng' that stands hand in hand around the maypole evokes the paganism of the classical world. There is a deliberate shading of the boundary between human and animal implied by the masks that they have donned:

> [...] the likeness of a bear, erect, brute in all but hind legs, which were adorned with silk stockings. And here again, almost as wondrous, stood a real bear of the dark forest, leading each of the fore-paws to the grasp of a human hand and as ready for a dance as the rest of that circle.[98]

Grotesque masks of distorted human form are worn; and the 'savage man', 'Girdled with green leaves' makes an appearance, as does, by his side, 'a nobler figure, but still a counterfeit' dressed as an Indian hunter. It is a scene straight out of the colourful revels of Tudor England, lent an American gloss by the implied sympathy with the Indian way of life (qualities which, as Zuckerman makes clear, did not endear the real-life Roger Morton to his Puritan neighbours). Liminality and lack of fixity can here be either freeing or sinister, depending on who is doing the observing:

> Had a wanderer, bewildered in the melancholy forest, heard their mirth, and stolen a half-affrighted glance he might have fancied then the crew of Comus, some already transformed to brutes some midway between man and beast, and the others rioting in the flow of this tipsy jollity that fore ran the change. But a band of Puritans, who watched the scene, invisible themselves, compared their masques to those devils and ruined souls with whom their superstitions peopled the black wilderness.[99]

The revels undertaken here find a more obviously sinister echo in the sacrificial rites discussed in the final section of this chapter. However, this particular recreation of Old World rituals in the New World setting is a more benign one than in most of the other instances that will shortly be discussed. The young couple whose marriage forms the centrepiece of the ceremony are so innocent that they even briefly touch the stern heart of Endicott, the Puritan defender who ultimately restores 'order'. The 'dismal wretches' from the nearby settlement of Puritans have an existence that is clearly much less enjoyable that that of the community they have descended upon, with a life that consists of little other than work and prayer. Even when they meet in conclave '[...] it was never to keep up the old English mirth, but to hear sermons three hours long, or to proclaim bounties on the heads of wolves and the scalps of Indians'.[100] Endicott and his fellow Puritans also have a very different relationship with the wilderness, and define themselves by exclusivity rather than replicating the 'anything goes' spirit of the maypole.[101]

The defiance of the rogue community at Merry Mount is clearly allied with the resistance shown by the land itself towards the Puritans. 'The Puritans affirmed that, when a Psalm was pealing from their place of worship, the echo which the forest sent back seemed often like the chorus of a jolly catch, closing with a roar of laugher.'[102] Endicott and his band of followers ride into Merry Mount, as much to stake *their* claim on the wilderness as to root out the pagan practices of which they so vehemently disapprove: 'But now shall it be seen that the Lord hath sanctified the wilderness for his peculiar people. Woe unto them that would defile it!'[103] Endicott hacks down the maypole with his sword, and we are told that tradition says that as it collapsed '[...] the evening sky grew darker, and the woods threw forth a more sombre shadow'.[104]

The revellers are bound to pine trees and whipped, and even the dancing bear is shot. Though they are spared the worst torments of their fellow travellers, Edith and Edgar, the young couple, are nevertheless forced to turn their backs upon the 'vanities' of their 'misspent youth'. The forces belonging to Endicott's 'own, well-ordered settlement'[105] have triumphed and brutal pragmatism has vanquished youthful idealism and sensuality. Zuckerman argues that the strong Puritan response to the real Roger Morton's 'violations' of their painfully imposed order had its roots in the very different ways in which the two groups of English settlers saw the land around them and their own relationship to the wilderness. Foremost amongst these was the fact that Morton and his men openly identified with the Indians:

> He and his men ate and drank with the Indians, spoke their language, and kept sexual company with them. All of this was too much for Bradford and his solemn band. It stirred the very spectre of instinctual abandon that they had hoped to exorcise in their movement to a new land. For if Morton and his cohorts could fall so easily into barbarism, might not even saints slip? Who was to say that the demonic descent into primitivity that had occurred at Merry Mount could not happen even in New England?[106]

Drawing on Slotkin, Zuckerman further suggests that the very existence of Morton's trading post challenged the resolve of the Puritan settlers to 'resist acculturation to the Indians world, and violated the aim of more "orthodox" settlers to "keep their distance from the natives psychically as well as strategically" '.[107] Order came from authority and from the policing of boundaries, and was facilitated by the swift and merciless repression of those who broke the rules.[108] Those who strayed were, therefore, automatically subject to suspicion:

> The pillars of the Puritan settlements held steadfastly to the precepts of order and authority and assumptions that only 'wild creatures' would 'ordinarily love the freedom of the woods'. They could not conceive of freedom except on terms of submission to masters and participation in the common fate. So men and women on their own were indigestive elements in the Massachusetts craw. As Winthrop would one day declare, those who 'lived under no government [...] grew very offensive'.[109]

Equally problematic, as 'Young Goodman Brown' (1835) illustrates, is the otherwise 'settled' citizen who for whatever reason decides to (even temporarily) leave the settlement and head into the wilderness in order to access dangerous or forbidden knowledge/experiences. Goodman Brown, after all, does not venture into the forest on any random whim, but because he has an *appointment*. This is also another story where 'the elders are doing the devils work while professing righteousness'.[110] In concluding my discussion of Hawthorne's work in relation to the wider theme of community relations within a wilderness setting, I will suggest that this 'Young Goodman Brown' further illustrates a contention which runs through the Rural Gothic, as a whole – that when the individual deliberately sets out to travel away from the moral and physical authority of the settlement, bad things happen. This is, as I indicated in my Introduction, not so much the story of a Puritan who finds Satan in the woods as it is about a man who finds Satan in *himself*.

Even though it is past sunset, and the wilderness is surely the last place any sensible young Puritan would wish to venture alone, Goodman Brown kisses goodbye to his pink-ribbon bedecked new wife 'Faith' and ignores her plea that he sleep in his own bed. As a resident of Salem Village, Brown should be hyperaware of the perils of venturing forth into the forest at night. As Brian Harding notes, the witch trials provide 'a historical reference for the story without which its metaphysical or psychological meaning cannot be understood'.[111] The question of who – or what – Goodman Brown has made an appointment with, and for what purpose, of course lurks at the back of the tale throughout, but we know this errand has an 'evil purpose'.[112] It is a sense heightened by the claustrophobic confines of the forest:

> He had taken a dreary road, darkened by all the gloomiest trees of the forest, which barely stood aside to let the narrow path creep through, and closed immediately behind. It was as lonely as could be; and there is this peculiarity in such a solitude, that the traveller knows not who might be concealed by the innumerable trunks and the thick boughs overhead; so that with lonely footsteps he may yet be passing through an unseen multitude. 'There may be a devilish Indian behind every tree!' said Goodman Brown to himself; and he glanced fretfully behind him as he added, 'What if the Devil himself should be at my very elbow!'[113]

Brown's thoughts evoke the reaction that the likes of real-life Puritans such as William Bradford and Mary Rowlandson had towards the wilderness, particularly their conflation of Indians and Satan.

The personified trees which 'barely stood aside' also bring to mind Rowlandson's evocative simile 'the Indians were as thick as the trees'.[114] Then there materialises Goodman Brown's 'not wholly unexpected companion', who functions as a kind of sinister alter-ego.[115] The mysterious older man leads Brown further into the wild expanse, noting, 'We are but a little way in the forest yet.'[116] It is made clear that the old man, who may or may not be the Satan himself, has 'a very general acquaintance here in New England':

> I have been as well acquainted with your family as ever with one among the Puritans; and that's no trifle to say. I helped your Grandfather, the constable, when he lashed the Quaker woman so smartly through the streets of Salem; and it was I that brought your father a pitch-pine knot, kindled at my own hearth, to set fire to an Indian village, in King Philip's War.[117]

As well as disabusing him of any illusions that he had cherished about the piousness of his ancestors, what Brown's foray into the forest forever undermines is his faith in the individuals and the institutions that underpin the community of Salem Village. His catechism teacher, Goody Cloyse, is revealed a witch; the minister and the deacon pass by on some sinister errand.[118] And, most horrifying of all, 'the aptly named Faith' is detected amidst the 'unseen multitude' of voices 'heard daily in the sunshine at Salem Village, but never before now from a cloud of night' (as in *Antichrist,* a husband finds that the association between the forest and his wife has sinister implications).[119]

'Young Goodman Brown' is one of the earliest examples of the paranoid conspiracy narrative manifesting itself in American popular culture, as seen in the likes of Jack Finney's *Invasion of the Body Snatchers* (1954), Ira Levin's *Rosemary's Baby* (1967), *The Truman Show* (1998) and *The Village* (2004) – all stories in which the protagonists, like Brown, gradually realise that everyone he or she knows and trusts is part of some sinister, all-encompassing conspiracy. In Hawthorne, the conspiracy reflects the most paranoid meanderings of the Puritan mindset. Dashing further and further into the dark heart of the forest, Goodman Brown is said to be 'rushing onward with the instinct that guides mortal man to evil'.[120] With desperate bravado, he cries: 'Think not to frighten me with your deviltry. Come witch, come wizard, come Indian powwow, come Devil himself. And here comes Goodman Brown. You may as well fear him as he fears you.'[121] Most significantly of all, we are told:

'In truth, all through the haunted forest there could be nothing more frightful than the figure of Goodman Brown.'[122] He is '[...] himself the chief horror of the scene'.[123]

Horror also lies in seeing the very rituals that bind the community together being subverted by the forces of darkness – in hearing, as Goodman Brown does, a church bell ring out, 'distorted', in the depths of the forest. It is a moment that aptly illustrates that, as the most notable line from *Antichrist* suggests, 'Nature is Satan's church'. Here, 'all the sounds of benighted wilderness pealing in awful harmony together' can be heard, a rock serves as an altar, and four blazing pines burn 'like candles at an evening meeting'.[124] What they illuminate is a scene which functions as a horrific subversion of 'Godly' Puritan worship. Brown comes across 'a grave and dark clad company' which constitutes a virtual 'Who's Who' of Salem society.[125] The discovery vindicates his most paranoid fears – the hierarchical and moral structures that shape his community have been completely overthrown:

> [...] irreverently consorting with those grave, reputable and pious people, those elders of the church, those chaste dames and dewy virgins, there were men of dissolute lives and women of spotted fame, wretches given over to all mean and filthy vice, and suspected ever of horrid crimes. It was strange to see that the good shrank not from the wicked, nor were the sinners abashed by the saints. Scattered also among their pale-faced enemies were the Indian priests, or powwows, who had often scared their native forest with more hideous incantations than any known to English Witchcraft.[126]

Even Brown's own mother and father are present. 'Sinners' and 'Saints' consort together, the pious gather to worship Satan, and Indians mingle with colonists. Brown's horror is compounded when his companion insists upon revealing the darkest secrets festering in the village. 'This night it shall be granted you to know their secret deeds.'[127] After reciting a litany of crimes committed by those present, he commands the congregation to look at one another: 'Depending on one another's hearts, ye had still hoped that virtue were not all a dream. Now are ye undeceived. Evil is the nature of mankind. Evil must be your only happiness. Welcome again, my children, to the communion of your race.'[128]

Though Goodman Brown and Faith resist being fully baptised into this dread congregation – perhaps because they cannot bear to fully know each other – and Brown suddenly finds himself all alone, 'amid calm night and solitude', the effect is profound.[129] It doesn't matter whether what he experienced was a dream, an exceptionally vivid hallucination, or, in fact, reality: the effect upon him is the same, regardless. Now that he has received his unwelcome yet secretly longed-for insight into the 'true' nature of mankind, the rites and rituals that he once perceived as sacrosanct have been forever sullied, and his relationships with the community – and, even more significantly, with *himself* – will never be the same again. No wonder then, that as Hawthorne concludes, '[...] they carved no hopeful verses upon his gravestone; for his dying hour was gloom'.[130]

The attitude towards the community expressed by Hawthorne throughout his oeuvre brings to mind two observations made by Yi-Fu Tuan in *Landscapes of Fear*. The first lies in the fact that, as the Puritans recognised:

> Strength lies in numbers and organisation. By acting together, people are able to master the local environment and create a more or less stable environment in which they feel at home. In the past and among tribal societies, this humanized world was perceived to be a small pocket or order and safety surrounded by a host of threats. The wall of a house or of a town provided both physical protection and magical defence against human enemies, demons, violent weather, and disease.[131]

Yet, safety in numbers and in boundaries has its negative aspect as well. Part of this lies in the claustrophobia and domestic insecurity that Douglas Anderson and others have identified as hallmarks of Puritan writing. The rest of it comes from the fact that, as Tuan argues, the human fear of the natural world lessens significantly once control over the environment tightens. This means 'The greatest single threat in the city is other people. Malevolence, no longer ascribed to nature, remains an attribute of human nature.'[132] Goodman Brown may be (justifiably) wary of the forest as both a physical and a psychological space, but ultimately, the most horrifying things of all come from within himself, and from within his community. Salem Village is certainly no city, but Goodman Brown, whose Grandfather was one of the original settlers (indeed, his family history strongly echoes that of Hawthorne himself), belongs to a generation who believe themselves to be the masters of the land that surrounds them. He is, therefore, as culpable as any of his ancestors for choosing not to face up to the reality of their conduct in subduing the 'New World', as well as for his own arrogance and moral frailty.

Black boxes: ritual and sacrifice in the modern 'Community in the Wilderness' narrative

The trope of the isolated rural community which mindlessly replicates the attitudes and behaviours of previous generations has become a notable strain in the American horror and Gothic tradition, and often revolves around the idea of ceremonial human sacrifice. One of the most notable examples can be found in Shirley Jackson's 'The Lottery' (1948). As Faye Ringel (1995) observes,

> though Jackson never indicates where 'The Lottery' takes place, presumably the names of the characters, their willingness to follow old customs even when they no longer understand why, and their ability to slaughter innocent scapegoats and then return to daily life as though nothing had happened, made readers assume a New England setting.[133]

Jackson wrote a non-fiction account of the Salem witch trials intended for children entitled *The Witchcraft of Salem Village* (1956).[134] She was very familiar indeed with the dark history of her adopted region (the setting for almost all of her novels and short stories).[135]

A great deal has been written about the various interpretations which can be applied to 'The Lottery' – it is easily Jackson's best known story – and many of these articles consider it 'in terms of the scapegoat traditions of anthropology and literature, pointing out its obvious comment on the innate savagery of man lurking beneath his civilized trappings'.[136] However, the story also belongs to the long tradition of the fatally flawed utopia in American fiction. 'The Lottery' has also been hugely influential: many of the narratives discussed here have clearly been directly or indirectly influenced by the story and elements of the premise can even be detected in the likes of *The Hunger Games* (2008), which also revolves around the concept of random scapegoating as a means of brutally reinforcing communal bonds. Even *The Cabin in the Woods* (2011), one of the most important horror films of the past decade, dramatises similar ideas about the scapegoat and the supposed necessity for symbolic human sacrifice.

In summary, 'The Lottery' is about a small community that meets every year on 27 June to decide who which of their number will be sacrificed to ensure that the crops remain fertile. It ends as housewife Tessie Hutchinson is stoned to death by the neighbours with whom she had been exchanging pleasantries a few moments before. One of the story's most disturbing conceits is the suggestion that the lottery is by no means an isolated occurrence:

> [...] in some towns there were so many people that the lottery took two days and had to be started on June 26th, but in this village, where there were only about three hundred people, the whole lottery took less than two hours, so it could begin at ten o'clock in the morning and still be through in time to allow the villagers home for noon dinner.[137]

Although 'the original paraphernalia for the lottery had been lost long ago' and the ritual chant forgotten decades before, the lottery remains as important a highlight of communal life as it ever was. It is clear that it is the binding ritual of community life even if, crucially, no one knows for sure what its origins are. The black box in which the lots are placed before being drawn is a resonant symbolic representation of the hold that history and tradition still have over the townsfolk:

> There was a story that the present box had been made with some of the pieces of the box that preceded it, the one that had been constructed when the first people settled down to make a village here. Every year, after the lottery, Mr. Summers began talking again about a new box, but every year the subject was allowed to fade off without anything's being done. The black box grew shabbier each year; by now it was no longer completely black but splintered badly along one side to show the original wood colour, in some places faded or stained.[138]

The village's most senior citizens scoff at the very idea that the lottery might be an outmoded ritual:

> 'They do say,' said Mr Adams to Old Man Warner, who stood next to him, 'that over in the north village they're talking of giving up the lottery'. Old Man Warner snorted. 'Pack of crazy fools,' he said. 'Listening to the young folks, nothing's good enough for *them*. Next thing you know, they'll be wanting to go back to living in caves, nobody work anymore, live *that* way for a while. Used to be a saying

> about 'lottery in June, corn be heavy soon'. First thing you know, we'd all be eating stewed chickweed and acorns. There's *always* been a lottery, he added petulantly'.[139]

'Old Man Warner' represents the unthinking adherence to traditional rites and attitudes that has kept the whole barbaric custom alive, even though he and his fellow villagers no longer have any real idea about what it means, and many of the ceremonies other elements – such as 'a perfunctory, tuneless chant that had been rattled off duly each year' and a 'ritual salute' have been modified or dropped altogether. What matters is that the box, and the three-legged stool that it sits on in the middle of the square remain, and that the unthinkable act of collective savagery that will bind the community together for at least another year, endure.[140] It is also significant also that the ritual contains echoes of the Old World paganism that characterised the more benign revels seen in 'The Maypole at Merry Mount'. Old Man Warner explicitly links the sacrifice which is about to occur with the belief that blood must be shed so that corn can grow.

This premise alludes to the kind of rituals outlined by Sir James Frazer in *The Golden Bough* (1890) with which Jackson was very likely familiar. The most notable onscreen example of this 'sacrificing for the crops' plotline can be found the cult British horror film *The Wicker Man* (1973), in which a deeply religious policeman is sent to investigate the disappearance of a young girl on an isolated Scottish island. He is shocked to discover that the community, led by Christopher Lee's kilt-wearing, opera-singing, cross-dressing Laird, is a hot-bed of enthusiastic paganism, and ultimately falls prey to a fiery and unforgettably horrific type of martyrdom. The film was rather disastrously remade by American writer/director Neil Labute in 2006, with the action moved to an island off the coast of Washington State. The crop cultivated by the natives this time round is honey rather than apples (which makes it all the more unfortunate that Nicholas Cage's traffic-cop protagonist is fatally allergic to *bees*), and the island is a matriarchal society in which men are considered useful only in terms of their physical strength and reproductive potential. An interesting but neglected precursor to *The Wicker Man* is *Eye of the Devil* (1967), which starred David Niven as a French aristocrat who sacrifices himself in order to save his community's dying vineyards. However, even before Niven is willingly impaled by a dozen arrows, the sharp-eyed viewer will have suspected that all was not well. After all, Donald Pleasence plays the (secretly pagan) local priest, whilst doomed starlet Sharon Tate, soon to be savagely murdered in real life at the hands of the Manson family (who, like Jim Jones, were a twisted offshoot of the utopian idealism of 1960s radicalism), features in a minor role.

There have also been some notable horror fiction variations on this theme. Thomas Tryon's bestselling 1973 novel *Harvest Home* is set in an 'ancient New England village' whose residents, like Jackson's townsfolk, have an unusual way of ensuring a good harvest. The title refers to the time around 25 September when European peasants traditionally celebrated the harvest by hosting a mock sacrifice in which a large wickerwork figure, believed to contain the spirit of the corn, was set alight.

In *Harvest Home,* the naïve city dweller who accidentally stumbles upon the community's terrible secret is Ned Constantine, a former ad executive. Ned moves his wife and daughter from New York City to the village of Cornwall Coombe so that he can follow his dream of becoming a successful artist. As in Jackson's village, life in Cornwall Coombe is still determined by the old ways:

> Tradition [...] was the important thing here; tradition and custom, customs that had been preserved through the villager's lineage since olden times. They were a tightly knit, insular group, these corn farmers, apparently determined to cut themselves off from the rest of society in an effort to preserve their old folkways, much as had the Amish in Pennsylvania, the Mennonites in Ohio. What had been good for a man's father and Grandfather was good enough for him; what they had worn, he wore; the tools they used, he used – a scythe to mow the hay, a sickle to cut the corn.[141]

Ned and his family initially find the village and its people charming. His daughter's asthma is cured by the local wise woman and his wife Beth's depression begins to lift as she becomes more and more involved in the community. The villagers are descended from farmers who came from Cornwall 300 years before, and brought with them the belief that 'Corn was king'.[142] As S.T. Joshi notes, their archaic way of life and devotion to the old ways evokes parallels with sects like the Amish and the Mennonites.[143] Harvest Home, is 'when the last of the corn comes in, when the harvesting's done, and folks can relax and count their blessings'. The Harvest Lord, the village's finest young man, is treated like royalty until his reign ends after seven years. His fate is to be sacrificed in order to prevent a failure of the corn crop.

Ned grows increasingly wary as the summer progresses and the date of the ritual approaches: significantly, however, Beth and his daughter seem to be becoming increasingly involved in local life. We are rather ominously told halfway through the novel that 'Beth was open to influence', and good at adapting to her surroundings, something due in part to her strict Christian upbringing. As in the remake of *The Wicker Man*, as well as 'Young Goodman Brown', active female participation in religious ritual is a dangerous development.[144] Ned sneaks into the cornfield on the night of Harvest Home to observe the community's secret rituals. The only other man present is Justin, the oblivious Harvest Lord, who is drugged, coerced into having sex with the Corn Maiden, and murdered. Ned is captured, forced to watch this terrible ceremony (in which his own wife has taken part), and then punished in a suitably horrible fashion. In a line which echoes the final words in 'The Lottery': '[...] and then they were upon her', we are told that 'the women fell upon me'.[145] The final chapter finds Ned completely dependent upon the women of his family because his eyes and tongue have been gouged out. In Cornwall Coombe, the relentless cycle of the seasons carries on as it has for centuries. As well as its similarity to other small-town New England narratives concerned with the relationship between ritual and community, Tryon's novel can be read in parts as a reflection of male anxiety regarding the rise of feminism. The family breadwinner ends up thoroughly emasculated whilst the women in his life embrace the old, matriarchal ways and live happily ever after. His wife has comprehensively rejected her fundamentalist upbringing and instead embraced another form of fanaticism, one in which women pull all the strings.

A ceremony in which corn is planted according to rituals and techniques combining both Native American and Old World paganism can also be found in T.E.D. Klein's sadly neglected *The Ceremonies* (1984), one of the best American horror novels of the 1980s, which combines the by now familiar 'naive city dweller ends up amidst rural religious fanatics' plot with a 'return of the Elder Gods' storyline consciously indebted to H.P. Lovecraft and Arthur Machen. In the novel, as Joshi notes, Klein plays up the 'city-country dichotomy' to an even greater extent than in his 1972 novella 'The Events at Poroth Farm' (which the novel is descended from).[146] This time, the outsider is Jeremy Freirs, a smug young academic (he specialises in Gothic literature), who decides to spend the summer renting accommodation on an isolated farm in New Jersey owned by a friendly young couple who belong to an Amish-style sect: he wishes to complete his dissertation amidst the peace and quiet of the countryside. The dominant local crop is corn, because

'That's what this land is made for'.[147] After watching the annual planting ritual, which involves tearing apart loaves of bread baked in the shape of a man, Jeremy reflects that, for all their religiosity and apparent friendliness towards him,

> Beneath his neighbour's sober-sided piety he had glimpsed the painted face of the savage; behind the evening's quaint observance he had seen a blood-stained altar and a figure stretched naked upon it like a five-pointed star. He had witnessed the ritual slashing of the throat, the rending of the limbs; while his friends had enjoyed their evening meal, he'd had a vision of frenzied hands tearing at a thing without a head [...][148]

Religious fanaticism again comes to the fore in another tale descended from 'The Lottery': Stephen King's 1976 story 'Children of the Corn'. In this case, the corn sacrifice is explicitly rather than covertly associated with Christian fundamentalism and the setting is for once not a New England one (though the main protagonists are from Massachusetts). This narrative follows a familiar pattern, as city dwellers find themselves threatened by rural religiosity. Burt and Vicky, a bickering married couple, find themselves hopelessly lost whilst navigating the back roads of rural Nebraska. Their argument, punctuated by doom-laden pronouncements from a Bible-bashing radio station, is violently interrupted when a child stumbles out of the corn and into the path of their car. The discovery that the child was probably dead even before they hit him provides little comfort: Burt, a Vietnam veteran, finds that the boy's throat was cut and realises that the killer – or killers – lurk nearby. He insists that they drive into the nearby town of Gatlin, which resembles 'a set from a movie about the depression' and has everything but a sign saying 'BAD PLACE' hanging at the entrance.[149] Nevertheless, he perseveres in his search for a local authority figure. Instead, he discovers within the ruins of the church a mural which suggests that religious observance in Gatlin has taken an unexpected turn: 'It looked like a comic-strip mural done by a gifted child – an old testament Christ, or a Pagan Christ that might slaughter his sheep for sacrifice instead of leading them.'[150]

As Burt's investigation continues, evidence of some kind of strange religious mania mounts: he finds that the last officially registered birth took place in 1964 (12 years previously) and that in the time since, the all-American, secular names of the children born prior to that date have been scribbled out and replaced by Old Testament monikers such as 'Amos' and 'Micah'. He realises that, '[...] something had happened in 1964. Something to do with religion, and corn... and children'.[151] In fact, the children of Gatlin, inspired by their teenage prophet Micah, rose up against the adults of the town and massacred them.[152] Instead of running away to San Francisco, these kids have embraced good old-fashioned religion. Believing that adulthood is synonymous with corruption, they decree that none of their number may survive past the age of 19, and now live 'alone under the eye of God... a God of corn, grown old and strange and hungry'.[153]

Burt soon comes to regret his decision to leave Vicky alone whilst he indulges in a spot of amateur sleuthing: when he emerges from the church she is gone, and he finds himself surrounded by fanatical youngsters armed with sharp farming implements. Though able to evade capture for a while, he finds himself back in the cornfield, and makes a terrible discovery. Vicky has been crucified, her mouth filled with corn husks: mounted beside her are the desiccated remains of the town minister and police chief – the most potent representatives of adult authority. Having, like the reader, taken the meaning of the phrase 'he who walks behind the rows' metaphorically, Burt is unpleasantly surprised when 'something green with terrible red eyes the size of footballs' bears down on him – this 'God of corn' actually exists.

As well as belonging to that fertile sub-genre of American horror which delights in placing unwary city dwellers amongst primitive, violent rural folk – a tendency which will be further explored in Chapter 4 – King's story, like the others discussed here, articulates the anxiety often felt by the more secular, urban sections of American society towards those parts of the nation perceived as subscribing to a rather different set of values. Flannery O'Connor famously wrote about what she termed the 'Christ-haunted' South, but American religious fundamentalism has always been of a much greater geographical extent: and indeed, as Ralph C. Wood has noted, '[...] American fundamentalism, is in fact, an urban rather than a rural phenomenon'.[154] Nevertheless, these urban outsiders who stumble across rural communities for whom intense religious observance is not merely a matter of course but a matter of life or death can be seen as representing the feeling that the only thing scarier than a redneck with a chainsaw is a redneck with religion.

It is also very fitting that corn plays such a key role in all three texts just discussed. It was the most important crop of the original inhabitants of the American continent; it has for thousands of years played a role in rituals which both pre-date and helped shape Christianity, and it remains one of the most important crops in American agriculture (Alistair Cooke notes that 'The United States abounds, as you have heard, in maize, so much so that like the English with their wheat, the Scots with their barley, and the Australians with their oats, they have adopted for it the usual counter-word for the staple crop: corn').[155] The presence of corn in these stories means that the sacrifices depicted here are connected with the continent's pre-European past, the pagan rituals of pre-Christian Europe, and the US's (mainly) Christian present. Even the residents of Merry Mount stage ceremonies in which corn is of central importance: '[...] they made an image with sheaves of Indian corn, and wreathed it with autumnal garlands, and bore it home triumphantly'.[156] More recently, Joyce Carol Oates's novella 'The Corn Maiden: A Love Story' (2005) articulates similar ideas about the significance of sacrificial ritual in the modern world.[157]

The domestication of maize accompanied the rise of the high civilisations of pre-Hispanic Mesoamerica. It only arrived in Europe after the Spaniards and other European interlopers began to export the plant during the fifteenth and sixteenth centuries. Maize had been cultivated by the native inhabitants of the American continent for more than 4,000 years and became a vital component of their culture and societies, with sacrifices to the corn god becoming a key rite in the religious systems of the Maya, Aztec, and Incan civilisations. *The Golden Bough* claimed that ancient Mexicans sacrificed human beings at all stages in the growth of maize, with the age of the victims corresponding to the age of the corn. Of course, we should take many of these accounts with a large grain of salt, given that tales of the brutality and bloodthirstiness of the continent's earliest inhabitants originated with invaders who had a vested interest in portraying those whose lands they had just stolen as violent savages. Nevertheless, what particularly interested Frazer were the obvious analogies between such rites in the US and ancient harvest customs in Europe and the rest of the world, a connection which, as we have seen, is often made directly in fictional narratives which dramatise these rituals.

Shirley Jackson's husband, academic Stanley Edgar Hyman, was teaching a course in folklore at the same time that she wrote 'The Lottery'. The story is to some extent obviously a modern-day fictionalisation of such rites. Although Jackson's villagers perform their ritual in order to fulfil distinctly pagan rites, they have chosen a particularly biblical method of execution, known as 'lapidation'. Now most associated with repressive Islamic theocracies, stoning is specifically mentioned in both the Old and New Testaments. There is also the fact that the sentence is carried out by the entire community, which reinforces one of Jackson's most notable recurring themes: the idea that community spirit isn't necessarily a good thing. Acts of communal togetherness in her work generally involve mob violence and her villages are never more united than when they close ranks against an outsider.

Tessie Hutchinson becomes a symbolic outsider through random selection, but as some critics have suggested, her fate may be telegraphed by her name.[158] In 1637, Anne Hutchinson was expelled from the Massachusetts colony for her antinomian beliefs: Hutchinson is a name associated with female rebellion and punishment. Therefore, whilst the ritual carried out in 'The Lottery' may seem to have little initial connection to Christianity, both the method of execution and the name of the scapegoat suggests a link between pagan ritual and the Christian appropriation of such rites.

Nebeker argues that the black box '[...] suggests the body of tradition – once oral but now written – which the dead hand of the past codified in religion, mores, government, and the rest of culture, and passed from generation to generation, letting it grow ever more cumbersome, meaningless, and indefensible'.[159] The villagers unthinkingly replicate the rituals of their ancestors despite the fact that they were clearly established at a time when there clearly existed a very different set of historical and practical circumstances. Though the ritual has evolved, it is clear that the fundamentals remain intact: '[...] they still remembered to use stones'. The next generation has been indoctrinated already: the piles of stones used to execute Tessie are assembled by the excited little boys of the village, and her youngest child is even given a few pebbles so that he can participate like the others.[160] Not only have Tessie's children been deprived of a mother, but also they have been encouraged to actively participate in her communally sanctioned murder, thus ensuring that the rituals of the past will continue to perpetuate themselves in the present.

Although human sacrifice doesn't directly feature in the storyline, black boxes again loom large in writer/director M. Night Shyamalan's *The Village* (2004), which has much in common with the other narratives discussed here. The trope of the isolated small town/village with something to hide is an extremely common one in American popular culture, and in addition to high-profile releases such as *The Village*, it has also manifested itself in more than a few relatively obscure films doomed to appear only as made-for-TV movies or to be released in straight to DVD format. These include *Skeletons* (1996), in which small-town New England religious fanatics murder those whose lifestyles do not conform to their strict codes of behaviour and morality; *The Spring* (2000), in which immortal youth is bestowed upon small-town residents with the inevitable caveat that they can never leave; *Black River* (2001) (which is interesting in that the plot's climactic revelations bring it into the realm of technologically created utopian fantasy-turned-nightmare stories such as *The Matrix* and Philip K. Dick's 1959 novel *Time Out of Joint*); and more recently, *Population 436* (2006) and *Jug Face* (2013).[161]

Population 436 is particularly interesting in that it owes such an obvious debt to the stories outlined earlier in this section. Inevitably, it is depicted from the perspective of an outsider who happens to stumble upon the community's terrible secret and must die or become part of the conspiracy himself. In these stories, as in the backwoods horror subgenre discussed in Chapter 4, the wandering outsider is the one who is under threat from the rural community, and not the other way round.[162]

Here, the outsider is a census taker named Steve Kady (Jeremy Sisto) tasked with finding out just why a town ironically named 'Rockwell Falls' has a population total that remains the exact same, decade after decade. Each birth appears to be perfectly balanced out by a death, and, as one of the residents cheerily remarks, 'Everything tends to stay the same around here' (the safeguarding of stasis is a common feature of the Rural Gothic). It eventually transpires that the town's obsessive interest in 'equilibrium' has its roots in a founding father's fascination with biblical numerology. The appearance of a black box – which contains the ballots the men of the town vote with when deciding who has to die in order to maintain the status quo – makes the debt to Jackson rather obvious. Kady is told that a woman who has just been publicly hanged in the local square has 'sacrificed herself for the good of the community'. Though he repeatedly assures the locals that he's just 'passing through', Kady inevitably realises that getting out of Rockwell Falls is a lot more difficult than it looks, and he is killed whilst trying to flee. In a twist reminiscent of the final moments of 'The Children of the Corn', the climactic intervention of supernatural forces adds another layer to the murderously ritualistic behaviour of the locals.

By way of contrast, one of the two major revelations to emerge in *The Village* is the discovery that the supposedly 'supernatural' threat which keeps the inhabitants corralled between strictly enforced boundaries turns out to be one that has been entirely fabricated by the community's elders, who want to keep their children 'safely' separate from the rest of the world. It is entirely fitting then that like *Wieland*, *The Village* is set in rural Pennsylvania, for not only is the film about setting up your own idiosyncratic world far from outside authority, but it is also a narrative about the relationship between parents and children, and the unintentional harm caused by the fanatical idealism of the older generation. Just as Theodore and Clara Wieland discover that they have much more in common with their ill-fated father than they had even suspected, so too do the trio of young adults who serve as the main focus of Shyamalan's film ultimately find themselves actively colluding in the strategies of concealment and evasion which maintain the status quo.

It is notable that the film begins with the burial of a child. Although the date of death on the boy's headstone reads '1897', and everything about the setting and the dress, demeanour, and ponderously stilted language of those gathered around the grave would seem to suggest that this is a historical drama, the audience, like the young people of the village, have been misled. In fact, it is the twenty-first century, and the village was founded in the 1970s by a group of like-minded individuals who had all lost loved ones to the violence and disorder of the city of Philadelphia (euphemistically referred to here as 'The Towns'). Having met at a grief-counselling centre, the group decided that the only way to keep their children safe amidst the chaos of modern life was to leave that world entirely and build their own community in the depths of the Pennsylvanian woods. It is a dream made possible by the wealth and political influence of a young history professor named Edward Walker (William Hurt), whose billionaire father was murdered by a business partner. The plutocrats of the late nineteenth century had a fondness for establishing their own private worlds outside the 'immoral' cities where they actually made their money (Jackson's *The Sundial* [1956] and *The Haunting of Hill House* [1959] are both set in houses which originate in this fashion). Walker's project represents an insanely ambitious scaling up of this instinct, revolving as it does around the creation of an entire community based on the assumption that an idealised and simulated American past is far superior to the nation's problematic present.

The existence of the village, therefore, hinges upon an audacious lie buttressed by the creation of a non-existent threat whose presence is used as a rationale for its isolation. For the first half of the film, the viewer, like the community's young people, is led to believe that the 'Covington Woods' are inhabited by dangerous creatures euphemistically referred to as 'those we do not speak of'.[163] There apparently exists a tenuous truce between the elders of the community and the creatures, which depends upon the strict enforcement of territorial boundaries. In an obvious echo of the garrison mentality experienced by early English settlers, we are told that the woods which encircle the neatly cultivated fields and wooden houses of the settlement are not to be entered under any circumstances. To do so will provoke the 'creatures'. There are even occasional animalistic screams heard in the distance, a literal evocation of the 'howling wilderness' so loathed by Bradford and Rowlandson.

> In building his utopia, Professor Edward Walker has chosen to replace Indians – those terrifying lurkers in the woods, those who have language but not one that the dominant white culture understands, those whose primitive responses to bold colours and supernatural ability to sense good and evil intentions frighten us and mark otherness – with monsters.[164]

Walker has clearly modelled the community upon early colonial settlements and attitudes towards the wilderness. Even though conventional religious observance seems to be absent (there is no mention at all of God during the funeral service, and although someone says 'God bless you' after the marriage ceremony that takes place later on, this seems more like a platitude than an expression of faith), the antiquated clothing, rudimentary farming techniques, and simple way of life practised by the villagers also brings to mind the many 'utopian' religious communities established in the US during the nineteenth century, particularly those by the Amish, Quaker, and Shaker sects.

An entire code of behaviour and set of ritualistic ceremonies has grown up around the constructed mythology of 'those we do not speak of'. Red is to be shunned (because it attracts them). Yellow is said to serve as a kind of creature-repellent. There is a strong attachment to communal celebrations and rituals, such as the 'Fall Festival' and the 'Ceremony of Meat' (during which a freshly slaughtered animal carcass is left at the edge of the boundary between the village and the forest as an offering). This ceremony is carried out by a quartet of young people. Their parents know that the whole thing is a sham, but as with the other rituals, the act helps bind the community together and reinforce their children's dread of the outside world. Defending the settlement against outsiders – be they Indian, demonic, or simple non-conformists – again plays a vital role in reinforcing the bonds of collective identity in a rural setting.

As previously noted, Pennsylvania was a popular destination for religious groups seeking freedom from persecution and outside interference. Theology aside, Walker's project has arisen from similar motives, but most particularly from the abhorrence which he and the other elders feel towards the greed and violence of the modern city. The community, therefore, represents a complete rejection of the values and modes of living found in the late twentieth-century US. It is an entirely artificial construct founded by damaged individuals who have cherry-picked what they perceive to be the most attractive elements in American history in order to create their own orderly, insular little world. This means that when one watches the film for a second time, elements that initially seemed like irritating lapses in historical accuracy – the stilted, euphemism-heavy language, the fact that the villagers way of life seems too antiquated for even an isolated rural community in the late nineteenth century, and the gender-balanced council of elders (it is worth noting that every single person in the community is white, however) – make more sense.[165] From the outset, there's something not quite right about its evocation of the past, and we eventually realise that this is because it isn't actually the 'past' at all. The elders are essentially role players who have invested everything they have in an artificial world. The village is a simulacrum, a copy of something that never quite existed in the first place. It could even be argued that the village is a perfect version of the 'achieved utopia' that Jean Baudrillard discusses in *America* (1988):

> What do you expect a 'successful' revolution to look like? It is paradise. Santa Barbara is a paradise; Disneyland is a paradise; the USA is a paradise. Paradise is just paradise. Mournful, monotonous, and superficial it may be, it is paradise. There is no other. If you are prepared to accept the consequences of your dreams – not just the political and sentimental ones, but the theoretical and cultural ones as well – then you must still regard America today with the same naive enthusiasm as the generations that discovered the New World.[166]

Quoting Octavio Paz, Baudrillard notes, 'America was created in the hope of escaping from history, of building a utopia sheltered from history, and that it has in part succeeded in that project, a project it is still pursuing today.'[167] Walker's village is self-consciously historical – a nostalgic vision that necessitates leaving the 'real' world behind. He has used his wealth to insulate the community from all influences save those which he and the other elders have created – buying up vast tracts of land on the pretence that he is creating a private nature reserve, securing the territory with fences and guards, and even bribing the Federal Aviation Administration to ensure that no planes fly overhead. If we exclude the threats they have created themselves, there are no outside forces for the villagers to fear. As a result, the greatest danger of all, inevitably, is that which comes from within – from the generation who know no other life but that which has been presented to them by their elders. As Cotton Mather knew only too well, it is in the second and third generations after its establishment that a community is most vulnerable (just as family businesses seldom survive into a third generation). Whilst it was material prosperity and the confluence of outside influences which put paid to Mather's hopes for the maintenance of what he considered the 'model' Puritan community,[168] in *The Village*, the community is threatened by fears that isolation is placing its residents in physical danger due to the lack of access to modern medical expertise.

The film's plot concerns as a series of events involving Ivy Walker (Walker's daughter), Lucius Hunt (Joaquin Phoenix), and Noah Percy (Adrien Brody), young people brought up knowing no other life than this, who threaten to unravel the fabric of lies their elders have woven. In different ways, the action of all three initially challenges but ultimately reinforces the isolationist policies of their community. It is significant that both Noah and Ivy have already suffered because of the village's rejection of modern medicine and that Lucius will do so later on. Noah, though in his mid-twenties, clearly has the mental capacity of a child, and whilst he is seemingly sweet natured he is prone to outbursts of violence (indeed, it is his aggression that drives the last third of the film). His perpetually childlike state serves as an obvious metaphor for the state of intentional ignorance which the elders have imposed upon their children. Noah will always be a child trapped in the body of a man, just as his contemporaries have been prevented from ever gaining full knowledge of their circumstances. His stasis – he will never mentally mature, or marry, or have children of his own – also replicates the arrested development of the village itself. It may, supposedly, be '1897', but the village is so shut off from the political, economic, and technological realities of twenty-first century life that for its young people it may as well be 1897 *every* year.

Noah's refusal to stay within the strictly delineated boundaries of the village manifests itself at first in the form of forays into the forest. When an animal-like howl is heard during the funeral feast, the others look around them in fear: he laughs and claps delightedly. When Ivy and Lucius recoil in terror from a red flower (this taboo against 'the bad colour' may reflect the abhorrence towards bloodshed that prompted the village's creation), Noah picks it up and presents it to Ivy. We later realise that he shows none of the fear displayed by the other youngsters because he has in his own way realised that it is all a hoax – 'a farce', as Walker later puts it. Because of his disability, however, Noah lacks the ability to properly process this information, and is unable to communicate it to anyone else. Presenting the red flower to Ivy may be his way of showing that there is nothing to be afraid of.

Noah's transformation into the very 'monster' that he alone of all the second-generation villagers knows to be a controlling lie is an inevitable consequence of the fact that he possess forbidden knowledge that he is unable to pass on. Like Goodman Brown, he becomes 'the chief horror of the scene' when he repeatedly stabs Lucius. The attack may first of all be the result of his frustrated romantic/sexual feelings towards Ivy (it happens soon after the she and Lucius have become engaged), but it could also be seen as an expression of anger at the fact that he and his entire cohort have been lied to for their whole lives.

Noah's attack on Lucius prompts Edward Walker to compromise, for the first time, the isolationist policy central to the survival of the village in its current state. We first encounter Lucius at a village meeting where he stands up in front of the assembled elders (including his mother, Alice [Sigourney Weaver]) to ask their permission to travel into the nearest 'town' in order to 'gather new medicines and information of what has happened in the world'. His belief that those who are 'pure of intention' will be safe is based on the fact that Noah has been able to venture into the forest without coming to harm. His request is refused, but the scene reinforces the film's suggestion that Lucius is a kind of fully functional counterpart to Noah. Although there is no suggestion that either he or any of the other young people suspect the true nature of their 'reality' (and they remain obedient and respectful towards their parents/elders throughout the film), the fact remains that Lucius is an able-bodied and intelligent young man who has clearly devoted much thought to their situation. It stands to reason that sooner or later, someone like him would begin to question the rules, and be tempted to traverse the boundary between forest and settlement, a misdeed that he publicly confesses to when he admits to 'crossing the forbidden line'[169] in a meeting called after an incursion supposedly made by the creatures. Noah's exploration of the forest, therefore, represents the first crack in the community's facade, and his attempt to murder Lucius widens it even further, by further illustrating elder August Nicholson's observation, 'You may run from sorrow, but sorrow will find you.'

Both Noah and Lucius love Ivy, although in very different ways. Though Edward Walker has more than one daughter, she is obviously his favourite. Her loss of sight as a child causes him considerable guilt – as with Noah's condition, the unspoken question of what could have been done for her back in the real world always hangs in the air. Ivy's obvious bond with Noah – shattered when he tries to kill Lucius – must be at least partially due to the fact that both have disabilities which mark them out as 'different'.

Ivy's blindness also proves exceptionally convenient for the elders (and Shyamalan). It is she who is chosen to go into the 'towns' in order to procure the antibiotics necessary to improve Lucius's chance of survival. Before she embarks upon her journey, Walker takes her to 'the shed that is not to be used', shows her the elaborate costumes that facilitates their ruse, and tells her the truth about 'those we do not speak of'. Crucially, he says nothing about the true nature of 'the towns'. When explaining his unilateral decision to the other elders, Walker claims that Lucius's case is different from that of the other youngsters who have died from the lack of modern medical care because his injuries were the result of violence. However, his own unexpressed love for Alice, as well as the fact that Lucius is engaged to his favourite daughter, obviously have more to do with the decision, which rather undermines the supposedly democratic principles of the village. Walker has acted in his own interests, not those of the community. He attempts to gloss over this fact by gravely connecting Ivy's quest to the very fate of the entire venture: 'If this place is worthy she'll be successful in her quest.'

Ivy is soon abandoned by her cowardly escorts – two young men who refuse to believe that the bag of 'magic rocks' she carries will protect them from harm. Her painstaking trudge through the woods soon becomes a suspenseful cat-and-mouse chase with the 'creature' that suddenly appears despite all of Walker's assurances to the contrary. It is a moment that wrong-foots both the character and the audience. It also resembles a life-and-death re-enactment of the games of tag and hide-and-seek Ivy used to play with Noah. This is, of course, intentional: the 'creature' *is* Noah, who has escaped from the room where he had been confined following his attack upon Lucius. His association with the forest is now complete, and we realise that the mutilated animals left strewn about the village must have been killed by him, and that he was responsible for the 'rogue' creature incursions that so concerned the elders. Unbeknownst to anyone until he tried to murder Lucius, Noah is a deeply disturbed individual dangerously empowered by his awareness that all is not as it seems. The hoax perpetuated by the elders literally allows him to run wild. Once again, therefore, the Rural Gothic trope of the individual who somehow becomes separated from the community and whose freedom of movement threatens its safety is replicated here.

Though she ultimately vanquishes her attacker – Noah is impaled in a pit filled with branches – and gets the medicine for Lucius with unconvincing ease, by the end of the film, Ivy is still only privy to part of the truth about the village. She literally cannot see what is right in front of her when she climbs over the fence that surrounds the woods and encounters the security guards employed by her father's company. We may see the various details which reveal that these events are taking place in the present day, and learn that the forest is actually a vast nature reserve owned by the Walker family but she, obviously, cannot (which is why she was allowed to cross the boundary in the first place). Like Noah, whose death, Walker implies to his devastated parents, is not in vain because he has helped 'make our stories real', Ivy's ordeal in the wilderness and triumphant return help give credence to the lies that underpin the community's very existence.

As Collier notes, by revealing the truth about the 'creatures', 'Walker has anointed his daughter to the elite of the village's second generation, a position for which she then shows herself worthy by passing the test in the woods'.[170] Given that the ruse can only be perpetuated if at least some members of this cohort are enlisted into the conspiracy, it seems likely that both Ivy and Lucius will soon become active participants in the supposedly benign ruse that will keep their contemporaries – and any children they might have themselves one day – in line. As Walker says, 'It is in them that our future lies. It is in Ivy and Lucius that this way of life will continue.' However, whilst the status quo has likely been preserved for another generation at least, it is at the cost of the considerable suffering endured by Lucius, Ivy's trial in the wilderness, and Noah's death. As in the other Rural Gothic texts discussed in this chapter, therefore, the actions of the older generation have dire consequences for their children. Furthermore, in *The Village*, we once more encounter youngsters who find themselves obliged – or compelled – to replicate the rituals practised by their parents in order to reinforce a deeply problematic status quo designed to keep the community in the wilderness together at all costs. To return to the painfully ironic adage which was erected on a sign in the centre of Jonestown (perhaps the most devastating real-life example of the toll that creating a new community in the wilderness can take, and of the collective tunnel vision, fanaticism, and in this instance, downright insanity, that so often accompanies such an enterprise), *The Village* ultimately demonstrates once more that 'those who do not remember history are condemned to repeat it'.

3
'Going Windigo': 'Civilisation' and 'Savagery' on the New Frontier

'The path to civilisation is not always civilised,' reads the tag line for Kelly Reichardt's revisionist western *Meek's Cutoff* (2010). The film is about a party of settlers in an 1840s wagon train bound for the new frontier. Theirs is a journey that, in real life, was repeated countless times by those who saw the West as 'another name for opportunity'.[1] Yet as the film makes clear – whilst the expanding frontier and the opportunities that it presented were enticing, the dangers were considerable. *Meeks Cutoff* presents an evocative and often eerie portrait of people moving through a landscape they do not understand. The group's blustering, buckskin-wearing guide, Stephen Meek (Bruce Greenwood), initially presents the travellers with an image of the West familiar to them from dime novels and newspaper clippings, but he is actually a murderous fool who has led them dangerously astray. Indeed, the film opens with the sight of one of their number disconsolately carving the word 'lost' into a tree trunk.

Though based on the story of the real 'Meek's Cutoff', the film is implicitly haunted by a much more infamous story of hardship on the Oregon trail: that of the Donner party, who were also victims of poor navigation, inclement weather, and unforgiving terrain. However, whilst the pioneers who made up Meek's wagon train were assailed by hunger and thirst as they meandered across the salt flats of the Oregon high desert, they never had to resort to the truly desperate measures of their snowbound contemporaries, who ended up eating the corpses of their travelling companions.[2]

As we have seen elsewhere in this book, the consumption of substances that would, in other, more 'civilised' circumstances, be considered abhorrent is a recurrent trope in American horror and Gothic narratives in which the wilderness or rural setting is significant. In Mary

Rowlandson's captivity narrative, as in the other historical accounts discussed in this chapter, the rigours of the journey through the wilderness forces white travellers to act in ways that would normally be seen as unacceptable. This chapter will discuss the compromises and, most of all, the adaptations that accompanied the movement from east to west, paying particular attention to the frequency with which the trope of cannibalism – both in the literal and in the metaphorical sense – manifests itself. As in previous chapters, the impact of certain real-life historical episodes upon such narratives will also be considered: the stories of the Donner party and of Alfred Packer are, as we shall see, particularly relevant here. I will also discuss the ways in which the Native American Windigo myth is appropriated in *The Shining* (1977, 1980) and *Ravenous* (1998) in order to critique the imperialist assumptions underlying the doctrine of 'Manifest Destiny'.

'We are starved!': cannibalism in colonial Jamestown

Cannibalism was a feature of the European relationship with the Americas from the very earliest days of exploration and colonisation. As Shirley Lindenbaum observes, 'even the very word "Cannibal" is said to be a legacy of Columbus's second voyage to the Caribbean in 1493':

> Referring originally to the Caribs in the Antiles who were identified as eaters of human flesh, the term was subsequently extended as a descriptive term for flesh eaters in other populations (Hulme, 1993, p.16). The discourse of cannibalism, which began with the encounter between Europe and the Americas, was to become a defining feature of colonial encounters in the New World, and especially the Pacific, during which the image of the 'noble savage' suffered progressive degradation. As a prime symbol of signifier of 'barbarism' the cannibal was central to the construction of the cultural 'other', and to Enlightenment notions of refinement, modernity, and Western civilisation.[3]

As Lindenbaum and scholars such as Jeff Berglund and Maggie Kilgour have suggested, the subject of cannibalism has, therefore, in recent years often been used 'by authors and cultural producers to critique imperialist policies and the ideologies of race, gender, sexuality and class that support them'.[4] There can be no quicker way than to dismiss another society as barbarous and savage then by characterising them as eaters of human flesh, and as such, doing so has often proven a convenient justification for aggressive European colonisation.

Berglund further notes, 'Defining the Other as a barbaric cannibal, one who may extinguish your life, clearly distinguishes the boundaries between good and evil, between *me* and *you*.'[5] It is an observation that brings to mind Roy Harvey Pearce's suggestion (1953), 'The Indian became important for the English mind not for what he was in and of himself, but rather for what he showed civilized men that they were not and must not be.'[6] What interests me here are not accounts, however, of the barbaric 'Other' eating human flesh, and acting in ways which violate one of the principal tenets of 'civilisation' – the unspoken (because it hardly need be said) understanding that other people are not food (or as Malcolm Bradbury once put it, that *Eating People Is Wrong* [1960]). Instead, I will focus on narratives featuring survival cannibalism undertaken by white Americans of European descent, and consider how this trope relates to the conflict between order and chaos, 'civilisation', and 'savagery' that lies at the very heart of the Rural Gothic. (cannibalism of a somewhat different nature will also be discussed in the next chapter.)

Recent archaeological research has conclusively confirmed the longstanding allegation that cannibalism occurred during one of the earliest attempts to establish a permanent colony in the New World. After John Smith was expelled from Jamestown in 1609, the settlement underwent a period of hardship so severe that it almost died out all together. The winter of 1609–10 was later referred to as 'The Starving Time'. The most vivid recollections of this period come from George Percy, who served as governor during this period 'during which more than 400 colonists died'.[7] Percy's account is not entirely unbiased, given that, as Rachel Hermann notes, he had a vested interest in presenting the events as a freak occurrence rather than as a result of bad leadership and a lack of proper preparation,[8] but nevertheless, it is based on first-hand experience. Percy describes in considerable detail the unpalatable substances that the colonists ate as the winter went on:

> Then having fed upon horses and other beasts as long as they lasted, we were glad to make shift with vermin as dogs, cats, rats, and mice. All was fish that came to net to satisfy cruel hunger as to eat boots, shoes, or any other leather some could come by, and, those being spent and devoured, some were enforced to search the woods and to feed upon serpents and snakes and to dig the earth for wild and unknown roots, where many of our men were cut off of and slain by the savages.[9]

Eventually, some of the colonists are said to have resorted to eating the dead:

> And now famine beginning to look ghastly and pale in every face that nothing was spared to maintain life and to do those things which seem incredible as to dig up dead corpses out of graves and to eat them, and some have licked up the blood which has fallen from their weak fellows.[10]

In John Smith's second-hand account of that winter, it is the grave of a 'savage' that is plundered in this manner, but Percy, tellingly, doesn't specify whether the corpses consumed are European or Indian. Once the taboo against violating the graves of the dead and eating human flesh is violated in this manner, we are told by Percy that one man, 'Collines' [sic], took things even further:

> [...] one of our colony murdered his wife, ripped the child out of her womb and threw it into the river, and after chopped the mother in pieces and salted her for his food. The same not being discovered before he had eaten part thereof, for the which cruel and inhumane fact I adjudged him to be executed, the acknowledgement of the deed being enforced from him by torture having hung by the thumbs with weights at his feet a quarter of an hour before he would confess the same [...][11]

Robert Appelbaum argues that the story of Collines and his ill-fated wife was retold again and again in the literature of early Virginia, because '[...] it served as a symbol of absolute extremity – the end not only of the natural means of human sustenance but of the natural restraint on human impulses that would several centuries later be discussed so compellingly in Conrad's *Heart of Darkness*'.[12] He further suggests that the fact that the English initially refused to adapt the 'food system' that had sustained them back in Europe contributed to their deprivations. In other words, Indian patterns of consumption were notable for their variety, and they moved around in order to maximise their ability to find sustenance. The English stayed in one place, and outside of feasts, tended to eat the same thing day after day, albeit with some seasonal variation.

Appelbaum also notes that in order to facilitate this settled lifestyle, the English salted and preserved animal products rather than eating them on the spot. Collines the cannibal, therefore, follows standard

English procedure when it comes to fresh kills. In a detail oddly reminiscent of Rowlandson's refusal to eat a foetal deer, he discards the unborn child ripped from his wife's womb, and salts his bounty. 'Even when practicing cannibalism, the Englishman attempts to reproduce the conditions of a society without hunger. Indeed, in refusing to gorge himself at the site of his kill, he practiced not only providence but moderation.'[13] Many of the most horrific moments in horror and Gothic narratives that feature cannibalism relate to exactly this kind of brutal utilitarianism expressed towards the human body. It is bad enough for a starving, insane, or 'possessed' individual to consume the body – living or otherwise – of another human being, but this kind of behaviour could be viewed as something akin to a wild animal attack. As we shall see in Chapter 4, we enter another realm of nastiness when a person who is slain for their flesh is systematically and carefully butchered.

Memories of 'The Starving Time' acted as a cautionary tale that shaped both Virginia's future and that of English settlement in North America in general, as 'Jamestown became America's first creation myth'.[14] European settlers expected to encounter cannibalism when they travelled to the New World because they'd already heard so many stories about man-eating natives.[15] What they didn't expect, of course, was to end up as cannibals themselves.

As Berglund observes, Indian captivity narratives such as Rowlandson's contain numerous references to cannibalism.[16] 'Such captivity tales explicitly explore estrangement from the familiar (and familial) and mark the concomitant terrors of destruction and incorporation into another alien body or group of people.'[17] Rowlandson genuinely fears that she will be eaten by her captors: they exacerbate her terror by pretending to have already devoured her son. Yet, Rowlandson's growing familiarity with and acceptance of the Indian way of life, and of *eating*, highlights the rapidity with which conventional European mores can be overthrown by the will to survive. What is further emphasised here is the fact that survival in the 'New World' can only come about through adaptation. However, the question of what is lost – and just what is gained – once this process has taken place is one that surfaces repeatedly in the Rural Gothic. The individual who has been changed by their ordeal in the wilderness may find themselves irrevocably distanced not only from their community, but also from themselves. It is a trope which is particularly notable in Charles Brockden Brown's *Edgar Huntly* (1799).

Killing Indians and eating panthers: *Edgar Huntly*

Wieland (1798) may have been subtitled 'An American Tale', but the protagonists still had one foot in Europe, and the heroine ultimately reversed the journey from the Old World to the New made by her ill-fated father. Whilst the complications of life in Europe still surface in *Edgar Huntly* – mainly in the person of Clithero, the Irish servant whose suspicious behaviour kicks off the whole plot – this is, nevertheless, an even more defiantly *American* text. It is also the first Brown novel in which the action largely takes place outdoors.[18] Most interesting of all is that the novel also makes a connection between starvation (allied with entrapment in an unfamiliar wilderness) and the rapid erosion of 'civilised' sensibilities.

Edgar Huntly begins his journey from refined young farmer to panther-eating, Indian-killing renegade when he follows Clithero (the Irish servant whom he believes has murdered his best friend, Waldegrave) into the Pennsylvanian wilderness and locates him in a mysterious cave. Edgar observes that the path through the cave was '[...] a maze, oblique, circuitous, upward and downward [...]'.[19] When Clithero suddenly disappears, Huntly presumes that he has fallen to his death, and unlike Hawthorne's Rueben Bourne, considers it his solemn duty to give the man a 'proper' burial. However, this is complicated by the fact that the landscape beyond his homestead is, for the white man, essentially unknowable. 'Perhaps no one was more acquainted with the wilderness than I, but my knowledge was extremely imperfect.'[20] Nonetheless, he becomes a reluctant trailblazer, and claims, 'Since the birth of this continent, I was probably the first who had deviated this remotely from the customary parts of men.'[21] Of course, he's wrong on two counts: the local Indians, are more than familiar with the territory, as is Clithero, who isn't dead at all, but has become an unhinged 'Wildman' in 'scant and coarse garb' who flatly refuses to leave his new home.[22]

There has long been an association between the Indian and the Wildman in the American cultural consciousness, because both are perceived to occupy

> a position on the other side of the strictly maintained boundary between civilized and savage [...] Wildness is lack and the Wildman's lack of language, religion and family threatened these institutions, the self-authenticating definition of the civilized. By the same token,

the very idea of 'civilized' depended on the idea of the other, of what 'civilized' was not.[23]

There are also considerable resemblances between the Wildman and the Indian *killer*, who is similarly 'without something', in this case, 'a settled life and a self-defining civilized identity'.[24] Edgar, as we shall see, is changed by his time in the wilds of Pennsylvania from well-bred young gentleman to first, Wildman, and then, Indian killer.

Edgar resolves to carry food back to Clithero so that he won't starve to death, and eventually gets to hear his story. Whilst he claims to be responsible for the death of the woman he loved (hence his guilty demeanour), Clithero denies all involvement in Waldegrave's death. This revelation, as well as the fact that Edgar faces a terrible dilemma in his own personal life (he has promised Waldegrave's sister, his own fiancée, that he will copy her brother's letters, but previously vowed to their author that he would never share them)[25] soon takes a powerful toll on the young man's already fragile psyche. One fateful night, he suddenly wakes up in the darkest, deepest recesses of the cave with no memory of how he got there. Like Clithero, he '[...] becomes a somnambulist, separated from his betrothed, and reduced to Clithero's elementary condition'.[26] (The dramatic possibilities of sleepwalking also form the basis of Brown's short story 'Somnambulism: A Fragment' [1797].)

Edgar soon finds himself struggling to control his most primal impulses. Though he tells us that 'My temper never delighted in carnage and blood', he nevertheless especially despises rattlesnakes and cougars, and sees it as his duty to 'exterminate' them whenever they are found – an attitude that will soon extend to his dealings with the Indians.[27] The weak and delusional young man is soon reduced to a truly desperate state, in which hunger and thirst dominate above everything else:

> My hunger speedily became ferocious. I tore the lining of my shirt between my teeth and swallowed the fragments. I felt a strong propensity to bite the flesh from my arm. My heart overflowed with cruelty, and I pondered the delight I should experience in rending some living animal to pieces, and drinking its blood, and grinding its quivering fibres between my teeth.[28]

Edgar's hunger prompts him to consider autocannibalism, thus making the collapse of boundaries identified by Berglund as being one of the most unsettling things about cannibalism ('in being consumed, *You* become *Me, I* become *You-Me*'[29]) even more destabilising. He considers suicide, and is uncontrollably excited by the thought of drinking his own blood. However, he is saved from either prospect when he is forced to battle two panthers that have also discovered the cave.[30] One falls off a ledge, but Edgar kills the second at close quarters with his trusty 'Tomhawk' [sic],[31] and reluctantly accedes to the inevitable, albeit not without a Rowlandson-style bout of self-justification:

> My hunger had arrived at that pitch where all fastidiousness and scruples were at an end [...] I will not shock you by relating the extremes to which dire necessity had driven me. I review thus scene with loathing and horror. Now it is past I look back upon it as some hideous dream [...] If this appetite has sometimes subdued the sentiments if nature, and compelled the mother to feed upon the flesh of her off spring, it will not excite amazement then that I did not turn from the yet warm blood and reeking flesh of a brute.[32]

Edgar has difficulty keeping his unorthodox meal down, and experiences near-fatal stomach pains. However, like the symbolic pangs of spiritual rebirth that they are, his suffering abates, and he is able to follow the light from a fire that he sees in the depths of the cave to an exit. His ordeal is far from over, however. The fire is surrounded by the same Indians who made 'frequent and destructive inroads into the heart of the English settlements'.[33] His parents were murdered by this very band. As a result, Edgar '[...] never looked upon, or called up the image of a savage without shuddering'.[34] Yet, like many of the protagonists discussed in this chapter, Edgar will soon become the thing that he fears most. Though he considers sneaking outside, his natural chivalry comes to the fore when he spies a helpless white woman who has been taken captive. He steals a musket and hatchet from the Indians, and, overcoming his naturally mild manner, quickly kills them. Throughout, he is gripped by a terrible thirst that he assuages as soon as he gets outside and finds water.

Edgar and the girl flee though what is, as Toles notes, an oddly unexpressive, 'sterile' landscape, which no longer seems even slightly familiar. He is, quite literally, *bewildered*. 'I scarcely knew in what region of the globe I was placed in.'[35] As in Rowlandson, hope springs from seeing evidence of the white presence on American soil, such as the '[...] obscure paths made by cattle'. Having followed such a path, he comes upon a dwelling, and has a moment to look over the weapons that he seized from the cave. He is horrified to discover that the musket is his own, which had been left in the house of his uncle (in which his younger sisters live as well). Deducing that the last vestiges of his family had been 'assailed by these inexorable enemies', he finds that the remorse experienced after the death of the Indians has vanished, and been replaced by the desire for vengeance.[36] From this point on, the narrative takes on an increasingly nightmarish tenor.

Soon thereafter a rescue party happens upon the field of battle, and after witnessing the young woman being reunited with her father, Edgar falls so deeply unconscious that the rescuers think he is dead and leave him behind. When he awakes he finds that he has been lying on 'the breast of him whom I had shot' and that his own 'dishevelled locks were matted and steeped in that gore which had overflowed and choked up the orifice [i.e. the bullet hole]'.[37] After gathering ammunition from the dead Indians, a battered and bloodstained Edgar heads for home once more. He is, again, in the grip of a severe thirst, and a bubbling spring that he happens upon provides him with 'unspeakable' refreshment. Now 'satiated and gorged with slaughter', he hopes that the necessity for violence has passed.[38] However, an Indian from the earlier attack has survived, and Edgar must again rationalise the killing of another human being: 'Should he be spared, he would still roam the wilderness, and I may still be fated to encounter him.'[39] What's more, 'He will live only to pursue the same sanguinary trade; to drink the blood and exult in the laments of his unhappy foes, and of my own brethren.'[40] He shoots the Indian, but his foe does not die straight away, and Edgar must stab him with a bayonet. Having left his tomahawk in the cave, Edgar takes one from his dead enemy, finding that a contradictory welter of emotions are raging in his mind: 'Horror, and compassion, and remorse were mingled into one sentiment.'[41] In order to stay alive, he must cultivate recklessness and primal aggression, and 'strike blindly at every danger in his path – trusting entirely to his instincts – or risk destruction'.[42] In other words, he must let 'savagery' overcome his more 'civilised' instincts.

Edgar's journey through the American 'Heart of Darkness' has a truly relentless quality. 'Nowhere is he permitted to reorient himself, to find a provisional stability in which he can calmly reassess his situation. Instead, he is propelled from horror to horror, in a forced circulation that threatens to be endless.'[43] Although moving headlong through the wilderness makes the possibility that one will lose all sense of rational, 'civilised' self all the more probable, standing still even for a moment is an even worse idea, because when he does so, like Clara in *Wieland*, he 'finds himself paralysed and vulnerable to attack'.[44]

As Edgar nears home he encounters a powerful matriarch of the local tribes nicknamed 'Old Deb', 'a foreign presence in the otherwise sophisticated society around the Huntly farm who also symbolises "property lost and family resentment"'.[45] Edgar understands the Delaware language spoken by Deb, 'for in deeper ways than he knows, Edgar understands, sympathises and joins with Old Deb's dislocation, her loss, her resentment, and perhaps even her vengeance'.[46] It is she who has incited her fellow Indians to rise up against the settlers, and this, in fact, is why Waldegrave was murdered.[47]

Edgar finds even when he returns to 'civilisation', everything has been tainted. The first 'proper' white home that he comes across is inhabited by an insane, drunken father who is trying to burn the place down (shades here of *Wieland*, in which the domestic scene similarly becomes one of violence perpetrated by an unstable patriarch). In a turn of events that further evokes Rowlandson, the Edgar who finally makes it home alive has been changed utterly by his experiences – to the extent that he wonders if anyone will even recognise him:

> The sleek locks, neat apparel, pacific guise, sobriety and gentleness of aspect by which I was customarily distinguished, would in vain be sought in the apparition which would now present itself before them. My legs, neck and bosom were bare, and their native hue were exchanged for the livid marks of bruises and scarifications. An horrid scar was upon my cheek, and my uncombed locks; hollow eyes, made ghastly by my abstinence and cold, and the ruthless passions of which my mind had been the theatre, added to the musquet [sic] which I carried in my hand, would prepossess them with the notion of a maniac or ruffian.[48]

The return home also brings with it two major plot developments. Edgar's uncle and sisters are still alive, and second, that the men who had most lately pursued him though the wilderness were, in fact, friends who had mistaken him for an Indian attacker. As Grabo notes, this mistake is understandable: 'As he caroms from cavernous depths to mountain precipices, Edgar himself is a confused menace, disorientated, displaced. Prying into Clithero's savage guilt, he discovers his own. *His own people mistake him for a savage because he is a savage*' (my italics).[49]

It is an important observation, and one that that brings to mind Pearce's discussion of the 'Renegade', the man who deliberately 'gives wilfully over to savagism and deliberately turns against civilization' as a recurring figure in American literature.[50] Such figures reinforced the perception that 'the men who were the instruments of bringing civilisation to the frontier ran the danger of becoming savages and semi savages'.[51] It is, therefore, significant that *Edgar Huntly* is set in Pennsylvania, in 1787. From the time that he was granted his charter by the future King James II in 1682, Penn, a devout Quaker, tried his best to deal fairly with the local Indians (by the standards of the time), 'not permitting colonisation to begin until he negotiated the right to settle and purchased the land'.[52] Like all colony founders in the early years of European settlement, he 'faced a formidable task in overcoming people's deep-seated fears of the wild wood' of his new territory.[53] One way in which to lessen the primal wariness people felt towards the forests was to try to present them in the best light possible, and so the new settlement was named 'Pennsylvania' – 'Penn's Wood' – in the hope that the name would 'banish dread from a prospective colonist's mind, conjuring up instead visions of sun-dappled groves'.[54] In fact, early settlers found the thick forests so imposing that they quickly divided their new territory into two separate domains: 'the woods'[55] and 'the inhabited part of the country'.[56] The latter was the area where they, the Europeans lived, whilst 'the woods' was seen as an *empty* space, despite the fact that large numbers of Indians lived there. What is even more interesting is that, as Merrell notes, the Indians did exactly the same thing, but in reverse: for them, 'the woods' was where, according to the Iroquois, the 'Garr Hagon' – the 'inhabitants of the forest or remote lands' – i.e. the *English* – lived.[57]

The so-called 'long peace' that followed the initial colonisation of Pennsylvania stretched from 1682 to the mid-1750s.[58] However, as the number of settlers increased, 'the borderlands became a more complicated, more contentious place', and the dubious 1737 'Walking Purchase' created an atmosphere of ill-feeling that soon spilled over into outright war. After 1750, Merrell writes, 'Penn's Woods became an abattoir.'[59] Another reason for the growing hostility was that the Indian population was decreasing as the white one was rapidly expanding. In the first decades of the eighteenth century, the English colonies doubled in population roughly every generation.[60] There were 250,000 colonists in 1700, and 1.3 million 50 years later, thanks in part to the fact that the settlers usually had lots of children, there was a relatively low fatality rate, and food was abundant. The death rate was between 15 and 20 per cent lower than that in Europe.[61] The colonists spread outwards from Virginia and Massachusetts, and could soon be found all along the Appalachians, from Pennsylvania south to the Carolinas.[62] In doing so, 'they laid claim to the lands of Indian peoples, who found themselves pressed to the mountain walls'.[63] New immigrant groups such as the Germans and the Scotch Irish increasingly made their way into the back country of the Eastern Appalachians and the Shenandoah Valley. These locales were actually the first sight of the US's 'West' (a term that was, like the expression 'frontier' not necessarily geographically fixed, as it expanded outwards with each new wave of settlers pushing it further across the continent).[64]

Hostility between the two populations was by no means merely an eighteenth-century development. The first major conflict between the New English and the Indians, the so-called Pequot wars, erupted in 1637. The trouble began when Colonial leaders demanded that the Pequot surrender their children as hostages, and pay tribute. This attempt to extend English authority was refused, so as a result, the colonies of Connecticut, Plymouth, and Massachusetts declared war on the Pequot, and pressured rival tribes into joining in (encouraging civil war amongst the Indians was a common tactic).[65] Whereas the Indians still thought of themselves as members of particular bands, or tribes, the English were willing to put aside grudges to unite against a common enemy.[66] The English were at this stage also much more ruthless in their tactics. For instance, they ambushed a Pequot village in May 1637 and massacred a sleeping band of mostly old people, women, and children, leaving only 5 out of 400 still alive.[67] Such actions contradicted existing Indian custom, but were seen by the Puritans as perfectly justifiable.

By the early 1640s, most of the Pequot had been killed, captured, or sent to the West Indies as slaves. However, a generation later, the colonial leaders decided to counter the powerful Narragansett tribe by encouraging discontent amongst the remaining Pequot. The result was the next major Indian war, 'King Philip's War' (1675–76). After the Plymouth colonists executed three Indians accused of murdering an informant, the young warriors of their tribe unleashed a devastating onslaught. Between the summer and autumn of 1675, they attacked 53 of New England's 90 towns, destroying 12 completely, and often killing or capturing entire families.[68] The attacks were a massive blow to colonists, who, for decades, 'had laboured to remake the New England landscape by constructing churches, houses, fences, and barns [...] to reverse the alienation of their land, the Indian rebels systematically burned, killed, mutilated and desecrated all of those marks of English civilisation'.[69] As noted in Chapter 1, the moment that the first colonists landed on North American soil, they began to change the landscape around them in ways intentional and unintentional, most particularly by attempting to recreate the physical landscape and patterns of life familiar to them from Europe. The fact that the Indians were able to raze so many English towns to the ground during the conflict seriously undermined their sense of security. The conflict also played a major part in creating the psychological conditions that gave rise to the Salem witchcraft trials.[70]

Just as the Indians had decided that their best chance to attack the interlopers on their own terms was by adapting their tactics of 'Total War', the Puritans soon realised that 'in order to defeat the Indian enemy, you had to become more like the Indian enemy'.[71] To that end, Indian tactics, such as the preference for stealth, dispersion, ambush, and a focus on individual marksmanship, were adopted, and after 1676, the tide turned decisively in their favour.[72] The cost, however, as Taylor notes, had been very high for both sides: about 1,000 English were killed, along with roughly 3,000 Indians (a quarter of the population), and many Puritan settlements, like Rowlandson's home of Lancaster, had been devastated.[73] The costs were much higher for the Indians of New England, who, due to war, disease, hunger, and other social causes (such as the rising levels of alcohol abuse) were almost wiped out of the region entirely by 1750.[74]

It was, as Slotkin notes, that in Benjamin Church's 'Entertaining Passages Relating to Philip's War' (1716), that we can begin to see the potent prototype of the heroic Indian fighter begin to emerge. 'In the course of his hunt for the Indian King, Church became more and more like the Indian. Furthermore, he not only accepted this amalgamation of white and Indian characteristics: he actively and enthusiastically sought it.'[75] Church was of the first generation of colonists to be born in America, and as such, viewed the landscape around him in a rather different way than his predecessors, who still, in many ways, had one eye on Europe. For Slotkin, he is 'a pivotal figure in the transition between two cultures and two generations in the colonies': a man who was born and educated in the conventional Puritan manner, yet who also made his living as a farmer, hunter, and soldier.[76] He was part of the growing body of settlers who wished to explore the wilderness, and as such is 'closer to the frontier hero of later literature than to the Puritan victim-hero of the seventieth and early eighteenth century. He is totally at home in the new environment [...] his adaptation to the wilderness has not cost him his civilisation and his self-possession.'[77]

Again, note that *adaptation* is the key word here. Unlike many of the other explorers discussed here, Church still remains a rational, 'civilised' man in full possession of his faculties. The key for Church, at least as Slotkin sees it, lies in facing the terrors of the forest head on. 'Do not flee from them, but master them, and make them your own power. And if this requires you to become an Indian, then do so.'[78] A similar necessity was described by Frederick Jackson Turner in 'The Significance of the Frontier in American History' (1893, 1920), in which he argued that American history thus far had been the history of the colonisation of an ever-expanding western frontier, the 'meeting point between savagery and civilisation'. This compelled those doing the colonising to reconfigure almost every aspect of themselves:

> The peculiarity of American institutions is, the fact that they have been compelled to adapt themselves to the changes of an expanding people – to the changes involved in crossing a continent, in winning a wilderness, and in developing at each area of this progress out of the primitive economic and political conditions of the frontier into the complexity of city life.[79]

Between 1689 and 1760, there were no shortage of wars for Indian fighters such as Church to take part in, as Indians displaced by the Pequot wars and subsequent conflicts repeatedly joined forces with France in order to attack English settlements.[80] The 1763 Treaty of Paris meant that France gave its North American territories, and as a result, all land east of the Mississippi (save New Orleans) was claimed by the British.[81] By Royal proclamation that same year, the Trans-Appalachian frontier was officially designated 'Indian country', which meant that Crown authorisation was supposedly needed before lands on the Indian side of the proclamation line were purchased.[82] This didn't stop settlers moving ever further away from the original sites of English colonisation and towards the western edges of the frontier.[83] The 1783 peace treaty between the Americans and the British meant that 'Indian Country', along with its 541 million acres and countless native inhabitants was now part of the new US.[84] The Land Ordinance Act of 1785 decreed that all of the land in the 'Western territory' would be divided up into 'Townships of six miles square' drawn from a giant grid.[85] The national survey, which ensured clear boundaries and firm titles, had its drawbacks, in that it 'imposed upon the land a uniformity that took no account of contrasting valleys, different climates, or individual people who might wish for other arrangements'.[86] The act created a system that enabled the conversion of the western lands over to private ownership.[87] These incursions into Indian lands did not always go smoothly, and as a result, the figure of the Indian killer took on an ever more resonant import as a 'mediating' figure bridging the gap between old and new.[88] The effect of the western wilderness upon the colonist was profound, according to Turner:

> The wilderness masters the colonist. It finds him a European in dress, industry, tools, modes of travel, and thought. It takes him from the railroad car and puts him in the birch canoe. It strips off the garments of civilisation and arrays him in the hunting shirt and the moccasin [...] before long he has gone to planting Indian corm and plowing [sic] with an Indian stick; he shouts the war cry and takes the scalp in orthodox Indian fashion. In short, at the frontier the environment is at first too strong for the man. He must accept the conditions which it furnishes or perish, and so fits himself into the Indian clearings and follows the Indian trails. Little by little he transforms the wilderness, but the outcome is not old Europe [...] The fact is, that here is a new product that is American.[89]

This process of 'Americanisation' also had its dark side, in that the 'Indianised' European could take on the 'savage' proclivities associated with the wilderness, even if these tendencies were often rendered acceptable by the fact that the victims of this violence were Indians themselves. A good post–*Edgar Huntly* example of the figure of the 'Indian-hater' can be found in Robert Montgomery Bird's *Nick of the Woods* (1837). Set in the then new territory of Kentucky, the novel tells the story of Nathan Slaughter, who embarks upon a bloody campaign of vengeance when his family is killed by a local tribe. Not only does Slaughter, in the guise of his alter-ego 'Nick of the Woods', kill every Indian that he comes across, but he also takes great pleasure in carving a cross into their flesh. Like some kind of Indian-hating superhero, Nathan hides behind his original identity – that of the mild-mannered Quaker mocked by other settlers for his pacifism – whilst secretly prowling the woods in search of Indians to exterminate. What saves him from becoming a bogeyman figure to the whites is the fact that the Indian-hater

> fights on the side of civilisation, not against it. [...] good is accomplished through evil; for only by living as a savage is he able to destroy savages and thus, consciously or not, to contribute to the advancement of civilisation. In his evil life as a savage he must be destroyed; but since he accomplishes good, his fate and its meaning must be comprehended and celebrated as one of the tragic or celebrated works of progress.[90]

Nick of the Woods, like *Edgar Huntly*, also in broad outline conforms to the template for that most American of 1970s-era B-movie narratives: the story of the previously mild-mannered everyman who, having been pushed too far by rampaging bad guys, becomes a frighteningly effective dispenser of vigilante 'justice'. Like Charles Bronson's architect in *Death Wish* (1974), the fish-out-of water mathematician in *Straw Dogs* (1971, 2011),the middle-class parents in *Last House on the Left* (1972, 2008), or the mute seamstress in Abel Ferrara's *Ms. 45* (1981), Brown's protagonist, like Bird's, is obliged to become just as bloodthirsty as those he is compelled to hunt down and kill. A similar desire for retribution also motivates Benjamin Martin, the tomahawk-wielding, British-hating protagonist of Roland Emmerich's Revolutionary War movie *The Patriot* (2000). Though some of these vigilantes undertake their task with a certain calculated cold-bloodedness, Edgar Huntly's actions, like those of the protagonist of the original version of *Straw Dogs*, are a reaction to events happening to him at that very moment. By way of contrast, the actions of Nathan Slaughter are carried out at some remove from original events and are, therefore, more calculated. In fact, certain aspects of Brown's novel are rather similar to elements found in one of the most controversial American horror films of the past decade: Eli Roth's *Hostel* (2005).

In both narratives, 'civilised' young men discover themselves trapped in dangerous and unfamiliar territory. Edgar Huntly goes to sleep in his own bed and wakes up in a cave, finding himself, quite literally, bewildered. Josh (Derek Richardson) and Paxton (Jay Hernandez), the college student protagonists of Roth's film, take a detour from the 'safe' itinerary of their hedonistic trip around Europe, only to end up in supposedly 'war torn' Slovakia. After some drinking and casual sex, they are drugged by local women in the pay of the 'Elite Hunting' organisation, which makes the most dangerous game available to jaded businessmen looking for a new thrill. Each young man wakes up to find himself chained to a chair in a labyrinthine industrial complex (surely the urban equivalent of a cave), in the same room as someone who is about to torture them to death. After he finally makes his way out of the cave, Edgar Huntly stops to rescue a young woman. Similarly, when Paxton, who, unlike his friend Josh, has managed to kill his would-be torturer and make his way through the complex (he even manages to kill an attacker wearing a Minotaur mask), he risks his life to go back to rescue a young Japanese woman. Like Edgar, Paxton must kill or be killed: in fact, he kills more people during the course of the film than the evil organisation he is trying to escape. Having finally made his way to onto a train and across the border into Austria, Paxton comes across the German businessman who killed his friend. Following him into some public toilets, he ambushes his prey in one of the stalls, mutilates him (just as he himself has been mutilated), and cuts his throat, before heading home.

Hostel, therefore, tells a very familiar American story – that of the righteous avenger who becomes as savage as those he or she is hunting down – but uses Eastern Europe as a stand-in for an American setting. As such, the film, perhaps, suggests that now that the American continent has been 'tamed', the threat to its citizens lies not within national borders, but back in the 'Old World'. Eastern Europe serves the same purpose that the American South does in the backwoods horror film: it is a place where resentful and violent locals like to take their frustrations out on more privileged outsiders, and well-brought up young gentlemen must become remorseless, vengeance-fuelled killers in order to survive.

'Eat or die': Antonia Bird's *Ravenous* (1998)

For Frederick Jackson Turner, the West was the place where American development, by necessity, had to return to primitive conditions. 'This perennial rebirth this fluidity of American life, this expansion westward with its new opportunities, its continuous touch with the simplicity of Primitive society, furnish the forces dominating American character.'[91] As Howard Kushner has noted, Turner's thesis became so influential because it offered a seemingly persuasive explanation for the importance of the West in American life; the frontier was a safety valve for urban unrest, and it was a place where American democracy could continually be renewed. Most famously, Turner asserted that after 1890, the frontier was closed.[92] Though now largely discredited, Turner's assertions still exert considerable influence, most likely because they 'reflect both the actual experience and ideological underpinnings of American expansion'.[93] The frontier thesis persists, in other words, because it tells Americans something they would very much like to believe about themselves:

> Although its character may vary, the frontier myth retains an essential narrative: migrants with traditional old world and/or urban habits and values conquered and then dominated the savage wilderness and, in the process were themselves transformed into pragmatic individualists. The lesson learned from this encounter with nature is that any man willing to expend the energy and sacrifice old ideas can transform himself into anything he wants to be.[94]

In the section that follows, I will discuss *Ravenous*, a 1998 horror film that dramatises many of these ideas about transformation and adaptation in a manner that directly critiques the doctrine of 'Manifest Destiny'. It also draws upon real-life historical incident (specifically, the cases of Alfred Packer and of the Donner party), as well as Native American folklore. The 1790 federal census – the first – found that less than 100,000 Americans lived west of the Appalachian Mountains.[95] By 1840, seven million – 40 per cent of the total population – resided there.[96] Faragher and Hine suggest that one of the main reasons why the British triumphed over the French in North America was because the British had more settlers. In fact, 'Settlement was the key to America's conquest of the continent.'[97] The discovery of gold in the Northern Georgia Hills in 1829 and the notorious Indian Removal Act of 1830 helped make the steady trickle of settlers a veritable flood. Indian tribes in the East were 'encouraged' to exchange their ancestral lands for government territory west of the Mississippi. Addressing Congress several months after the act passed, President Andrew Jackson discussed the plan in terms that made it very clear that the original inhabitants of the continent were surplus to requirements:

> Philanthropy would not wish to see this continent restored to the condition in which it was found by our forefathers. What good man would prefer a country covered with forests and ranged by a few thousand savages to our extensive republic, studded with cities, towns and prosperous farms, embellished with all the improvements which art can devise or industry execute, occupied by more than 12,000,000 happy people, and filled with all the blessings of liberty, civilisation, and religion? [...][98]

The Indian nations known as the five 'civilised' tribes, were not amongst the 12 million happy citizens that Jackson spoke of: not only were they being referred to as though they were already extinct, but they were being forced to leave their homelands behind and venture into unknown territory already occupied by rival tribes. The Cherokee Nation, who would shortly thereafter be forced to embark upon the notorious 'Trail of Tears', issued a dignified response which stated, in part,

> We wish to remain on the land of our fathers. We have a perfect and original right to remain without interruption and molestation. [...] But if we are compelled to leave our country, we see nothing but

> ruin before us. The country west of the Arkansas territory is unknown to us.[99]

Their pleas fell on deaf ears. It had already been decided at the highest levels – and, indeed, by providence itself, as newspaper editor John L. O'Sullivan put it, in the 1845 editorial in which he coined the phrase 'Manifest Destiny' – that the new republic was going to encompass the entire continent.

By 1840, 'Oregon Fever' had struck, and thousands of Americans, attracted by the territory's high-quality land, timber, and fur (as well as its proximity to Puget Sound) made their way there to settle.[100] In accordance with the Oregon Treaty in June 1846, the territory was divided by simply extending the existing boundary between the US and Canada – the 49th parallel – further westward. As well as providing a tempting prospect for prospective settlers, the 'Oregon Trail' also provided a convenient thoroughfare for those wishing to make their way to California, which it was (rightly) believed that the US would soon be able to wrest from Mexico. By 1846, word of a swift new wagon route to the 'Promised Land' beyond the Sierra Nevada had made its way east, and a new influx of emigrants headed west.[101] Amongst them was the Donner party (named after their initial leader, George Donner), whose lengthy ordeal left a lasting impression upon American popular culture, most particularly because their story so vividly illustrated the horrible necessities that extremity could force upon ordinary men and women. Indeed, for George R. Stewart (whose novel *Earth Abides* (1949) will be discussed in Chapter 5), the Donner party were 'a microcosm of humanity, to be tested with a severity to which few groups of human beings have been subjected, destined to reveal the extremes of which the human body and mind are capable'.[102]

The story of the Donner party further illustrates that bad things happen to white people interacting with the American landscape when they are forced to deviate from their original plans. The trouble started with the fact that, like all travellers who hoped to make it through the Oregon Trail alive, they had a narrow window of time in which to make their journey.[103] The group's downfall came courtesy of a book entitled *The Emigrants Guide to Oregon and California*, by one Elijah White, who had settled in California and was determined to attract other settlers. He was determined to promote a new shortcut west, despite the fact that he had never travelled it himself.[104] It was on his advice that the Donner party chose to traverse the so-called 'Hastings Cut-off'. They had already had an onerous journey even before reaching the edges of the Sierra Nevada range, but by then had completed all but the last 100 miles of their 2,000-mile journey.[105] It seemed as if the end was in sight. Nature had other plans. Having reached Truckee Lake, which represented their last major obstacle, the weary travellers decided to rest for a short time rather than head straight into the mountains. That very night, it snowed so heavily that they had no choice but to wait out the long winter at the lake.[106]

Eighty-eight settlers left Independence, Missouri, in the spring of 1846. Six had died en route, one had been left to die, and three had crossed the mountains ahead of the snow (and would later be instrumental in leading the relief parties back to the main group later that winter). Seventy-eight were now left huddled in makeshift shelters at Truckee Lake.[107] Faced with rapidly dwindling stores, the Donner party were forced to consume the only source of protein left: the bodies of those who died. In addition, in a detail that is often curiously underplayed in accounts of their ordeal, Rarick notes that two Indian guides sent to help them later that winter were probably murdered before being eaten, and a group of 15 who set off to seek help also resorted to cannibalism and murder.

The sight that greeted the first relief party to make it to the lake (almost four months after the group became trapped) was a truly ghastly one:

> Some of the emigrants were still alive, but around their hovels lay partially butchered corpses, 'fleshless bones and half-eaten bodies of the victims of famine'. Limbs and skulls littered the ground, even the hair of those who had been consumed. When they moved on to the Alder Creek site, they found the children of Jacob Donner eating his heart and liver raw, the blood still on their chins.[108]

Yet, although the rescuers surveyed the scene before them with abhorrence, they knew only too well that anyone trapped in the same circumstances would have had no choice but to resort to similarly desperate measures. What the ordeal undergone by the travellers had vividly illustrated was the way in which the body's need for sustenance could override moral and cultural taboo. As Rarick notes, perceptions of the Donner party evolved as the story became widely known. Initial newspaper reports overstated the incidence of cannibalism at the lake (of the 45 survivors, half had eaten human flesh).[109] Stories of mothers who let their children starve to death and then ate the bodies were circulated, and as reports spread all over the US, ever more bizarre details were added to the original tale.[110] Not that this had any impact on the steady stream of settlers making their way west: between 1840 and 1860, a quarter of a million people crossed the continent, and very few indeed ended up eating each other (it is estimated that only about 4–6 per cent died on the journey).[111] Early accounts often blamed the Donner party themselves for the calamity:

> The last thing anyone in California wanted to suggest publically was that a harrowing catastrophe was simply an intrinsic – if highly unlikely – risk of westward migration. In the early years, therefore, the public imagination took on a twofold perception of the Donner Party – first that they were ghouls, second that they bore a substantial responsibility for their own misfortune. Together, these two ideas intertwined into an ugly and depressing perception of the emigrants. Some survivors rarely spoke of the events, almost as if they were hiding a shameful family secret.[112]

It was only a generation later, with the publication in 1879 of a book about the tragedy that downplayed the extent of the cannibalism, that the Donner party began to be seen in a more sympathetic light: as exemplars of the pioneer spirit even, who deserved their own monument.[113] For Stewart, writing in 1936, their story was ultimately an uplifting one: 'For though despair is often close at hand, it never triumphs, and through all the story runs, a sustaining bond, the primal force which humanity shares with all earthly creatures, the sheer will to live.'[114]

There was another, equally well-known and even more notorious incidence of cannibalism (and probable murder) which took place 27 years later. This case is the real-life origin of *Ravenous*. In April 1874, a bedraggled prospector named Alfred (sometimes spelled 'Alferd') Packer turned up at the Los Pinos Indian Agency in Gunnison, Colorado. He claimed to have been abandoned by his companions, and to have survived for several months in the mountains.[115] Suspicions were aroused by the fact that Packer looked oddly healthy, and had had arrived back with far more money than he had left with.[116] Several months later, the mutilated bodies of Packer's party were found in the mountains, and although Packer initially tried to pin the blame for their deaths on another member of the group, he later admitted to having eaten them in order to survive. In 1885, he was sentenced to 40 years in prison – at that time, the longest sentence ever handed down by an

American judge. Diana Di Stefano suggests that Packer's crimes aroused such strong public disapproval not only because of their severity (it was believed that he had deliberately led his party astray to kill them), but also because his actions so strongly violated the codes of behaviour deemed essential in the wilderness. 'Packer's alleged behaviour threatened an emerging cultural code among Western prospectors that relied on trust and reciprocity to lessen the risks of mountain living. Anger towards Packer stemmed not from what he ate but from the miners' perceptions that Packer broke the codes that governed behaviour in the mountains.'[117]

In a place where the winter season could last for up to nine months, and sudden storms and avalanches made living and working in the mountains particularly dangerous, shared codes of behaviour, Di Stefano argues, took on huge importance. If one trapper or prospector got into trouble in the mountains, he could, ideally, depend upon the community to dispatch a rescue team. He knew also that he could be called upon at any time to join a team going to help someone else. Packer, the false guide who led his companions to disaster, violated the rules upon which mutual survival depended. The process of adapting to the harsh new landscape had taught settlers and explorers that the chances of surviving were greatly increased if they could rely upon each other (even the sorry tale of the Donner party illustrated the heroism of the rescue teams who aided them). Packer's actions pulled the rug out from under these comforting assumptions, and in doing so, suggested that one's fellow travellers could be as dangerous as the weather.

This is certainly the case in *Ravenous*, which has the tag line: 'Survival is the only option'. The story begins during the Mexican–American war (1846–1848), which ultimately brought vast new territories fully into the US, amongst them Texas, California, New Mexico, Nevada, and Arizona.[118] The victory over Mexico helped 'promote the nation from a third-rate to a second-rate power that would have to be reckoned with in its own region'.[119]

We first encounter the film's protagonist, US Army Captain John Boyd (Guy Pearce) as he is being awarded a medal for heroism. As his fellow officers and superiors sit down to dine, Boyd looks anything but happy at the prospect of eating the oozing slab of beef in front of him. Repulsion compels him to dash outside and vomit. It is at this point that we get a flashback to the battle that brought Boyd his medal and an explanation for why both the food and the ceremony so sickened him. Rather than support his comrades in their assault on an enemy position, Boyd passed out, and, like Edgar Huntly, was mistaken for a dead man. Awakening to find himself in a pile of dead bodies, Boyd accidentally ingested the blood of his commanding officer. The blood appeared to give him both new life, and a renewed zeal for combat, which allowed him to single-handedly take the position. As Di Marco has noted, this scene 'provides a broader context for reading the film as a cultural commentary on the disaster brought about by a policy of manifest destiny and war'.[120] Boyd's refusal to fight could be seen as a form of tacit resistance to his nation's imperial ambitions, as could his inability to eat the food that is placed in front of him (a motif in the film).[121] Whilst Di Marco's reading is a persuasive one, I will also be arguing that the obsession with consumption and cannibalism seen in the film is also a recapitulation of a preoccupation seen even in the earliest days of American literature and popular culture. Namely, the awareness that leaving behind the familiar and travelling into the geographical unknown necessitates an adaptation in order to be truly successful, and that the transformations this process engenders are often unsettling ones.

Because his squeamishness does not reflect well upon the army, Boyd is sent to serve at Fort Spencer, an isolated fort built by the Spanish. The fort serves as a way station for wagon trains making their way through the Sierra Nevada, and is populated by a motley crew of misfits, including an alcoholic surgeon (Knox), a religious fanatic (Toffler), and a layabout who seems to have 'gone native' (Cleaves). The commanding officer is the genial Colonel Hart, who notes that Boyd must be seeking escape to end up in as dismal a place as this, and presciently adds, 'Funny thing about escape though – you might end up someplace worse.' The fort is also home to two Ojibwa Indians, siblings named George and Martha, of whom it is dismissively noted 'they came with the place'. Shortly after Boyd's arrival, in a development that has clearly drawn on the Packer case, a stranger (played by Robert Carlyle) is found collapsed outside in the snow. He is placed by the fire to warm up (where he lies ominously close to the cooking pot that feeds the entire fort), and after he regains his senses, claims to be a settler named 'F.W. Colqhoun'. Speaking with a strong Scottish accent, 'Colqhoun' tells the story of how his party of six, guided by the 'detestable' Colonel Ives, left the East in April, having believed the Colonel's assurances that he knew a shortcut through the Sierra Nevada. He was wrong, and they were still 100 miles from safety (like the Donner party) when the snow began, and were forced to shelter in a cave. In a familiar litany of desperation, the travellers finished off their scant supplies, then ate the dogs and the horses, before turning to roots, shoes, and belts. When asked how he survived for three months without food, Colqhoun responds, 'I said no food. I didn't say there was nothing to eat.'

According to Colqhoun's story, one of the group died, and when he returned to the cave after gathering wood, he found that the others had 'cooked his legs for dinner'. However, the 'meat' only lasted a week, and they found that it made their hunger 'more severe... savage'. Ives, Colqhoun claims, killed and ate two more survivors, before he fled into the wilderness in a bid to escape the same fate. Though Colonel Hart and the others accept the story, George tells Hart that Colqhoun is what the Objiway call a 'Windigo'. As Hart translates for the benefit of Boyd, George explains in his own language: 'A man eats another's flesh and he steals his spirit. And his hunger becomes insatiable. And the more he eats, the more he wants to, and the more he eats the stronger he gets.' 'George, does this still happen?' Hart asks, to which George responds, 'White man eats the body of Jesus Christ every Sunday.'

As David Gilmore observes, whilst there are many monsters that haunt the woods of North America, none is more terrible than the spectre of the Windigo.[122] The Windigo is described in any number of ways in Native American folklore, although some constants remain: it is a creature of superhuman size and strength, filled with rage and the hunger for human flesh. The Windigo is human-like in appearance, but also monstrous, with bulging eyes and claw-like hands, as well as a heart of ice (one sure way to kill the creature is to melt the heart).[123] The most terrifying thing of all about the Windigo, however, is that humans can, very easily 'turn Windigo' themselves – and one sure-fire method, as George's story illustrates, is to eat human flesh. As Margaret Atwood wrote in *Strange Things: The Malevolent North in Canadian Literature* (1995), 'Fear of the Windigo is twofold: fear of being eaten by one, and fear of becoming one.'[124] Indeed, that fear is so strong that so-called 'Windigo psychosis' is a long-recognised, if controversial, psychiatric disorder specific to the people of the Northern tribes of the Algonquian-speaking Indians, who had a particularly strong belief in the creatures.[125] As Di Marco notes, George is a descendant of just such a tribe.[126]

The disorder was the subject of a 1960 monograph by Morton Teicher named *Windigo Psychosis*, which compiled reports of as many recorded instances as the author could find. There were apparently numerous outbreaks of Windigo psychosis in the Northern US and Canada right up until the 1950s, and it has been posited that such symptoms derive from the fact that to the Indians, the desire to eat human flesh was seen as incomprehensible except as a result of sorcery or possession by an evil spirit.[127] On the other hand, it has been said by commentators such as Marano (1982) that so-called 'Windigo Psychotics', i.e. insane individuals who expressed or acted upon the urge to eat human flesh never actually existed, and that whilst there were cases of insanity, and also of murder and cannibalism, amongst the Indians, these latter were motivated entirely by famine.[128] Carolyn Podruchny has suggested that this 'bogeyman for adults' was a way to scare people into continuing to fully participate in society (the Windigo is distinguished by his hermit-like ways) and into following rules designed to ensure their safety and those of others (such as the taboo against eating one another, no matter how hungry you are).[129]

In *Ravenous*, Bird draws upon American history and combines it with Indian folklore to establish '[...] a concrete correlation between the iconic Windigo myth and the metaphorical cannibalism of manifest destiny'.[130] Central to this connection is the complex relationship between Boyd, the reluctant soldier, and Colqhoun, the identity-shifting cannibal who both fascinates and repulses him. Because Colqhoun claims that the rapacious Colonel Ives is still in the cave with an innocent member of their party, Hart forms a rescue party, and, led by the stranger, they head into the mountains. It soon becomes clear that their new companion is not to be trusted. He's shifty and evasive, and has an insatiable thirst for human blood. His behaviour becomes even more bizarre when they reach the cave. Boyd and another soldier, Reich (the one other competent member of the rescue party) enter and find it filled with body parts. Discovering a skeleton clad in the uniform of a colonel, Boyd realises that Colqhoun was the real murderer, and they rush outside. It's too late, however: the cannibal has fatally stabbed Colonel Hart, and gutted Toffler. After a chase during which he seems to exhibit superhuman speed and strength (as well as utter insanity), Colqhoun stabs Reich. Though the mad man is shot by Boyd, he simply will not die: the Captain has no choice but to throw himself off a cliff, and lands on top of the unfortunate Reich.

Now trapped in a hole in the ground with no supplies, a badly broken leg, and a cannibalistic murderer on his trail, Boyd finds himself contemplating what would, in other circumstances, seem utterly unthinkable. After several days of restraint, he surrenders to the survival instinct, and eats part of Reich's body. As before, the ingestion of sustenance from another soldier gives him the strength to carry on, and he is able to make his way back to the fort. Upon his arrival, we find the settlement under new command: that of the highly respected 'Colonel Ives', who is, in fact, the man previously known as Colqhoun, albeit with a snappy new uniform, neatly tended moustache, and, significantly, an American rather than a Scottish accident.

No one at the fort, (apart from Martha, who tells him, 'To stop Windigo, you must die') heeds Boyd's objections to this development. Boyd looks like a Wildman, he can produce no evidence to support his story (there are four missing soldiers, and no dead bodies), and the only authority figure who can corroborate his claim that the new Colonel and Colqhoun are the same person is Knox, who is such a drunkard that he is unable to remember what the man looked like. In fact, they all suspect that Boyd must have done something to the other men. It doesn't help that he has begun to experience terrible nightmares in which he kills and eats his comrades, a clear warning sign, according to legend, that he is about to become a Windigo himself.

It is from the moment of Boyd's return to the fort that the film's critique of the young nation's imperial ambitions and ceaseless appetite for new territory really clicks into high gear. Before, Colqhoun had conformed to a familiar stereotype in the American popular consciousness, that of what Denis Duclos calls the 'Blood Thirsty Vagrant', a close relative to the berserker figure in Norse mythology.[131] Though he is still all of these things, now that he possesses the authority of a US Army officer, Colqhoun/Ives is even more dangerous. His own sinister appetites have found a corollary in the expansionist tendencies of the nation itself. When the two of them are alone, Colqhoun tells his kindred spirit Boyd that, until recently, he had been gravely ill with tuberculosis (commonly known, of course, as *consumption*). Whilst on his way to a sanatorium out west, he heard the legend of the Windigo, killed and ate the Indian guide who told him the story, and then killed and ate another five men over the next three months, with the result that both his spiritual and physical malaise lifted completely.

But, Colqhoun/Ives notes, it is 'lonely being a cannibal', and, understandably, 'hard to make friends' – which is why he intends to turn Boyd into a Windigo as well. Indeed, Colonel Hart has become just such a creature, having been force-fed human flesh, with the result that 'by the time I regained my senses, there was no turning back. Now I feel terrific.' Colqhoun/Ives' plan is to turn the fort into a kind of monstrous parody of the US itself. Throwing out terms like 'Manifest Destiny', and 'Westward Expansion' as he gazes out at the mountain range which will (literally) provide a free meal ticket, he makes his agenda clear to Boyd: 'We just need a home. And this country is seeking to be whole.

Stretching out its arms, and consuming all it can. And we merely follow.' Although Boyd immediately responds 'Not me', his jailor insists, 'You're already one of us – almost [...] You just won't resign yourself to it.'

As Colqhoun/Ives knows, Boyd is a coward for whom 'morality is the last bastion'. To make the decision of whether or not to become a cannibal a more urgent one, he slashes Boyd in the guts, and leaves a stew made with human flesh before him. 'Famine or feast. Live or die' is the stark choice. In the end, Boyd convinces himself that it is only by eating the stew that he can act to frustrate the plan to turn the fort into an abattoir. This will be accomplished by converting General Slauson, who is in overall charge of the region. (Here the film evokes a common trope of the backwoods horror narrative: that of the settlement in the middle of nowhere populated by individuals who see those passing through as lambs to the slaughter.)

As the next scene opens, we see that spring has finally come to Fort Spencer. It is only a matter of time before fresh meat starts passing through. Boyd, now returned to health, desperately tries to convince Hart to let him go, so that he can kill Ives. Hart does so, but only on the condition that Boyd first kills *him*: he no longer wants to live like this. There follows a brutal final reckoning between Boyd and Colqhoun, each of whom recognises the other for what he truly is. Ultimately, they end up in a final, fatal embrace, impaled by the giant bear trap that Boyd has manoeuvred them into. Both know that whoever manages to outlive the other, and eat of his flesh, will find the strength to break free. As Colqhoun, who may be insane, but is always insightful, puts it in the film's final line, 'You know, if you die first, I am definitely gonna eat you. The question is, if I die, what are you gonna do?' As audience members, we already know that Boyd's sacrifice has been rendered obsolete. General Slauson has just unwittingly consumed human flesh anyway (that cheerfully bubbling communal cooking pot was his downfall). No wonder then that the final shots of the film find Martha, the only survivor of the fort's original company, leaving the fort and walking towards the wilderness. She knows that the ceaseless appetite for territory, power, and indeed, human life itself, will, like the wagon trains themselves, relentlessly rumble on. 'Even though Boyd dies a hero – he has ended his own cannibalistic urges – viewers see that the unquenched, limitless desire is a systematic problem that can't and won't be solved so easily.'[132] As Chief Sitting Bull once said of the white US, 'The love of possession is a disease with them.'[133] If this is indeed the case, few narratives have dramatised this disease in as original and as pointed a manner as *Ravenous*.

Consumption, chaos, and family values in *The Shining* and *The Road*

In this final section, I will discuss two well-known horror narratives which further dramatise the preoccupations and anxieties regarding consumption, the frontier, and the American sense of self. They are, first, Stephen King's 1977 novel *The Shining* and its 1981 film adaptation, and Cormac McCarthy's 2007 novel *The Road*.

The Shining is one of King's best-known novels, whilst the film version, though widely considered a commercial and artistic failure upon initial release, has in recent years been enshrined in the popular imagination as one of the greatest horror films ever made. Given the high profile and richness of the source material, it is hardly surprising that both versions of the story have been written about at considerable length.[134] One reading has, however, been oddly overlooked: it seems to me rather obvious that King's novel – and Kubrick's film – are each, in their own way, the story of a man who transforms into a Windigo. As such, it has much in common with the texts just discussed. For a start, this is another story that begins with a move from east to west. Though the Torrance family are living in Boulder, Colorado, when Jack is offered the job as winter caretaker at the Overlook Hotel, King makes it clear that they have recently moved from Vermont, where Jack was a teacher at an exclusive prep school until his explosive temper cost him his job. The family's move across the country replicates the wider pattern of American history. 'I think the place forms an index of the whole post World-War II American character',[135] Jack declares in the novel, and he's more right than he knows. What he has missed, however, is the fact that the Overlook's connection to the national character actually goes back much further than that. It is a connection that King repeatedly highlights. When, for instance, Danny is left alone in the family car (the modern equivalent of a wagon, of course – in fact, it actually is a *Volkswagen*), he examines the maps used during the family's journey. 'Colorado, Nebraska, Utah, Wyoming, New Mexico. He loved road maps, loved to trace where the roads went with his finger. As far as he was concerned new maps were the best part of moving west.'[136] Similarly, Wendy sees the hotel's crotchety old janitor, Watson, as epitomising what 'the west was supposed to be about' (an ironic sentiment, considering that Watson's grandfather, Robert Townley Watson, built and then lost the place. Clearly, the West has not been all that it was cracked up to be for that family, nor will it be for the Torrance clan).[137]

Danny, like Wendy, was perfectly happy with life in Vermont, but he has no choice but to accompany his parents. Wendy, of course, *does* have a choice, but she has decided to try to save her marriage. Though Jack is excited by the thought of living in the Overlook and sees it as his last chance to make something of himself (by reconnecting with his family and completing his long-in-gestation writing project), her reaction to the move, like Danny's, is lukewarm. In fact, her mind keeps turning to the horrible possibilities that can await those who lose their way in the mountains and to one infamous example in particular: that of the Donner party. Their fate is first referred to on the journey across the mountains: 'They were beautiful mountains but they were hard. She did not think they would forgive many mistakes. An unhappy foreboding rose in her throat. Further West in the Sierra Nevada the Donner Party had become snowbound and had resorted to cannibalism to stay alive.'[138] Later in the drive she asks Jack, 'You're sure the larder is fully stocked', still thinking of the Donners.[139] Once they arrive, and she is being shown around the hotel's lavishly supplied larder by resident cook (and saviour) Dick Halloran, the abundance that she is being confronted with, again, paradoxically, arouses thoughts of extremity and isolation:

> The food supplies amazed her but did not reassure her as much as she might have thought: the Donner Party kept recurring to her, not with thoughts of cannibalism (with all this food it would indeed be a long time before they were reduced to such poor rations as each other) but with the reinforced idea that this was indeed a serious business [. . .].[140]

Again, Wendy is seized by feelings of foreboding as the family are ushered into the lift by Ullman, the hotel's manager. 'Wendy had a vision of the four of them being trapped like flies in a bottle and found in the spring. . . with little bits and pieces gone. . . like the Donner Party.'[141] The final overt reference comes much later on in the novel, when Jack's deteriorating mental state and the severe weather conditions begin to make her worst presentiments of catastrophe seem increasingly prescient. The inane chatter of two radio DJs vocalises her anxiety. 'And don't go anywhere you don't have to. Remember,' the announcer added jocularly, 'that's how the Donner Party got into trouble. They just weren't as close to the nearest Seven-Eleven as they thought.'[142]

Whilst Jack continuously downplays the dangers of spending almost half a year in the Overlook (the same amount of time that the Donner party spent at Truckee Lake), Wendy's mind repeatedly returns to the worst-case scenario of historical record. As well as being a cautionary tale about what happens to those who overestimate their own ability to successfully navigate in unfamiliar territory, the Donner story is that of family members who become hopelessly trapped in each other's company, and must consume one another in order to survive. Danny may be the one with psychic powers, but the fact that she returns repeatedly to the fate of the Donner party suggests that Wendy, on a subconscious level at least, knows from the start that the hotel is, as King would characterise it, a very 'bad place'. Literal cannibalism never occurs in the Overlook, but food, consumption, and appetite are referred to throughout the novel, and, the malevolent entity that represents the true face of the hotel transform's Jack into a lurching, murderous ogre who says things like, 'The giant has come to eat you all up in your beds.'[143]

In the novel, Jack Torrance's greatest flaws are his arrogance, temper, and inability to control his longing for booze. Though his depiction here is a good deal more sympathetic than in Kubrick's film – King's Jack actually seems to like his wife and son, and he sacrifices himself so that they can escape – it is these weaknesses which allow evil forces to gain a foothold in his fragile psyche. When told, for instance, about what happened to the Gradys, the last family to spend the winter at the Overlook, he arrogantly believes that his superior intelligence will make such a scenario unthinkable, because, 'A stupid man is more prone to cabin fever, just as he's more prone to shoot someone over a card game or commit a spur-of-the-moment robbery. He gets bored [...].'[144] The trouble is, the hotel uses Jack's intellect as a means of entrapment. It appeals to the writer in him. When Wendy asks him why he's been spending so much time in the basement, poring over old newspaper clippings and scrapbooks charting the history of the hotel, Jack jokingly replies, 'Trying to find where the bodies are buried, I suppose', but he's not as far from the truth as he thinks.[145]

Once immersed in the Overlook, Jack rapidly undergoes a metamorphosis into a Windigo-like figure ('Windigo' of course sounds like 'Wendy, Go' and by giving his heroine this name, King might be subtly pointing up the folkloric roots of her husband's transformation).[146] Like the monster, he is defined by his uncontainable appetite. There is never a moment when he isn't craving a drink 'or a thousand of them'.[147] He reflects on the fate of Grady, who came to stay with a generous supply of cheap whisky, and concludes, 'He shouldn't have been here. And he shouldn't have lost his temper', but sees no parallels with his own situation. This lack of self-awareness will ultimately prove disastrous.

As the novel progresses, Jack goes through the stages which precede transformation into a full-blown Windigo. When thinking about his lifelong inability to control his temper, he realises that savagery has never lain too far from the surface of his 'civilised' behaviour. 'Passively, with no say, you ceased to be a creature of the mind and became a creature of the nerve endings; from college-educated man to wailing ape in five easy seconds.'[148] In folklore, those most likely to become a Windigo are male hunters after an unsuccessful winter: deprivation, isolation, and icy weather are also important factors.[149] Though not a hunter (although he does, unsuccessfully, tackle a wasps' nest), Jack is the one who led them to the Overlook in the first place, the one who makes the trip in to town for supplies (by way of contrast, in the film, Jack's *lack* of movement is notable). The human-turned-Windigo in Algonquian mythology finds himself increasingly subject to the prompting of supernatural spirits who appear to him in dreams.[150] As the novel progresses, Jack finds himself caught up in the fantasy world created by the hotel, and increasingly willing to carry out its orders, until he finally becomes an unthinking puppet of the 'management'.

In an observation that again can be said to apply to King's novel, Hay argues that the relationship between the affected individual and those around him is key to regulating Windigo psychosis:

> If those around him have such good control that they are not frightened by his symptoms of loss of control, they treat him in ways which both strengthen and reduce the intensity of his cannibalistic impulses. If the self-control of those around the incipient Wendigo is less secure, so that they are frightened by his symptoms then their behaviour tends to exacerbate his symptoms, and they usually give in to the desire to eat human flesh.[151]

We already know that Wendy and Danny have severe reservations about the Overlook, and it is clear from the very outset – as Jack struggles to maintain a polite demeanour during his interview with Ullman – that he has serious anger-management issues. The revelation that he is a recovering alcoholic, as well as a child abuser (he broke Danny's arm and physically assaulted a student who vandalised his car) suggests that to his family, he is already a figure that inspires wariness. Because he has previous bad form, Jack's descent into murderous insanity is even more terrifying to Wendy and Danny because that lack of self-control had always been there. If Hay's argument regarding Windigo psychosis holds true here, then their entirely understandable fear of Jack may actually exacerbate his symptoms. Jack is turning into the monster that he had always been in their worst imaginings.

This thread of the narrative becomes even more obvious in the film, partially because Kubrick's Wendy is very different from King's version (as is his version of Jack). King's Wendy is blonde, conventionally pretty, assertive, and seems to have a more equal relationship with her husband. Kubrick's Wendy (Shelley Duvall), is a timid, dowdy brunette who is obviously terrified of her mercurial spouse. She is, in fact, an almost textbook caricature of an abused wife: 'She is clearly afraid of him, and her shaky, chain-smoking, emaciated, wrecked expression places her in a position of passive subservience.'[152] It may be that in the film version, in particular, therefore, that her fear has accelerated Jack's transformation into the axe-wielding ogre.

In both novel and film, Jack's degenerating physical appearance highlights his degeneration. King repeatedly mentions the fact that Jack has a very specific tic that worsens as he digs into the hotel's history: he wipes his mouth with a handkerchief so often so that his lips begin to bleed (again, as in Rowlandson and Brown, blood on the face signifies a descent into savagery in a Rural Gothic narrative).[153] The gesture is a reminder of his alcoholism, but also of his similarity to the Windigo, who in Native American folk art is often depicted as having no lips (in a form of autocannibalism worthy of *Edgar Huntly*, they've been chewed off). 'When a human goes Windigo, observable changes happen. First, the affected persons size increases and he or she becomes coarsened and wild-looking, with a maniacal snarling look. Then, the victim's heart freezes over and becomes ice [...].'[154] In the novel, we are told that Jack's complexion has changed, and that he looks 'slightly lunatic', and that he also constantly chews aspirin (another sign of uncontrollable appetite).

At the end of the novel, Jack rampages through the hotel with a roque mallet. According to Indian lore, the Windigo leaves a trail of destruction in its path, and will sometimes rip up a tree to use as a club or walking stick (in the film, of course, the mallet becomes an axe). At the end of the film, Jack freezes to death (which means that his heart becomes ice), whilst in King's novel, he is killed in a fiery explosion (the only sure way to kill the Windigo is to melt its heart). Ultimately, the novel makes it clear that whilst Jack's weaknesses made him particularly vulnerable to manipulation, the monstrous creature that he becomes in the final chapters is, in fact, an avatar of the 'huge dark shape' that occupies the land on which the Overlook is built. When he sees his father for the last time, Danny realises, 'It was not his father. The mask of face and body had been ripped and shredded and made into a bad joke.'[155]

As Tony Magistrale has noted, whilst the novel tends to focus on Danny, his supernatural abilities, and the Overlook's attempts to absorb the boy's powers for itself, Kubrick's version (co-written with novelist Diane Johnson) centres on Jack.[156] As a result, his descent into savagery is rendered in even more detail. From the outset, as noted, Nicholson's Jack is much less sympathetic. Even as the family drive to the hotel, he appears to be filled with barely repressed frustration, staring straight ahead, as though to lose concentration for a moment would mean lashing out. Even before the family arrives at the Overlook, we have the sense that this is a man barely keeping himself under control. Another element highlighted in the film is the role played by the natural landscape. It opens with that famous overhead shot of Jack's little car threading its way through the beautiful but merciless mountains. The road – the only marker of human presence – is a small grey line in the midst of an unforgiving autumn wilderness. As the journey progresses, we can see snow on the nearby peaks, a warning of what is to come. All the while, the sense of ominous detachment is increased by the strains of 'Dies Irae' (punctuated by eerie wails and tribal-sounding percussion) and the fact that the camera is speeding along like an uncanny higher intelligence (scenes in which the camera takes on the vantage point of a detached natural presence loftily gazing down on vulnerable humans also recur frequently in the eco-horror narratives discussed in Chapter 5):

> [. . .] the careful symmetry of the camera eye in slow forward motion, first following the mirrored surface of a placid mountain lake, then the serpentine line of that mountain road, upon which a barely perceptible car appears to crawl towards a looming, solitary hotel that sits, grey and sullen, high up in the Colorado Rockies. Viewers soon notice that the camera has implicated their point of view, following behind the car, forcing a predatory identification with a seemingly all-encompassing, overwhelming vision.[157]

The preoccupation with food and with consumption evinced in the novel (in which even the Overlook itself is ultimately seen as some kind of devouring entity, a characteristic King cribbed from Shirley Jackson's equally rapacious Hill House)[158] continues in the film, and is combined with the familiar Donner-party fixation, which first comes up in the following scene:

DANNY: I'm hungry.
JACK: Well you should have eaten your breakfast.
WENDY: We'll get something as soon as we get to the hotel, okay?
DANNY: Okay, Mom.
WENDY: Hey, wasn't it around here that the Donner Party got snowbound?
JACK: I think that was farther west, in the Sierras.
DANNY: What was the Donner Party?
JACK (enjoying telling the story): They were a party of settlers in the covered wagon times. They got snowbound one winter in the mountains. They had to resort to cannibalism in order to stay alive.
DANNY: You mean they *ate* each other up?
JACK: They had to, in order to survive.
WENDY: Jack...
DANNY: Don't worry Mom. I know all about cannibalism, I saw it on the T.V.
JACK (grins sarcastically): See, it's ok. He saw it all on the television.[159]

Kubrick and Johnston further highlight the connection by making sure that, as in the novel, food and its availability are referred to throughout. The first thing the family do when they arrive is have lunch. Whilst Jack is being instructed about his responsibilities, Wendy, as in the novel, is led on a tour of the kitchen by Dick Halloran (Scatman Crothers), she remarks, in a line that anticipates the climax, 'This place is such an enormous maze. I feel like I'll have to leave a trail of breadcrumbs every time I come in.' 'The presence of all the extra food ironically underscores the isolation of the small family, hearkening to other doomed families that set out for the west.'[160] Like Wendy, the audience can only look in amazement as the chef lists all that there is in-store. Kubrick makes sure that we pay particular attention to the pantry that will later serve as Jack's prison. Surveying the freezer, Halloran says:

HALLORAN: Now this is where we keep all of our meat. You got fifteen rib roasts – thirty ten pound bags of hamburgers. You got twelve turkeys, two dozen pork roasts and twenty legs of lamb.
(to Danny)
Do you like lamb, Doc?

DANNY: No.
HALLORAN: You don't? Well what's your favourite food then?
DANNY: French Fries and Ketchup.
HALLORAN laughs.

A lamb is, of course, an animal slaughtered before it reaches maturity. It may well be that Kubrick intends Danny's preference for non-carnivorous foods to foreshadow the scenes in which he is pursued by an axe-wielding father with slaughter on his mind. The fate of the Grady girls – whose ghosts manifest themselves to Danny as he pedals up and down the corridors (knowledge of which will later save his life) is another reminder that youngsters do not fare well in the Overlook.

As though subconsciously trying to forestall her husband's transformation into a Windigo, Wendy keeps bringing him food. When Kubrick cuts to a scene starkly titled 'A MONTH LATER', Jack is in bed even though it is 11.30 a.m. (an indication of the lethargy and apathy associated with the initial stages of 'Going Windigo'). Wendy brings him breakfast, and cheerily asks 'Any ideas yet?' Later, whilst he plays handball in the Colorado Room, Wendy and Danny explore the hedge maze (a feature absent in the novel). As his wife and son have fun figuring out the maze, in one of the film's most famous shots, Jack looms over the scale model of the attraction, and for a jolting, disorientating moment, it is as if the real maze and the model have merged, and an angry giant is gazing down at them.

As well as highlighting the link between the troubled recesses of the mind and the physical geography of the landscape around the Overlook, the scene also emphasises Jack's increasingly Windigo-like isolation:

> [...] Jack appears alone in scene after scene. Significantly, Jack elects to remain inside the hotel's corridors and rooms – especially within the Gold Ballroom, which appears to be the centre of the Overlook's 'brain' – while Wendy and Danny are free to explore its outdoor surroundings. Until the final chase through the snow-encrusted maze, Jack is never seen outside the hotel's interior.[161]

A little later on, Wendy interrupts Jack when he is typing, after being rebuffed, consolingly says, 'I'll come back with a couple of sandwiches'. In response, Jack utters the film's first profanity: 'Get the fuck out of here!' There is indeed, as Wendy senses, a void in Jack – but it isn't food that he craves, it's alcohol. Sure enough, it is when he fully gives himself over to the visions conjured up by the hotel, that this craving is satisfied by Lloyd the spectral bartender, who appears in response to the cry, 'I'd give my goddamn soul for a glass of beer.' The encounter happens just after Wendy has wrongly blamed him for the attack upon Danny that occurred in room 237, the dark heart of the Overlook. This act of perceived betrayal, combined with Wendy's pleas for them to leave, are what prompts Jack to return to the 'Gold Room', and wholly give himself over to the dark forces coming from within (his inner Windigo) and from without (the hotel itself). 'Drink up, Mr Torrance', urges Lloyd, but it is like Jack is drunk already, and from that point on he has become a leering, drooling, and increasingly non-verbal embodiment of rage. By the end of the film, when Jack's inability to correctly read the landscape leads him to his death in the maze (Danny, who already knows the route and also has the presence of mind to reverse his tracks, survives), he is only able to utter incoherent bellows of rage. For him, the maze, like the journey to the Overlook itself, really was a dead end.

Jack's transformation into a creature straight out of Indian folklore is further emphasised by the fact that Kubrick repeatedly reminds audiences of the fact that the near-destruction of the Indians lies at the heart of national history. Bill Blakemore suggested as far back as 1987 that *The Shining* wasn't about the murders at the Overlook at all, but about 'the murder of a race – the race of Native Americans – and the consequences of that murder'.[162] He points out that visual clues to this reading: Indian motifs on wall hangings and rugs serve as a backdrop to many key scenes (for instance, a baking powder can emblazoned with the head of an Indian chief is prominent in the scene in which Jack is locked in the pantry). And, of course, there's the fact that the hotel is built on an Indian burial ground. In a detail not present in the novel, Ullman tells Jack and Wendy that during construction (1907–09), there were even a few Indian attacks. Therefore, as Blakemore suggests, even though there are no Indians *physically* present in the film, we see signs of their existence in almost every frame. For him, the tidal wave of blood that runs out of the elevator during Danny's first vision of the hotel (and is also seen by Wendy at the end of the movie) '[...] is the blood upon which this nation, like most nations was built, as was the Overlook hotel'.[163]

It is a reading built on by Magistrale, who further suggests that Jack's violence towards Wendy 'signifies the enduring presence of patriarchal repression and its link to the doctrine of Manifest Destiny associated with white notions of masculinity and power', and which was anticipated by Frederic Jameson's take on the film as far back as 1981, which argued that Jack '[...] is possessed neither by evil nor by the "devil" or some analogous occult force, but rather simply by history, by the American past as it has left its sedimented traces in the corridors and disembodied suites of this monumental rabbit warren [...]'.[164]

If this is indeed the case, it is surely all the more appropriate that King's novel, and the film that followed it, should so obviously transform Jack Torrance into a Windigo, the creature whose appearance here, as in *Ravenous*, further critiques the greed and arrogance that helped fuel the nation's expansionist policies from the nineteenth century onwards.[165] The Overlook's existence in both versions of the story is testament to the fact that the nation's original inhabitants have been violently ousted from their territory, whilst the devastating costs of the journey west undertaken by the Torrances reminds us of the fact that those who replaced them sometimes had to pay a high price for venturing into unfamiliar terrain in the hopes of achieving a better life.

Although the figure of the Windigo is absent, even more so than the other narratives discussed here, Cormac McCarthy's *The Road* (2007) is concerned with the struggle for survival in a hostile environment, and, in particular, with the need to find food. What one eats – and what one *refuses* to eat – is again of considerable significance. McCarthy's protagonists, a father and his young son, seemingly represent the last exemplars of civilised humanity in a post-apocalyptic world in which every source of nourishment save for canned food (and human flesh) has long since been consumed. McCarthy provides us with scene after scene in which his protagonists painstakingly forage and strive to ration what little they do have. 'Mostly he worried about their shoes. That and food. Always food.'[166] 'The man' worries about food because, without it, he and the boy will die. Yet, he knows only too well that it is only a matter of time before they starve. He worries about their shoes, because their ability to keep moving, to traverse the car-strewn, corpse-littered highways, is what keeps them alive. All that is left of the old world is the road, and the dwindling hope that, somewhere, things are just a little better. 'We have to keep moving. We have to keep heading South.'[167] To stay in one place means certain death (when the father becomes so weakened by illness that he can no longer walk, we know he won't last long). At times, it almost seems as if the novel is intended as a bitter mockery of the ceaseless drive towards movement, exploration, and consumption that has so often shaped the national character. Because of the never-explained catastrophe that has befallen the US, there are no natural resources left to exploit. The trees have been chopped down for firewood, the birds and animals are dead, and even a lake which once generated electricity is said to sit 'Cold and grey and heavy in the scavenged bowl of the countryside'.[168]

The Puritans scorned the Indian way of life, along with the fact that they moved around the countryside rather than construct permanent settlements in one place. In McCarthy's novel, the few Americans that survive roam the denuded landscape like 'the walking dead in a horror film'.[169] The wintry conditions that trapped the Donner party at Truckee Lake and the Torrance family at the Overlook have become permanent. The atmosphere is so laden with ash that there aren't even any real colours anymore. Hell, even apostrophes are in short supply. As they push the shopping cart that contains their worldly possessions along the highway, father and son find that the distinctions between city and countryside, road and forest have become largely irrelevant: all that is left is one vast, dead wilderness, and the '[...] odd things scattered by the side of the road [...] things abandoned long ago by pilgrims enroute to their several and collective deaths'.[170]

The few vaguely uplifting moments in the novel all revolve around food left over from the time before. A can of Coca Cola fished out of an old machine represents a poignant reminder of the abundance there once was. When the father insists that the boy have the can to himself, he rightly observes, 'It's because I won't ever get to drink another one, isn't it?'[171] The one sustained sequence of calm in the entire story comes courtesy of the discovery of a bunker filled with 'Crate upon crate of canned goods'.[172] The description of this sight evokes Halloran's tour in *The Shining*:

> Tomatoes, peaches, beans, apricots. Canned hams. Corned beef. Hundreds of gallons of water in ten gallon plastic jerry jugs. Paper towels, toilet paper, paper plates. Plastic trash bags stuffed with blankets. He held his forehead in his hand. Oh my God, he said. He looked back at the boy. It's all right, he said. Come down.[173]

Although they spend a few days in the bunker, finally able to sleep in warm beds, to eat their fill, and to bathe, the father insists that they move on before they get too comfortable, and someone else – the bad guys, as he calls them – stumbles across the find. Later, however, it will be their gift (reluctant on the father's part) of tinned food to Ely, a mysterious old man who assures them that 'You don't want to know what I've eaten', that reaffirms the essential humanity of the pair, and in particular, the boy's position as a symbol of hope for the future.

Consumption of another sort also defines those who have taken the other path to survival: cannibalism. The father's greatest fear is that he and the boy will be butchered by the 'blood cults' that roam the countryside like a medieval army, picking off any straggler unlucky enough to stumble into their path. It is this prospect which prompted the boy's mother to kill herself. 'They are going to rape us and kill us and eat us and you won't face it. You'd rather wait for it to happen. But I cant. I cant' [sic].[174] This 'army in tennis shoes, tramping' is dressed in clothing of every possible description, the men are bearded, and carry spears and lances – primitive weapons – whilst the women (many of whom are pregnant) wear dog collars and walk behind in chains. We get a long description of a cannibal campsite, which has become a 'tableau of the slain and devoured' featuring 'A frieze of human heads'.[175] Worse even than the blood cult's halting site is what the father discovers when he and the boy enter a 'once grand house' in search of supplies. He breaks open a lock on the basement door and discovers men and women who are being eaten whilst they are still alive. 'On the mattress lay a man with his legs gone to the hip and the stumps of them blackened and burnt. The smell was hideous.'[176] In a more conventional narrative, the father would manage to free the prisoners, or at least contrive some means of ending their suffering, but here, there is no comforting resolution. Instead, when he hears the cannibals returning, the man grabs the boy and runs away, aware that if he tries to intervene, the two of them will likely meet the same fate.

McCarthy's cannibals, though undeniably monstrous (in a detail that would seem excessive even in the work of pulp horror novelists like Richard Laymon or Jack Ketchum, they even roast a newborn baby on a spit, although the 'tree of dead babies' in his 1985 novel *Blood Meridian* tops even this), have adapted to the circumstances around them in the most ruthlessly practical way possible. In a world in which there is hardly any food left and the only living things are other people, the decision to cast aside morality and view ones fellow humans as just another source of protein makes brutal sense. It also makes sense that the cannibals should play up their 'savagery', by creating a 'cult' that enshrines a ritual element within their eating habits (although other than describing the scarves they wear as a marker of collective identity, McCarthy never describes what form these rituals take). This is 'survival' cannibalism taken to its most excessive level, and as such, the cult members display an even more extreme version of the adaptability that has for so long characterised the white relationship with the American landscape. They are in that sense the most horrifying exemplars possible of the descent into chaos and savagery that the Puritans feared would overtake those who insisted upon making their own way in unknown territory. In McCarthy's post-apocalyptic world, chaos really does reign: in fact, embracing it is a viable survival strategy. For McCarthy's protagonists, the refusal to countenance such a possibility means that 'We're still the good guys'. It is hardly surprising then, following his father's death, when he is found by strangers – a man and a woman with a child of their own – the boy insists on querying their eating habits:

> You dont eat people.
> No. We dont eat people.
> And I can go with you?
> Yes. You can.
> Okay then.
> Okay.[177]

McCarthy finishes, however, with a paragraph that reminds us of the natural abundance that once existed in this now dead land:

> Once there were brook trout in the streams in the mountains. You could see them standing in the amber current where the white edges of their fins wimpled softly in the flow. They smelled of moss in your hand. On their backs were vermiculate patterns that were maps of the world in its becoming. *Maps and mazes.* Of a thing which could not be put back. Not be made right again. In the deep glens where they lived all things were older than man and they hummed with mystery.[178]
>
> [my italics]

Like the hedge maze in *The Shining*, or the labyrinthine cave that Edgar Huntly finds himself trapped in, *The Road*'s elegiac conclusion further reminds us of the tricks that the mind can play upon itself, and of the ways in which humans interact with the environment around them. We leave the novel with the sense of a landscape fraught with the potential for wonder and terror in equal measure, and an implicit reminder of the fact that the harm that has been done to the natural environment by humankind cannot 'be made right again'. The boy's story, nevertheless, finishes on what could arguably be considered a tentatively hopeful note, as he leaves with newcomers who appear to have preserved some vestiges of 'civilised' behaviour. However, we remain in no doubt as to the fact that, as in the other narratives discussed in this chapter, extremity caused by prolonged exposure to the wilderness can transform the traveller into a figure straight out of nightmare, and that the ceaseless appetite that propelled settlers across the continent had a monstrous side of its own.

4
Backwoods Nightmares: The Rural Poor as Monstrous Other

In Herschell Gordon Lewis's *Two Thousand Maniacs!* (1964) we find assembled for the first time many of the elements which would go on to feature prominently in the most formulaic sub-genre of the American horror film (save the slasher movie): the backwoods horror flick. There are cackling locals with a fondness for sporting overalls and bandanas. There are repeated shots of the Confederate flag, meant to reinforce, for the benefit of anyone not paying attention, that this is indeed 'THE SOUTH'. Then there are the other subtle signifiers of southern 'otherness': banjo playing, moonshine swilling, a scene in which the local band solemnly plays 'Dixie', and another in which someone yells, whilst looking at a dismembered body, 'I reckon we got ourselves the making of a barbecue!'[1] Apart from the fact that Pleasant Valley is of supernatural origin, and all of the murders carried out in the film are committed by the townspeople as a collective, *Two Thousand Maniacs!* helped establish a paradigm that would be replicated over and over again in the decades that followed, particularly once the success of John Boorman's film version of *Deliverance* (1972) and Tobe Hooper's *The Texas Chain Saw Massacre* (1974) ensured that these tropes infiltrated mainstream popular culture.[2]

David Bell (1997) has observed that alongside the many representations of 'idyllic' or idealised versions of rural life found in British and American popular culture, there exists a parallel tradition of films in which the countryside serves as a 'perfect backdrop for terror' which have spawned '[...] a peculiar species, usually referred to in US horror films as hillbillies, rednecks or mountain men. Trading on assorted cultural myths – of inbreeding, insularity, backwardness, sexual perversion (especially incest and bestiality), these rural "white trash" are familiar popular culture icons [...]', which serve as 'symptoms of social, cultural, and economic processes having profound impact upon rural regions in the USA [...]'.[3] More recently, in a reading of the 'hillbilly horror' film that links the sub-genres post-2000 resurgence to the Bush administration's 'War on Terror', Blake notes that '[...] the United States has a very long history of representing the inhabitants of its own isolated rural places or backwoods communities as monstrous, grotesque, diseased and polluted'.[4] The result of this 'urbanoia' as Carol J. Clover puts it, is the assumption, 'People from the city are people like us. People from the country [...] are people not like us.'[5]

The conception of the backwoods inhabitant is far removed indeed from that promoted by Thomas Jefferson, who '[...] believed that the open land and the act of working it had a civilizing effect, that it shaped people by providing them with the material means for sustenance, taught them to defend themselves, and thus nurtured them as citizens of a democratic society'.[6] Backwoods settlers '[...] constituted the vanguard of colonisation in the temperate wooded areas of North America, opening the way for less adventurous but more enduring peoples to follow and complete the occupation of the continent's forests'.[7] Even early on in the movement to the frontier, this group saw themselves (and were perceived) as being different from the dominant settler culture. According to Terry Jordan and Matti Kaups (1992), they saw themselves as an essentially classless society, had a lack of respect for centralised authority, high levels of personal freedom and individualism, were dominated by the nuclear-family units or small kinship groups, mixed with the Indians (both racially and culturally), and lived in log cabins in dispersed homesteads rather than in larger collective settlements.[8] 'Locational Instability' is also cited as one of their main characteristics.

As we shall see, the 'backwoods horror' narrative transforms the 'pioneer' spirit and rugged individualism welcomed by the likes of Jefferson into signifiers of resentfulness and savagery. Perhaps even more significantly, the backwoodsman's 'almost compulsive mobility' becomes stagnation and degeneration.[9] There is a sense that with the so-called 'closing of the frontier', energies that were once positive and necessary for the growth and expansion of the nation have nowhere left to go. '[...] Slotkin notes, "traits that had been productive and heroic might become antisocial and dangerous".'[10] With this change, the backwoodsman is transformed from '[...] an American Adam, building a democratic Eden in the amply legislated garden of the New World' and becomes, instead, '[...] one who inhabited the physical and conceptual margins of the nation, the abject territory of "outlaws, outcasts and paupers" '.[11] During the late nineteenth and early twentieth century, this conception of the backwoods inhabitant became particularly associated with the southern US.

This chapter will explore the reasons why it is that the post-1970 American horror film so often uses the city dweller versus evil rural folk paradigm, and more specifically, why the rural South is by far the most popular setting for such narratives. Indeed, as we shall see later on, the sub-genre generally focuses on a small pool of locations even within the southern region: of the many southern-set backwoods horror films watched for the purposes of this chapter, only one is set in a state outside of Virginia, Texas, or Georgia. I will also briefly discuss two films which have much in common with the southern-set backwoods horror movie, but are actually set in California: *The Hills Have Eyes* (1977) and *Motel Hell* (1980).

Although backwoods horror films tend to be set in South or South West (Texas), New England is the region which most often features in novels and stories of this type. Shirley Jackson's fiction often featured uncomfortable encounters between New England townsfolk and outsiders who inadvertently violate rigid local mores, as in 'The Summer People' (1950), which is one of her finest horror stories.[12] The writing of H.P. Lovecraft often featured fraught encounters between unwary travellers and degenerate country folk, as the likes of 'The Shadow over Innsmouth' (1936) and 'The Dunwich Horror' (1928). 'The Picture in the House' (1924) even urges the true 'epicure in the terrible' to esteem the 'ancient, lonely farmhouses of New England', and concludes with a memorably tense revelation of pagan ritual and cannibalistic practices.[13] The setting of Stephen King's epic small-town vampire novel *Salem's Lot* (1975) also becomes a no-go area for unwary travellers in later stories such as 'One for the Road' (1977). However, unlike as in King and Lovecraft, none of the films that I will discuss here have any supernatural element. The backwoods horror movies considered in this chapter eschew the fantastic in favour of violence perpetrated by humans. As a result, I will not be discussing films such as *The Evil Dead* (1981, 2013), *Monster Man* (2003), or *The Cabin in the Woods* (2011) in any detail, even though they contain many of the tropes I will be outlining. Their dependence upon overtly fantastic elements disqualifies them from my definition of 'backwoods horror'.

Jack Ketchum's *Off Season* (1980) is about a group of New York sophisticates who are taken captive by a clan of feral cannibals in the Maine Woods. There were two sequels: *Offspring* (1991) and (written with Lucky McKee) *The Woman* (2012). McKee's film version of *The Woman* is interesting in that it presents us with what is in essence a reverse captivity narrative. A cave-dwelling young woman (Pollyanna McIntosh), the last survivor of Ketchum's cannibal clan, is captured in the woods and chained up in the cellar by a self-righteous small-town lawyer named 'Chris Cleek' (Sean Bridgers) who is determined to 'civilise' her because, 'We cannot have people running round the woods thinking that they're animals.' Enlisting the help of his wife and teenage children, who are too cowed by his aggression to do anything but obey, he sprays the woman with a power hose to remove all traces of dirt, and tries to train her not to crave human flesh (in another plot element that evokes Rowlandson in reverse, his captive is forced to eat cooked food, which she finds disgusting). Needless to say, the supposed boundaries between 'savage' and 'civilisation' are soon shown to be meaningless, and the 'respectable' family man reveals himself to be a psychopathic misogynist who will ultimately pay a fitting price for his abusive ways.[14]

Richard Laymon's *The Woods Are Dark* (1981) is a California-set variation on the Sawney Bean plot, in which travellers are kidnapped, robbed, and tied to trees by forest-dwelling murderers known as 'the Krulls'. Edward R. Lee's 1997 novel *The Big Head* (about an inbred psychopath suffering from hydrocephalus who rampages through the backwoods of Virginia), manages the rare feat of making Ketchum's work look tame. Flannery O'Connor's 'A Good Man Is Hard to Find' (1953) provides an early example of the southern-set 'unwary travellers meet redneck killer' narrative. 'There was nothing around her but woods', we are told, as 'The Grandmother' awaits her death by the side of a road in rural Georgia, and the rest of her family are led one-by-one into a pine forest to be executed by escaped convicts. The story does differ from the classic backwoods horror story in one significant aspect: in this instance, both the victims and their killers are transient, whereas as we shall see, the sub-genre proper usually deals with encounters between travellers and those resentfully confined to one place.

The fact that the South serves as by far the most common setting for the backwoods horror story obviously has much to do with the manner in which the area is perceived by the rest of the US. Alison Graham observes that depictions of the region have long been notable for their 'creative paralysis':

> The American South, it seems, is frozen at its eroticized apex and nadir, relegated by tacit national consensus to a heaven-and-hell diptych of social types: sleepwalking belles and gentlemen of the Old South, and rampaging crackers and hillbillies of the Benighted South.

> But whether it is depicted as an agrarian idyll of Lost Causes and mistily rendered Belle Reves or a backwoods nightmare of lynch mobs and graphically sketched Tobacco Roads, the South of post-World War II popular imagination has embraced not only the polarized rural depictions of 'the country' but also, ironically '*the* country' itself. Howard Zinn claimed in 1964 that 'the Southern Mystique' was in fact simply an exaggeration of regrettable *American* traits; thirty-three years later in *The Redneck Manifesto*, Jim Goad put it more crudely: the South, he said, is 'America's cultural nigger rendered in geographical terms'. The 'dark' underbelly of the nation, the reversed image in the mass-media mirror, the South was and is America's repellent yet all to compelling Other.[15]

Graham's characterisation of the South as 'compelling Other' helps explain why it is so frequently depicted as a nightmarish region distinct from the rest of the US. Allain Mathé contends that this very particular kind of 'Otherness' allows a national audience to localise certain anxieties – mostly to do with race – without feeling threatened themselves. 'The region thus becomes a metaphor for the worst in America – violence, corruption, oppression – as well as the best – individualism, pride, self-reliance, honor and true grit.'[16]

To begin to understand how these perceptions of the South came about, and how they relate to the Rural Gothic more specifically, we first need to remind ourselves that there were two starting points for the European settlement of the US. The first was the fertile but malaria-ridden coast of 'Virginia' (the name which, between 1580 and 1620, the English applied to the entire mid-Atlantic coast between Florida and Arcadia).[17] It was not until a generation later that the New England colony began. Although the English had attempted to settle Virginia as far back as 1585, it took until 1616 for the colony to really begin to find a secure foothold in the 'New World'. The need for agricultural labour first required by the tobacco industry, and later, by the cotton industry, helped justify the introduction of slave labour.

Initially, farmers and planters had relied upon indentured servants from back home. The tobacco boom greatly increased their value particularly once a second southern colony was established in Maryland in 1632.[18] The European labour supply lessened in the 1680s and 1690s because the nascent American economy was weak, and there was increased competition from other, newer colonies such as Jamaica, Carolina, and Pennsylvania.[19] Yet, 'To be a great tobacco planter in Virginia, two things were required: plenty of cheap land to replace the acres wasted by soil exhaustion and soil erosion, the marks of inefficient agriculture, and cheap labour [...] Oppression of the Indians provided the first, oppression of the Africans the second.'[20] There were 13,000 African slaves in America by 1700: by 1750 they would represent 40 per cent of the population of Chesapeake.[21] There was nothing new or exceptional about the use of slave labour. The British Empire, 'like its rivals, was built on slavery', and the both colonial Pennsylvania and Boston owed much to the business of slavery.[22] By the time of the Revolutionary War, the largest ethnic group in America, apart from the English, was Africans, the majority of them slaves.[23] So the South was by no means alone in profiting from the use of slaves, even if the extent of its dependency did distinguish it from the North.

The last northern state to end slavery where it had previously existed was New Jersey, in 1804.[24] It would persist for another 60 years in the southern states, which had come to rely economically and psychologically on the practice. The South was an agrarian region (even at a time when most of the US was still rural rather than urban), and 'the rural community in much of the South was shaped by the institution of slavery'.[25] The market for cotton and other agricultural products fuelled the trend for agricultural settlement in the South and in the West, and attracted more and more colonists, many of them Scotch-Irish settlers who would feature prominently in future figurations of 'White Trash'. 'They were a proud, tough and independent people who contributed to the aggressive, rough-and-tumble nature of the Southern backcountry.'[26] The persistence of slavery in the South played a considerable part in creating the perception that the region was the problematic, uncivilised 'Other' to the urban, industrialised, and 'civilised' North. Indeed, in a formulation that has much in common with the relationship between 'civilisation' and 'savagery' considered in earlier chapters, '[...] "South" and "North" end up functioning rather like a photograph and its negative, in a mutually determining, reciprocally defining relationship: the South is, in these circumstances, whatever the North is not, and vice versa [...]'.[27]

It is important to consider the ways in which slavery affected the class structure of the South, because along with the issue of race – and, in particular, the position of African Americans within the southern US, and the various ways in which 'whiteness' sought to define itself, and was defined – class lies at the heart of the construction of the poor white as monstrous aggressor. Slave ownership was overwhelmingly concentrated in the upper strata of southern society, and the owners of large plantations derived a much greater benefit from slave labour than their poorer neighbours.[28] Wealth was overwhelmingly concentrated in the hands of an aristocratic ruling class whose dominance 'retarded the rise of a prosperous yeomanry', and helped ensure that the South remained a predominantly agrarian society.[29] It was in the best interests of the ruling classes to use their supposed racial 'superiority' as a means of creating a sense of shared purpose and of identity between whites.

During the antebellum period, a collective white identity which transcended class divides was shaped by the belief that whites were inherently superior to blacks, and as a result, 'A dark skin became synonymous with slavery, just as freedom became associated with whiteness.'[30] As well as providing a convenient justification for slavery – just as the characterisation of the Indians as depraved savages had provided a excuse for all manner of atrocities during the early colonial period – this connection 'obscured the persistent power of class distinctions between the common planters and the great planters', which became all the more significant in maintaining existing hierarchical power structures as the gap between the richest and the poorest whites widened.[31] Another factor that helped preserve the status quo was the fact that many poorer whites – and, in particular, thousands of relatively recent Scotch, Scotch-Irish, and German immigrants – were concentrated in the more mountainous and less profitable areas of the South.[32] These same poor whites and their descendants would often later be denigrated as 'hillbillies' and 'White Trash'. As Katherine E. Ledford illustrates, the 'Mountain South', in particular, became a site of considerable unease for travellers who '[...] encountered conditions that, when present in the West, aligned with expectations of frontier adventure and exploration. In the East, however, those affiliated conditions necessarily became markers of backwardness, coded as the backwoods and corralled into the Mountain South.'[33]

Rather than decisively upending pre-existing class structures for good, therefore, the Civil War simply reconfigured them. It had 'highlighted the essentially rural and agricultural nature of the country', but 'while there was a future for Southern agriculture, it was not as lucrative as in the past':[34]

> A free labour system replaced slavery, but those operating in it coped with severe social and economic constraints. The freed people remained free and benefited from freedom in many ways, but their class and race doomed them to the status of a degraded and oppressed caste in their native region. And the rural community of the South continued to be three communities as it had been under slavery – one

> biracial, one black, and one white. Well into the twentieth century, rural Southerners lived with the legacy of an institution that died in 1865.[35]

The Federal government had decided that the best way to 'fix' the South was to encourage the dismantling of the plantation system and instead focus on an agricultural system organised around the northern model of the family homestead and the small town.[36] The trouble was that, as Brogan elaborates, the end of slavery had eliminated the one major advantage that southern agriculturalists had over their northern brethren. The labour supply dropped by a third with emancipation and the subsequent 'Great Migration' to the northern cities, and as cheap new sources of cotton emerged in Egypt and India, the South sank deeper and deeper into financial crisis.[37] Because the best land remained largely under the control of the ruling class, the economic burden fell on the shoulders of those who were least equipped to cope.

The sharecropping system – under which tenant farmers worked land that belonged to their social and financial superiors, who in turn received a hefty cut of the profits – left many thousands of poor whites and recently freed African Americans hopelessly indebted to their landlords. A new form of slavery – debt slavery – became the norm for the vast majority of poor farmers, with the result that 'Southern Blacks were the only Americans with worse prospects than Southern Whites'.[38] It was during the reconstruction and after that the perception of the South as, at best, a backwards embarrassment, and at worst, a national disgrace, took hold. It didn't help that the 'Jim Crow' laws ensured that the often meagre gains that freed slaves and their descendants had been granted after the war were cancelled out by legislation intended to reaffirm their position at the bottom of the social and economic hierarchy.

By 1935, two-thirds of the nation's tenant farmers were in the South, of whom the majority were white.[39] Thirty-nine per cent of southern farms were managed by sharecroppers.[40] In 1938, Roosevelt declared the rural South US's 'Number One' economic problem,[41] and under the auspices of the New Deal, agencies such as the Farm Security Administration (FSA) were established in order to try and do something about the South, whose inequities had deepened considerably during the Great Depression.[42] However, the southern poor whites who would be the beneficiaries of much of this government aid, '[...] had negative associations in American culture that stretched back to the colonial period and which these agencies were obliged to address to cultivate and retain public opinion and political support for their expensive programs'.[43] One attempt to garner public sympathy involved commissioning photographers and writers to travel around the region, in a bid to acquaint the rest of the US with a region with which they were largely unfamiliar.[44] Yet, as Stuart Kidd notes, the media's response often perpetuated well-established conventions regarding the representation of the poor white southerner. In what had even then become a wearyingly familiar trend they were presented by the popular press as an 'alien people, confined outside the mainstream of a modernising America'.[45]

This perception that the South had been 'left behind' was exacerbated by the fact that it had a considerable basis in reality. 'The poverty of the rural South was much more than just a theoretical abstraction; it affected the lives of most people every day in many ways.'[46] Danbom highlights some of the afflictions that characterised the region during the early mid-twentieth century, amongst them: '[...] much higher infant mortality rates than in the rest of the country; lower life expectancies; the persistence of endemic health conditions such as hookworm and pellagra; poorly supported community institutions (due to lack of funds); poor schools, and as a result, ignorance and illiteracy; isolation and sorely limited horizons'.[47]

As we shall see, many of the most negative characteristics associated with the South (and with the Mountain South, in particular) would be absorbed into the backwoods horror sub-genre, resurfacing in ways that greatly exaggerated or otherwise appropriated existing stereotypes. In the backwoods horror film, the 'otherness' of the region is dramatised in ways which graphically reaffirm the sense that not only is the South an inherently problematic place, but also that the rural poor are themselves monstrous and degenerate.

Paupers, criminals, and imbeciles: eugenics and the backwoods horror film

In *White Trash: Race and Class in America*, Matt Wray and Annalee Newitz argue that:

> Americans love to hate the poor. Lately, it seems there is no group of poor folks they like to hate more than White Trash. [...] In a country so steeped in the myth of classlessness, in a culture where we are often at a loss to explain or understand poverty, the white trash stereotype

> serves as a useful way of blaming the poor for being poor. 'White Trash' is not just a classist slur – it's also a racial epithet that marks out certain whites as a dysgenic race unto themselves.[48]

While Wray, Newitz, and their contributors focus specifically upon recent figurations of 'White Trash', Dina Smith notes, 'America's fascination with "White Trash" is [...] not a new phenomenon [...].'[49] The older sense of the term is often anchored to racialised and occupational class status: '[...] the white trash sharecropper, the white trash miner, the white trash mill worker, *all of whom are stuck in place*. At once white and trash, a metonym for blackness, the term historically designated a border position between white privilege and black disenfranchisement' [my italics].[50] As we shall see, Smith's characterisation of the term as one that is tied to certain forms of manual labour undertaken by working-class men tied to their place of origin is absolutely crucial when it comes to achieving a proper understanding of the ways in which the rural poor are depicted in backwoods horror. Rural Gothic narratives, as we have seen, often pivot upon ill-fated encounters between people who are tied to one place, and those who are 'just passing through'. In the backwoods horror movie, outsiders are victimised by locals whose aggressiveness, resentment, and degeneracy is always linked to the fact that they tied to a deprived rural locale which epitomises the stagnation of what was once 'frontier territory'.

In their discussion of the term 'White Trash', Newitz and Wray trace it back to the early nineteenth century, and to a derogatory term used by slaves as a way of contemptuously referring to white servants. With the abolition of slavery, the original 'White Trash' category

> expanded and diffused to embrace a wide variety of white groups and communities, mostly rural, and became identified chiefly with the 'backwoods' yokels of areas such as the southern Appalachians – the 'hillbillies' of derisive folklore and, significantly, supposedly scientific studies undertaken at the end of the 19th century by the US Eugenics Records Office.[51]

The prejudices and biases these studies helped propagate persist in the backwoods horror movie, most particularly in its resurgent twenty-first-century incarnation, in which the backwoods aggressor is often depicted as being downright sub-human. As Newitz and Ray note, between 1880 and 1920, the Eugenics Records Office (ERO) produced 15 'Eugenic Family Studies' which sought to demonstrate that large numbers of the rural whites were 'genetic defectives'.[52] Their standard methodology was to begin with an individual who was already incarcerated, and then trace back their genealogy to supposedly 'defective' source – often an ancestor who was suspected of having 'mixed blood':[53]

> Some idea of the ways in which the 'degenerate' rural family was codified by the ERO can be gleaned from 'The Hill Folk: Report on A Rural Community of Hereditary Defectives' (1912).[54] The report, which investigated two family trees in a small Massachusetts town, aimed to show 'how much crime, misery, and expense may result from the union of two defective individuals' in order to 'throw some light on the vexed question of the prevention of feebleminded, degenerate individuals, as a humane and economical state policy'.[55] It focused upon a district known locally as 'The Hill', said to be populated by 'troublesome paupers' prone to alcoholism, reckless fecundity, and criminality. The inhabitants of 'The Hill' were descendants of two men, one English and one French, who settled in the area at around the same time (1800) and whose children and grandchildren intermarried: their many progeny spread through the town and beyond it, and everywhere 'made desolate, alcoholic homes'. Their degenerate condition was said to have been increased by the rural environment, for they had 'not been subjected to the social influences of a city or even of a large town' and their many negative traits had '[...] been modified by a less powerful social environment than those of urban dwellers'.[56]

Charles Davenport made it clear in the preface that while the 'Scientific' observations contained within were specifically about 'The Hill' and its inhabitants, communities of this kind were actually very common, and that it was in society's best interests to take steps to 'control' the problem:

> We are dealing with a rural community such as can be found in nearly if not quite every county in the older states of the union, in which nearly all of the people belong to the vague class of the 'feebleminded' – the incapable. The individuals vary much in capacity, a result which follows from the complexity of their germ plasm. Some have capacities that can be developed under proper conditions, but for many more even the best of environmental conditions can do little. They must remain a drag on our civilisation; a condition for which not they, but society, is responsible. It is to be hoped that a presentation of the facts will hasten the so much desired control by society of the reproduction of the grossly defective.[57]

In 1924, the Commonwealth of Virginia's law licensing the enforced sterilisation of those deemed by the state to be genetically 'defective' and/or 'feebleminded' was upheld by the Supreme Court. Famously, Justice Oliver Wendell Holmes said, 'It is better for all the world, if instead of waiting to execute degenerate offspring for crime, or to let them starve for their imbecility, society can prevent those who are manifestly unfit from continuing their kind.'[58] As a result of the Supreme Court's decision, the mass sterilisation of more than 50,000 Americans 'whose sole crime was to have, or be claimed to have, an intellectual impairment'– or who were deemed to have significant 'moral' or 'hereditary' failings – got underway.[59]

As the ERO's 'Memoir No 1' indicates, families living in impoverished rural areas were to become particular targets of these policies of institutionalisation and involuntary sterilisation. Edwin Black (2003) describes events that took place in the impoverished Appalachian community of Brush Mountain, Virginia, in the 1930s:

> On this day the Montgomery County Sheriff grabbed six brothers from one family, bundled them into several vehicles and then disappeared down the road. Earlier, the sheriff had come for the boys' sister. Another time, deputies snared two cousins. [...] From Brush Mountain, the Sheriff's human catch was trucked to a variety of special destinations, such as the Western State Hospital in Staunton, Virginia. [...] formerly known as the Western Lunatic Asylum. [...] By the time the Brush Mountain hillbillies were transported there, Western not only housed those deemed insane, but also the so-called 'feebleminded'. No one was quite sure how 'feebleminded' was defined. No matter. The county authorities were certain that the hill folk swept up in their raids were indeed mentally – and genetically – defective. As such, they would not be permitted to breed more of their kind.[60]

Though the racial theories that helped fuel this interest in 'genetic defectives' were entirely discredited in the late 1930s (largely due to their undeniably fascist, and specifically, Nazi associations)[61] they significantly influenced social and medical practice in the early twentieth century, and were an invaluable boon for conservative propagandists who disapproved of state-sponsored welfare programmes.[62] The offensive stereotypes these supposedly 'scientific' studies helped perpetuate left an imprint that lingers in popular culture until this very day. Part of the reason why these stereotypes were so resonant was because the

'Poor White Trash' category medicalised by the ERO drew upon two distinct and pre-existing categories of the rural white: the 'redneck' and 'the hillbilly'.

The term 'redneck' originated in Mississippi in the late nineteenth century, and in the twentieth became a pejorative term that characterised white male southerners who engaged in manual labour as poor, ignorant, reactionary racists.[63] Though it has in recent decades also been reconfigured a label to be worn proudly, marking the bearer out as a more authentic, pragmatic, 'real' American than the supposedly effete urban elite, like the frontier backwoodsman, the 'redneck' is frequently cast in negative, and at times, even monstrous terms. Though they have much in common, the 'redneck' and the 'hillbilly' do differ.

The hillbilly is specifically associated with the Appalachian and Ozark mountain ranges, whereas 'redneck' can be applied to any working-class white southerner. As Williamson notes, the hillbilly can seem either harmless or sinister, depending on the context:

> The hillbilly provokes a range of responses, from an odd kind of comfort to a real kind of terror. When he looks like [...] a harmless cartoon, we indulge him, even take on his identity in public and become boundary-crossing fools-for-freedom ourselves. But put the hillbilly in *Deliverance*, and he can fill us with horror.[64]

The past three years have seen a re-emergence of this idea of the 'hillbilly' or 'redneck' as an amiable buffoon due to the success of a number of 'reality' TV shows constructed around the concept. They include: *Bayou Billionaires* (CMT 2011–), *Buckwild* (MTV 2013), *Moonshiners* (Discovery 2011–), *Redneck Island* (CMT 2012–), *Duck Dynasty* (A&E 2012–), *Swamp People* (History Channel 2010–), and *Here Comes Honey Boo Boo* (TLC 2012–), all of which draw upon the stereotypes discussed here.

For Williamson, the hillbilly's resonance lies in the fact that he or she links Americans to their '[...] developmental past, an uncomfortable or unwelcome opening into a history we have tried hard to forget, or conflicted memory of the pain and heartache of living in the dirt on the frontier'.[65] The term first featured in print in 1900, in *The New York Journal*: 'A Hill-Billie [sic] is a free and untrammelled white citizen of Alabama who lives in the hills, has no means to speak of, dresses as he can, talks as he pleases, drinks whiskey when he gets it, and fires off revolvers as the fancy takes him.'[66] Although ways in which the term was used evolved, the fundamentals remained the same: a hillbilly was a mountain-dwelling southerner 'on the poor rural fringes of the economy who did not seem to be accompanying anyone else into the dawning of the thoroughly modern twentieth century'.[67] As both Williamson and Harkins note in their explorations of the ways in which the hillbilly has been depicted in American popular culture, it is their assumed detachment from modernity, their 'ignorance', and their disdain for conventional social and sexual mores that helps single them out from their more 'civilised' neighbours. These are a people who, like their region, have supposedly been left behind by modernity.

For Harkins, the persistence of the hillbilly trope can be explained by the fact that the typical hillbilly portrait 'stems from the dualistic nature of this cultural conception – which includes both positive and negative features of the American past and present'.[68] These positive features include: a pioneer spirit, strong family and kin networks governed by benevolent patriarchs, clearly defined gender roles, closeness to nature and the land, and authenticity (the similarity here to the definition of the backwoods settler provided by Jordan and Kaups earlier in this chapter is obvious). Their negative aspects 'show the anachronistic incompatibility of such values to twentieth century America'.[69] The pioneer spirit becomes social and economic backwardness; strong kinship ties become inbreeding (which is frequently implied in the backwoods horror film), domestic violence, and feuding; individuality means stubbornness and an inability to adapt to changing circumstances; and closeness to nature means savagery and promiscuity.[70]

This kind of mixed feeling about what the mountain-dwelling poor white really represents can be seen as far back as 1901, in Ellen Churchill Semple's article 'The Anglo-Saxons of the Kentucky Mountains: A Study in Anthropogeography'.[71] In it, she marvelled that:

> In one of the most progressive and productive countries of the world, and in that section of the country which has had its civilisation and its wealth longest, we find a large area where the people are still living the frontier life of the backwoods, where the civilisation is that of the eighteenth century, where the people speak the English of Shakespeare's time, where the large majority of the inhabitants have never seen a steamboat or a railroad, where money is as scarce as in colonial days, and all trade is barter. It is the great up heaved mass of the Southern Appalachians, which, with the conserving power of the mountains, has caused these conditions to survive, carrying a bit of the eighteenth-century into this strongly contrasted twentieth-century, and presenting an anachronism all the more marked because

> found in the heart of the bustling, money-making, novelty-loving United States.[72]

Semple applauded the racial purity of her Kentucky 'Mountaineers', claiming that their isolation had nurtured the preservation of 'the purest Anglo Saxon stock in the United States' which meant that despite the fact that '[...] these mountain people are the exponents of a retarded civilization and show the degenerate symptoms of an arrested development, their stock is as good as any in the country'.[73] Yet, for all their racial 'purity', Semple's 'Mountaineers' have 'retained little of the ruddy, vigorous appearance of [their] forebears'. The key phrase Semple uses here is 'arrested development'. It is precisely this sense of physical, intellectual, and even *moral* stagnation that infuses the backwoods horror film.

These films always depict attractive, wholesome, middle-class outsiders who fall victim to clannish, insular, psychotic, and physically repellent backwoods/rural inhabitants. This dynamic, as we shall see, illustrates the persistence in contemporary popular culture of ideas that have long since been stripped of any sociological or scientific credibility, but nevertheless endure in other, seemingly less harmful manifestations. This may in part be because they coincide so neatly with the long-standing perceptions of the South itself as aberrant 'Other' outlined at the beginning of this chapter, but it is also because they articulate even more long-standing ideas about the relationship between the representatives of 'civilisation' and 'savagery' in American culture.

A taxonomy of the backwoods horror film

I will now outline the most notable tropes, settings, themes, and plot developments of the backwoods horror film. It is my contention that the sub-genre can be divided into two main varieties. 'Type 1' is the *Deliverance* (1972) influenced narrative, in which the antagonists are resentful working-class men. As such, they can to some extent be considered a corrupt version of the positive figure of the frontiersman: the backwoods male gone rogue who takes out his economic and sexual frustrations on middle-class outsiders. This is why the 'Type 1' film so frequently plays out as a narrative in which duelling conceptions of masculinity – urban and rural – face off against one another against a wilderness backdrop. The antagonists in 'Type 1' films usually carry guns and often partake in the rape or sexual assault of their victims. This configuration was first established in *Deliverance*, but can also be seen in the remakes of *Straw Dogs* (2011) and *I Spit on Your Grave* (2010). It should also be noted that many of the films which I have classified as 'Type 1' backwoods horror movies could, in fact, accurately be described as rugged action thrillers, although they all contain horrific elements. Certainly, *Deliverance, Southern Comfort* (1981), and *Trigger Man* (2007) fall into this category. As Clover notes of *Deliverance*, '[...] its particular rendition of the city-country encounter has been obviously and enormously influential in horror [...]', and as such, it should certainly be discussed here.[74] The 'Type 1' backwoods horror story is less common than the 'Type 2' variety, which, as we shall see, always contains much more overtly horrific elements.

In the much more frequent 'Type 2' backwoods horror film, the antagonists are degenerate, savage, and often cannibalistic family groups. The foundational text here is *The Texas Chain Saw Massacre* which, unlike John Boorman's film version of *Deliverance*, is most definitely a horror film. The way in which the two films depict both their protagonists and the locals whom they encounter on their forays into the rural unknown differs significantly. For instance, in Boorman's film one can see, despite the harrowing ordeal undergone by his quartet of weekend warriors, a certain degree of sympathy towards both the soon-to-be-flooded Georgian wilderness as well as those who live in it (toothless rapists aside), even if this component is present to a much lesser extent than in Dickey's elegiac and sensitive source novel. By way of contrast, from the outset, the monstrous clan who terrorise the college kids in *The Texas Chain Saw Massacre* are depicted as terrifying embodiments of chaos, disorder, and malevolence. Although the setting in rural Texas is obviously important – it is, like all of the films discussed here, a variation on the frontier horror story – I would argue that the specific locale isn't quite as important as it is in later 'Type 2' films, because, as Christopher Sharret suggests, the film articulates a more general sense of '[...] a world dissolving into primordial chaos'.[75] Later 'Type 2' films often articulate how the rest of the US sees the rural poor, and the poor white southerner, in particular, but this is also a significant aspect of *The Texas Chain Saw Massacre* – Hooper's film is also about the failure of American history, and of modernity.

As well as owing a great deal to perceptions of the 'problematic' working-class family as a hive of crime, addiction, and degeneracy, the legend of Scottish cannibal Sawney Bean and his sprawling, incestuous, and murderous clan serves as 'the founding myth of the regional cannibal' and, therefore, also exerts some influence even within a specifically American context such as this.[76] If we look at two famous examples of 'backwoods' families that would come to popular culture prominence during the 1970s – the Waltons (from Earl Hamner Jr's 1972–81 semi-autobiographical TV show) and Hooper's cannibal clan (unnamed in the original film, but given the splendidly all-American surname 'Sawyer' in the tongue-in-cheek 1986 sequel), we can see the 'negative' qualities associated with one are merely the flipside of the 'positive' behaviours manifested by the other:

The 'good' backwoods family

1. Agreeable folks with their own homespun wisdom.
2. Family orientated.
3. Members of a close-knit rural community, even beyond the nuclear family.
4. Representatives of the 'real' US.
5. God-fearing and moral.
6. Poor, but happy.
7. Close to nature.
8. Hardy and physically resilient.
9. Pragmatic and proudly individualistic.
10. Proud owners of their own ramshackle but beloved homestead filled with cherished homemade furniture, furnishings, heirlooms, etc.
11. Self-sufficient – they rear their own animals, pickle and preserve their own fruits and vegetables, and do their best to survive on what they can.

The 'bad' backwoods family

1. Racist and ignorant/uneducated.
2. Inbred and incestuous.
3. Insular and xenophobic.
4. Representatives of the 'Other' US – and not in a good way.
5. Fanatical and intolerant.
6. Deeply resentful of those who have more economic power.
7. Feral, savage, and degenerate.
8. Physically and psychologically misshapen.
9. Brutal, callous, and psychotically idiosyncratic.
10. Deeply attached to a squalid, filthy, nightmarish, hovel furnished with Ed Gein–style human remains, trophies from previous victims, and other visual signifiers of deviancy (such as the oddly unsettling sight of a chicken in a tiny cage in *The Texas Chain Saw Massacre*).

11. They treat fellow human beings like animals and preserve their remains in the form of smoked meats, barbeque, or stashed away in dirty old jars. The line between human beings and other animals does not exist for them: everything and everyone is considered fit for consumption. They survive, but at the cost of their humanity.

Before I begin my discussion of the films themselves, it is important to note that women are often marginalised in the backwoods horror sub-genre, appearing only as victims from the outside world (though in more recent films, they often features as resilient Final Girl figures). Occasionally, as in *Motel Hell*, they show up as peripheral associates of the male villains, but *Timber Falls* is the only film of this kind I have seen in which a woman is a principal antagonist (and she is part of a couple, like Vincent's sister in *Motel Hell* [another female accomplice] – interestingly, both women are named Ida). The strong associations between backwoods horror and deviant white males seen throughout this chapter may help explain why the sub-genre is so focused on problematic working-class masculinity, to the frequent exclusion of notable female antagonists.

The protagonists

With the notable exception of *Tucker and Dale vs Evil* (2010), which is the only film discussed here in which the heroes are themselves rural southerners, the protagonists of these films are white, middle-class, and relatively young urban or suburban outsiders (*Deliverance* and *Southern Comfort*, which feature men in their 30s and 40s, are notable exceptions to this rule). A college education is often explicitly mentioned, or strongly implied. The 'Type 2' film tends to focus upon a mixed-sex group of college kids (the usual configuration is two couples and a single individual). The 'Type 1' film often features a larger, same-sex group, almost always male (except for the all-female groups found in *Mother's Day* (1980) and *The Descent* (2005), although the later doesn't really qualify as a backwoods horror film because the antagonists are inhuman cave-dwelling mutants). All-male groups who find trouble in the wilderness can be also found in the Arkansas-set city guys versus poachers film *Hunters Blood* (1986) (tag line – 'After *Deliverance*, comes… the ultimate test in Survival'); *Shoot* (1976) (another *Deliverance* knock-off made and set in Canada); *Rituals* (1977 – another Canadian film);[77] *Southern Comfort* (1981); and, more recently, *Trigger Man* (2007), which is set in Delaware.

Very rarely does a backwoods horror film of either variety focus upon the ordeal undergone by an individual rather than a group. The 2011 remake of *I Spit on Your Grave* is a rare example of this configuration, whilst both *Straw Dogs* (2013) and *Timber Falls* (2011) focus on couples (it could be argued this is because *I Spit on Your Grave* is more of a rape-revenge film than a backwoods horror film, although there is considerable overlap in this instance). Murderous backwoods dwellers, as far back as *Two Thousand Maniacs!*, therefore, seem to prefer to target groups (perhaps because they too seldom operate alone).

Setting

The general geographical setting of these films, as indicated, is usually the South, although there are a couple of notable exceptions. Three southern states dominate: Louisiana (*Southern Comfort* [1981], *Eaten Alive* [1977], and the 2010 version of *I Spit on Your Grave*); Georgia (*Deliverance* and *Two Thousand Maniacs!*); and Appalachian West Virginia, the setting for *Wrong Turn* (2007), *Timber Falls*, and *Tucker and Dale vs Evil*. Texas is home, of course, to *The Texas Chain Saw Massacre* and its various prequels, sequels, and remakes, as well as Rob Zombie's *House of 1000 Corpses* (2003) and *The Devil's Rejects* (2005). As noted earlier, the 2011 version of *Straw Dogs* moves the action from Cornwall, England, to small-town Mississippi. Both *Motel Hell* and *The Hills Have Eyes* are set in California, but, setting aside, have much in common with the southern-set films mentioned here, although I will not be discussing them in much detail. *Cabin Fever* is set in a generic, never specifically identified region of the Deep South, which is perhaps an indication that in more recent iterations of the sub-genre, regional specificity is less important than a pre-existing notion of problematic 'southern-ness' gleaned from earlier films.

The backwoods horror movie tends to employ the same basic locations: the cabin in the woods, the lonely old farmhouse, and the woods themselves (a locale in which the protagonists are hunted like animals). As noted in the first chapter, *The Cabin in the Woods* (2012) – a horror film about the way in which we construct and watch horror films – plays around with the idea that this particular setting is such a clichéd one. In a historical sense, the cabin in the woods as a specific structure is most particularly associated with the backwoods settlement (as outlined in much greater detail by Jordan and Kaups, who devote an entire chapter to 'backwoods folk architecture'). The major literary association is, of course, with Thoreau, whose 'house in the woods', constructed at a cost of only $28, represented independence and freedom from a world in which men had increasingly become '[...] tools of their tools'.[78] As we shall see, the same qualities of thriftiness and self-reliance valorised by Thoreau in *Walden* (1854) become signifiers of stagnation and dangerous insularity in the films discussed here.

The fact that *Deliverance, Southern Comfort,* and *Trigger Man* all take place almost mainly outdoors is a further indication of the fact that they are action thrillers with some backwoods horror elements rather than as backwoods horror films per se. The protagonists of 'Type 2' films always at some stage find themselves exploring a run-down rural dwelling. Even in films such as *Timber Falls* and *Wrong Turn,* in which the characters do spend significant stretches of time outdoors, the protagonists finally end up being brutalised indoors.

Both the generic cabin in the woods and the *Texas Chain Saw Massacre*-style creepy old farmhouse owe much to the Ed Gein school of interior design. As Jennifer Brown notes of newspaper coverage of Gein, 'Images of his ramshackle farmhouse abounded as frequently as his smiling face. The dirty kitchen, grimy stove top, and eviscerated bodies visually fulfilled a stereotype of the unhygienic hillbilly who cannot keep house and who butchers meat within the home.'[79] *The Texas Chain Saw Massacre* established the trend for Gein-inspired interiors (though Hitchcock got there first with the fruit cellar and the eerily preserved bedrooms in *Psycho* [1960]). These paradigmatic 'Terrible houses', as Robin Wood characterises the homestead in *The Texas Chain Saw Massacre,*[80] invariably feature all kinds of unconventional objects made out of human and animal remains. Amateur taxidermy is a standard visual trope. Animal heads and hides appear regularly, as do bear traps which, will, like Chekov's gun, invariably be deployed in the last act. One of the things that is disturbing about these dwellings is that they blur the lines between interior and exterior, human and animal. Wood notes of the house in *The Texas Chain Saw Massacre* that 'the borderline between house and slaughterhouse (between work and leisure) has disappeared'.[81] On the single instance I have come across in backwoods horror in which a cabin in the woods seems a cosy and well-maintained place (in *Timber Falls*), all manner of awfulness is actually going on in the mineshaft that lies under the property (as in the cellar in *The Evil Dead* [1981]). The same can also be said of the setting of *The Cabin in the Woods,* to which there is, as the poster art suggests, a great deal more than first meets the eye.

Opening the fridge in these films is never a great idea in the 'Type 2' film. They will invariably contain a corpse, or dismembered body parts and/or jars in which clumps of human tissue float like sinister pickles. Containers filled with teeth turn up as well. Occasionally, a saucepan is found merrily bubbling away on the stove: it will, of course, contain human remains (another nod to Gein). These movies also make it clear that when they're not out stalking college kids, backwoods killers like nothing better than to hoard junk that will then be strategically placed around their home in order to create an atmosphere of maximum creepiness. Old gramophones (scratchily playing as the protagonists warily enter) recur frequently, as do broken dolls, defaced photograph albums, filthy old quilts, and collections of missing-person posters or suggestive newspaper clippings.

This focus upon the pack-rat sensibilities of the backwoods aggressor emphasises the fact that mainstream American culture appears to find something inherently suspicious about the self-sufficiency of those who make their own belongings rather than buy mass-produced products in a store like 'normal' folks. The 'make do and mend' philosophy of those who recycle or salvage what others would throw out, though seen as admirable in narratives which emphasise 'positive rurality' (such as *The Hunger Games* trilogy and *Walden*) are here further markers of deviancy.

Finally, it is interesting to note how often lakes feature in both varieties of the backwoods horror film. The impetus for the canoeing trip in *Deliverance* is the creation of a lake that will swamp the whole area (Dickey's novel even concludes with this image). The cabin in the woods very often adjoins a lake, as in *I Spit on Your Grave*, *Cabin Fever*, *Tucker and Dale vs Evil*, and *Motel Hell*. The female lead in *Timber Falls* is kidnapped from a lakeside campsite. Even in films which do not otherwise conform to the classic backwoods horror template – such as *Let's Scare Jessica to Death* (1971), *Friday the 13th* (1980, 2009), *Don't Go into the Woods* (1981), the 2009 remake of *Last House on the Left*, and Michael Haneke's home invasion narrative *Funny Games* (1997/2007) – the lakeside setting becomes a crucial plot point. The frequency with which lake settings occur in these films is perhaps due to the fact that they attract tourists and outdoor-pursuits enthusiasts. In addition, a lake makes a great place to hide a dead body, provided you dispose of it in the correct manner.[82]

The reason for the trip

There are a few basic reasons given as to why the victims in these films have ventured into the backwoods in the first place. Sometimes, it's so that the protagonist(s) can have peace to work on a scholarly or creative exercise that emphasises their difference from the supposed anti-intellectualism of the rural community. Jennifer Hills (Sarah Butler) in *I Spit on Your Grave* (2011) is working on a novel; David Sumner (James Marsden) in *Straw Dogs* (2010) is writing a screenplay, and one of the protagonists in *House of 1000 Corpses* is working on a guidebook. More frequently, outsiders visit because they want to go hiking, or caving, or canoeing. There is an assumption that the local people do not experience the beauty of the wilderness in the same way that our well-educated outsiders do. The visitors use the outdoors for physical and spiritual enrichment. They are clad in expensive outdoor gear, carry tents and cameras and GPS systems and compasses, and remark upon the beauty of their surroundings.[83] They often see the countryside solely in terms of its suitability for recreational activities. In the remakes of both *Straw Dogs* and *I Spit on Your Grave*, there are scenes in which the heroine is seen jogging through the woods. In each instance, her skimpy clothing emphasises her vulnerability to sexual aggression, as well as her excellent physical condition, which contrasts with the slovenly demeanour of the locals.

The contrast between the ways in which locals and outsiders perceive their surroundings in these films brings to mind the questions asked by William Cronon in his 1996 essay, 'The Trouble with Wilderness':

> Why, for instance, is the 'wilderness experience' so often conceived of as a form of recreation best enjoyed by those whose class privileges give them the time and resources to leave their jobs behind and 'get away from it all'? Why does the protection of wilderness so often seem to pit urban recreationalists against rural people who actually earn their living from the land (excepting those who sell goods and services to the tourists themselves)?[84]

In a reflection of the contradictory perceptions surrounding the 'wilderness experience' that Cronon identifies in the real world, rural dwellers in the backwoods horror film almost always have a utilitarian and brutally pragmatic relationship with their surroundings. Their main forms of outdoor recreation are hunting and fishing activities which strongly evoke the definitions of the backwoods settler cited earlier.[85] The attire worn for these activities seldom changes much from the jeans/baseball cap/flannel shirt-style attire worn the rest of the time: these men (and as Clover notes, the local people in these films *are* almost always male) dress the same whether they're inside or outside the house.[86] They also tend to be boorish and disrespectful. Their hunts are often accompanied by the consumption of large amounts of beer or moonshine (*Deliverance, I Spit on Your Grave, Timber Falls*, and *Straw Dogs* all have scenes in which beer-drinking louts victimise visitors). When the outsiders themselves hunt – as in *Deliverance* – the method of hunting (bow and arrow) and the mist-shrouded reverence with which they carry out the act make it clear that their actions are motivated by higher reasoning than that of the crude louts who actually live in the area. This may partially be because the outsiders don't need to eat what they kill: their hunting is done for reasons other than brute necessity.

Occasionally, as in *Cabin Fever, Tucker and Dale vs Evil*, and the backwoods-set slasher *The Tripper* (2006), the outsiders (always arrogant college kids in this instance) see the countryside only as a convenient locale for partying: their revels, naturally, never go as planned. These kinds of characters are always depicted as being less sympathetic than the outsiders who want to commune with nature or engage in physical or intellectual pursuits. Some backwoods horror films feature protagonists who actually have no intention of stopping and are 'just passing through'. Inevitably, they are prevented from completing their journey by events which trap them in one place and subject them to the attentions of violent locals.

Last chance for gas

The ominous encounter at the local gas station is one of stock situational tropes of the southern-set backwoods horror movie. The reasons are simple: first of all, anyone who has travelled to a remote locale will need to refuel eventually. It is also the first location where the working-class southerner and middle-class tourist encounter one another. Buying gas necessitates a financial transaction, which feeds into the sense of economic resentment so often found in these narratives. The gas station also represents the last chance for our protagonists to turn back. It is the point at which they make the fatal choice to continue the journey that will lead them to disaster. Ominous warnings from grizzled old storekeepers/gas station attendants are a regular feature of the subgenre. It's a trope that mimics one of the stock situations in the horror film more generally: the moment when the innkeeper tells the unwary traveller not to continue their journey to some ill-omened castle on a hill. The proprietor of the last-chance-to-turn-back gas station is always an unsavoury older man (often wearing overalls).

Furthermore, early encounters at the gas station – which usually functions as the general store also – can kick-start the whole plot. If the youngsters in *The Texas Chain Saw Massacre* had been told that they'd have to wait around for a day until the fuel delivery arrived, they wouldn't have gone to see the old family homestead. What's particularly interesting about this scene is the fact that the attendant, who is later revealed to be a member of the cannibal family, specifically warns them *not* to go to 'the old Franklin place'. In *Wrong Turn*, Chris (Desmond Harrington) follows the map on a wall at a rural gas station despite the fact that it is also covered in missing-person posters. In *I Spit on Your Grave* (2011), the first meeting between newcomer and local at the gas station provides the impetus for the rest of the plot. When she stops to ask for directions to her rural retreat, Jennifer Hills encounters the three louts who will later attack her. Their ringleader, 'Johnny' (Jeff Branson), uses a cheesy pick-up line, but she laughs in response, and then accidentally spills water over him when they tussle for her car keys (an early indication of his latent sexual violence). By asking for directions, she has inadvertently let assailants know exactly where she lives, thus setting in motion the chain of events that will culminate in her gang rape and attempted murder.

During the rest-stop at the Aintry garage in *Deliverance*, each member of the group behaves in ways which will later prove decisive. Lewis (Burt Reynolds), well aware of his economic superiority, haggles with the local men he has hired to drive their cars from one part of the river to another; Drew (Ronnie Cox), the gentlest member of the group, whose body will, Roger Malvin-style, soon be disposed of in the wilderness, plays music with a local boy (Billy Raden). Bobby (Ned Beatty) treats the locals with disrespect, therefore lending his later rape/humiliation a certain level of inevitability, while Ed (John Voight) watches the scene with a quiet intelligence which helps establish him as the most sympathetic member of the group. The glimpse of the town itself is a deeply unedifying one: the locals are unkempt, toothless yokels, many of whom seem to have physical or mental disabilities (during the equivalent scene in Dickey's novel, Ed observes that, 'There is always something wrong with people in the country [...]').[87]

The gas station scenes in *Tucker and Dale vs Evil*, *Cabin Fever*, and *The Cabin in the Woods* depict comedic versions of the encounters just described. The gas station scene in *Cabin Fever* features an angelic-seeming blond child who sits quietly on the porch outside. When the most boorish of the college kids asks, 'Cat got your tongue?', the boy bites him and hangs on for dear life, until a baseball bat-wielding local intervenes, shouting, 'Everyone knows not to sit next to Dennis!' Inside the store, the clutter and griminess always associated with such places is present: the crazy old coot behind the counter is obsessed by his bottle collection, and the visitors (who buy several cases of 'Arrogant Bastard Ale') are condescending and ill mannered, thus telegraphing their certain doom. The college students who (with one notable exception) become the antagonists in *Tucker and Dale vs Evil* stop at a store called 'Last Chance Gas'. This is where the first in a series of increasingly outlandish misunderstandings between local and visitor take place. Won over by the beauty and pleasant demeanour of Allie (Katrina Bowden) one of the college girls, Dale (Tyler Labine), a shy but sensitive local man, is encouraged by his best friend Tucker (Alan Tudyk) to just be himself, and 'Whatever happens, just smile and laugh'. Unfortunately, Dale's typically 'redneck' attire, strained grin, and nervous giggling – together with the fact that he is absent-mindedly holding a scythe when he approaches her – mean that he conforms to every stereotypical ideal of backwards monstrosity. As a result, Dale's well-meaning overtures are interpreted as a threat. The gas station scene in *The Cabin in the Woods* is where the protagonists unwittingly pass the first major 'checkpoint' en route to their ritual sacrifice: it is inhabited by a crazy old man known as 'the harbinger', who is actually part of the elaborate conspiracy designed to lead them to their doom. Even in films where the gas station doesn't feature as prominently as in these instances there is usually some sort of stand-in location. For instance, in *Straw Dogs*, David makes a fool of himself in the local bar by trying to pay with a credit card and by ordering Bud Lite. *Timber Falls* features a ranger station which comes complete with missing-person posters, and a ranger who helpfully warns, 'We have a few generations of families that have called this place home. Most of them are friendly.'

'He's not retarded, he's misunderstood!': mutilation, deformity, and 'backwardness'

The presence of some kind of physical deformity amongst the locals is a given in the backwoods horror movie. At the very least, they will be toothless, physically repulsive (notable for their extreme leanness or gross obesity), and unhygienic. This contrasts with the higher standard of living enjoyed by the middle-class outsiders who can most likely afford health insurance. Here, the beautiful are also good, particularly if, like the Final Girls played by Eliza Dushku in *Wrong Turn* and Jessica Biel in *The Texas Chain Saw Massacre* remake, they spend much of the film clad in white tank-tops, which will later be besmirched with strategically placed smudges and tears. It is in this trope that we can see the underlying strain of eugenics so important to the construction of early twentieth-century figurations of the 'redneck' and the 'hillbilly' really come to the fore.

Historically, the poor in the South actually did have a propensity towards coarse complexions and skin disorders due to the prevalence of diseases of poverty such as pellagra and hookworm. Pellagra became particularly prevalent amongst the lower social classes from the early twentieth century onwards, when mass produced corn meal that had been stripped of its vitamin-rich exterior began to dominate the marketplace.[88] By 1912, the problem had become so severe that the government established a commission to investigate the disease, which caused lassitude, dermatitis, dementia, and diarrhoea.

Travellers passing through the South in the years following the Civil War often described poor white bodies as 'degenerate' and 'death-like'. Particular attention was paid to their excessive whiteness; one commentator noting, 'The [poor] whites…have a grey, earthy look, as if the Lord God had formed them of the dust of the ground.'[89] Pellagra and hookworm both caused changes to the physical appearance of the person afflicted, and their ubiquity helped give rise to the preconception that poor whites had a distinctively unhealthy 'look' about them. Whilst conducting a 1902 survey on the prevalence of hookworm in the South, parasitologist Charles Warren Stiles discovered that the disease was widespread, and noted that 'it might be possible for some of the proverbial laziness of the poorer classes of the white population'.[90] Stiles' observation soon caught on: in his 1925 article on 'The Poor Whites of the Ante-Bellum South', Paul H. Buck noted that clay-eating was historically associated with the poor whites (hence the prominence of epithets such as 'dirt-eater') and argued that the 'poor man's malady' of hookworm was the true cause of 'much of the trouble popularly associated to "dirt-eating", "resin-chewing", and even some of the proverbial laziness of the poorer classes of the white population'.[91]

The presence of so many 'sickly' looking specimens in the southern-set backwoods horror movie is not just, therefore, as Clover argues, 'the material expression of family wrongness (inbreeding being one obvious form of wrongness)'.[92] It also underlines the historical reality that the deprivation and economic marginality endured by the rural poor, particularly in the South, negatively impacted upon their physical appearance and health. The physically deformed/disfigured or mentally challenged local turns up in practically every backwoods horror film, beginning with the mentally disabled banjo-playing boy in *Deliverance* (the child is an albino in Dickey's novel), and Leatherface (Gunnar Hansen) in

The Texas Chain Saw Massacre (1974). Leatherface's physical difference is emphasised even more in the 2003 remake and the 2006 prequel *The Texas Chainsaw Massacre: The Beginning*, in which we are told that he was born on the floor of the slaughterhouse. The infant's facial deformities (characterised here as the result of skin disease) cause him to be abandoned in a dumpster, but he was taken home by a member of the deeply dysfunctional 'Hewitt' family and grows up to be a self-mutilating psychotic with impressive butchering skills. As his adoptive uncle, Charlie Hewitt (R. Lee Emery) notes, 'You don't have to look pretty to work down at the slaughterhouse!'

In the remakes of *Straw Dogs* and *I Spit on Your Grave* (as in the original, non-southern set versions), it is the actions of a mentally disabled young man which escalate the conflict between warped locals and naïve outsiders. Matthew, in *I Spit on Your Grave*, wrongly interprets the heroine's impulsive hug as a come-on, and when he's talking to his bullying 'friends' from the gas station, he inadvertently inflames their desire to humiliate her, thus precipitating her rape, in which he takes part. Jeremy Niles (Dominic Purcell) is the mentally disabled local associated with sexual aggression in the *Straw Dogs* remake. He panics when a teenage girl is flirtatious towards him and kills her, an act which leads to the film's climactic seige. Clyde and Ida, the husband-and-wife duo who kidnap the young couple in *Timber Falls* aren't obviously disfigured or disabled themselves, but cannot have children of their own, which is presented here as an indication of genetic 'wrongness'. They also keep the deformed foetuses Ida was unable to carry to term stored in jars in the cellar. Ida's younger brother Deacon is clearly mentally disabled, and is also associated with sexual aggressiveness: he attempts to rape the heroine, and it is implied that he did the same to other female captives. *Cabin Fever*'s witty take on the association between the rural resident and mental retardation finds expression in Dennis-the-biter, whilst in addition to Leatherface, *The Texas Chain Saw Massacre* remake features a buck-toothed, feral child named Jedidiah (David Dorfman) who occasionally pops up to make useful but grammatically suspect observations like 'Road don't go there'. Other indicators of physical and mental difference include obesity (more usually associated with the few rural women that show up, as in *Motel Hell* and the *Texas Chain Saw Massacre* remakes and prequel, although the original Leatherface is less than svelte). Clover also notes the prevalence with which male 'oral deficiency' surfaces, particularly amongst the perpetrators of sexual assaults, dryly observing, '[...] the country is a world beyond dentistry'.[93]

The most extreme depictions of physical difference amongst the 'locals' can be found in two relatively recent films, *Wrong Turn* (2005) and *Albino Farm* (2009). The cabin-dwelling antagonists in *Wrong Turn* are so misshapen that they barely even look human anymore and are distinguishable from each other only by the nature of their deformity (the villains are named in the end credits as 'Three Finger', 'Saw Tooth', and 'One Eye'). *Albino Farm* is about a group of college students investigating contemporary American myths and legends (clearly, they've seen *The Blair Witch Project*) who find themselves trapped in Shiloh, an isolated community in the Ozarks populated entirely by sinister locals with all manner of outlandish deformities. In some of the most recent films of this type, therefore, the genetically 'substandard' rural inhabitant no longer even really qualifies as human. Their 'degeneracy' has placed them entirely outside of 'decent' society. It is a figuration that has much in common with the rigid standards of genetic 'fitness' touted by the ERO a century before.

Sexual assault

One of the most significant differences between 'Type 1' and 'Type 2' backwoods horror narratives is that rape and sexual assault only occur in 'Type 1' films. There are some rare almost-exceptions – such as the scenes in which the heroines of *Wrong Turn* and *Timber Falls* are briefly slavered over by disfigured antagonists – but in both films, the threat of sexual abuse is quickly defused. Generally speaking, in the 'Type 2' film the sexual threat is entirely absent. This is, perhaps, so that the antagonists can avoid the kind of dilemma that meat factory scion Mason Verger projects onto his suave nemesis in *Hannibal* (2001): 'Does Lecter want to fuck her or kill her or eat her alive?' If anything, the fact that the villains in this variety of the sub-genre have no sexual interest in their nubile young victims actually renders them even *more* terrifying. When Sally desperately cries 'I'll do anything you want' in *The Texas Chain Saw Massacre*, and is repaid with hoots of derision from her captors, their reaction confirms that what we have here is a kind of monstrosity so far outside of 'normal' understanding as to be incomprehensible. These antagonists actually see their victims as little more than livestock.

By way of contrast, rape is a frequent occurrence in the 'Type 1' film. In both versions of *I Spit on Your Grave*, the heroine is raped by local men who see her independence and economic superiority as a personal affront. Another rape scene is central to *Straw Dogs*. Of course, the most infamous rape scene in the sub-genre involves a male victim: Bobby

Tripp in *Deliverance*. Rape metaphors in fact play quite a big role in both the book and the film, in which Bobby's violation and that of the natural landscape itself is linked.[94] Though Michael and Sheryl, the young couple in *Timber Falls,* are taken captive by locals who try to force them to have sex with each other, the sexual dimension to their ordeal isn't a result of the desire to express dominance or achieve gratification on the part of their jailers. Clyde and Ida want a child of their own, but are determined that it will be born to parents who have been 'properly married' in an impromptu ceremony of their own devising.[95] This leads to the film's one funny line: angered by Michael's refusal to have sex with his unconscious new 'bride', Clyde says, 'It was fine when penetration was a sin, but now that she's your wife, it's sick? Unbelievable.'

Trespass

There is frequently an element of trespass in the actions of the naive outsiders who feature in these films: after all, it is a given from the very beginning that they have entered an environment that is not their own. In *Deliverance, Southern Comfort, Wrong Turn, Timber Falls,* and *Cabin Fever,* we encounter forests inhabited by locals who see 'outsiders' as fair game. As in the first two films, the outsiders have often done something to arouse the ire of the natives. The river on which the suburban businessmen in *Deliverance* intend to spend an invigorating weekend will soon be no more, destroyed by a power company dam that will flood the region in order to fulfil the energy needs of the city. Although the antagonists never directly refer to this fact, and their actions also seem attributable to psychotic degeneracy (in the novel, Ed notes that they have clearly done something like this before), it is also not difficult to see what happens on the banks of the river as at least in part an expression of contempt for the city folks whose desire for more air conditioning has hastened the destruction of a much older and more authentic way of life. It's no surprise that later on, as the lone surviving local man stalks the protagonists from the undergrowth, his actions seem increasingly Indian-like. Clover also dwells upon this link, connecting the 'urbanoia' film with the settler-versus-Indian-western, and arguing that both redneck and Indian are figured as 'indigenous peoples on the verge of being deprived of their native lands'.[96] The local foe in *Deliverance* is only defeated when Ed becomes even more 'Indian-like' and engaged with nature than he is. However, the fact that neither we nor Ed can be completely sure that this is the same man who participated in Bobby's rape makes the justification for their actions highly problematic. To Ed and his pals, as to the audience, all 'rednecks' look alike. It is notable that the two 'Type 1' films discussed here, which are arguably more accurately defined as action thrillers rather than outright horror films (*Deliverance* and *Southern Comfort*), have a degree of moral and psychological complexity missing from many of the other films being considered.

The bickering National Guardsmen in *Southern Comfort* (which is often interpreted by critics as a Vietnam War allegory) do even more to provoke their rural antagonists than Boorman's white-collar professionals.[97] First, they commandeer a boat belonging to local poachers (whose livelihood clearly depends on getting around in the swamps), and then one of their number fires a heavy machine gun loaded with blanks at the Cajuns, provoking a lethal return of fire which kills the unit's commanding officer. It's little wonder that pragmatic newcomer Hardin (Powers Boothe) soon looks even more disgruntled with his comrades in arms than with the Cajuns. The soldiers behave in every respect like an ill-informed and xenophobic invading force, even congratulating themselves on having completed a successful 'raid', when all they have done is blown up a shack. As their Cajun 'POW' (the understandably peeved owner of the shack) later warns: 'We live back in here. This is our home. And nobody don't fuck with us.'

Violation of the domestic space – both by outsiders and by locals – is another common feature of the backwoods horror movie. Jennifer's retreat in *I Spit on Your Grave* is invaded first by the trio of thugs, and then by the vile local sheriff. She later repays the favour by terrorising both of them in *their* own homes. Told to steer clear of 'the old Franklin place', catastrophically, the college kids in *The Texas Chain Saw Massacre* visit it anyway. It may be the old family homestead to Sally and Franklin, but the house just behind it is not, as Leatherface's rapid dispatch of Kurt (the first trespasser to set foot inside) makes clear. As Kim Newman notes, 'In Texas, you are legally allowed to shoot dead someone who steps on your lawn. The kids are trespassing, so this murder spree probably isn't even against the law.'[98] This is thanks to the 1868 Cattle Ranchers Law, still in effect, which states that a landowner can shoot anyone that trespasses upon their territory. The outsiders in *Tucker and Dale vs Evil* not only enter the titular duo's rundown 'vacation home' without asking permission, but they also burn it down. Similarly, both *Wrong Turn* and *Cabin Fever* have scenes in which the protagonists creep around in houses that don't belong to them. An attempted home invasion drives the action of the final third of *Straw Dogs*. In this instance, the climax is foreshadowed by scenes in which the antagonists, who at that point are employed by David to do building work, violate his personal space by playing their music loudly, drinking his beer, and traipsing around the house. It is all leading up to other, more sinister forms of trespass: the killing of a cat, Amy's rape, their attempt to murder David during a hunting trip, and the siege itself.

As Clover notes, breaches of etiquette and violations of conventional notions of cleanliness and dress frequently feature in the rural horror film.

> What is threatening about these little uncivilities is the larger incivility of which they are surface symptoms. In horror, the man who does not take care of his teeth is obviously a man who can, and by the end of the movie will, kill within his kin, commit incest, and or/eat human flesh [...].[99]

Similarly, trespassing, whether it is carried out by the protagonists or antagonists, is invariably a signifier of naiveté (and hence impending doom) on the part of the former, and nefarious designs on the part of the latter.

Hunting

Hunters and hunting (both of animals and of other human beings) looms large in backwoods horror, though most prominently in films of the 'Type 1' variety. The hunting of wild animals – usually deer – provides the most obvious reason why working-class men would be roaming around the woods in the middle of the day (almost none of the outdoors encounters between locals and outsiders take place at night). This also emphasises that when local people enter the backwoods in these narratives, it is seen to be for pragmatic rather than aesthetic reasons. Ed reverently stalks a deer in *Deliverance* because he longs to get in touch with a primal kind of masculinity that will help shake him out of suburban banality. For the backwoods local, hunting often serves a practical purpose: '[...] they kill not for fun but for a living', Clover observes of *Deliverance* knock-off *Hunter's Blood* (1986).[100]

In these films, the line between hunting animals and hunting humans is frequently crossed, as in *Deliverance, Southern Comfort, Cabin Fever, Straw Dogs, I Spit on Your Grave,* and *Motel Hell*, in which agreeable villain 'Farmer Vincent', clad in typical hunting garb, even sets traps for passing motorists. Scenes in which a connection is made between stalking deer and hunting humans are a staple of the sub-genre. Aside from

Ed's transition from unsuccessful deer hunter to ice-cool man killer in *Deliverance*, this connection is made most notably in the *Straw Dogs* remake, which intercuts a scene in which David is on a hunting trip, with events back at the farmhouse, where his wife is being raped by her ex-boyfriend Charlie (Alexander Skarsgård) and his buddies. *Deliverance* and *Trigger Man* both have scenes early on in which the main protagonist has a chance to kill a deer, but misses: such moments are always recalled later when they establish their superior will to survive by killing a human. Bear traps are also frequently deployed on humans. It is a further reminder of the fact that one of the defining characteristics of the backwoods settler was a dependence upon hunting and trapping: in the horror film, what was once a sign of self-reliance and practicality becomes often indicator of cruelty and brutal utilitarianism.

Law enforcement

The forces of law and order in these films are at best ineffectual, and at worst, openly collude in the brutality being meted out to our protagonists. It is, perhaps, no surprise that the figure of the southern sheriff, in particular, should be depicted in such a negative way: after all, the civil rights struggles of the 1960s enshrined in popular culture the stereotype of the racist, baton-wielding southern cop whose job it is to reinforce the corrupt status quo.

Law enforcement is largely absent or irrelevant in *The Texas Chain Saw Massacre*, *Deliverance*, and *Southern Comfort*, but does play an important role in some more recent films. Indeed, the remakes of *The Texas Chain Saw Massacre* and *I Spit on Your Grave* make the small-town sheriff a figure of pivotal importance. In the remake of *The Texas Chain Saw Massacre*, Charlie Hewitt has facilitated the cannibalistic proclivities of his clan by killing Hoyt, the real sheriff, then donning his uniform, and stealing his patrol car. To all outside appearances, he actually *is* the sheriff, and his hippie-hating tendencies, tobacco chewing, and penchant for casual profanity make him such a natural for the job that no one has ever seen fit (or survived) to question his credentials. Sheriff Storch (Andrew Howard) in *I Spit on Your Grave* also abuses the authority that the position bestows upon him (a tendency worsened by the fact that, unlike Hewitt, he is the real thing). He uses his power to humiliate and discredit the victim of a serious assault, and then actively participates in Sarah's rape, attempted murder, and the cover-up that follows.

Sometimes, the local cop is honest, but incompetent. The minute he shows up in *Wrong Turn*, the lone police officer sent to help is shot dead.

Straw Dogs (2011) briefly looks as if it might actually combine two rare backwoods-horror character types in one character – the heroic black guy (he's a morally upstanding Gulf War II veteran) and the good sheriff, but he soon gets a shotgun blast to the face. Stoner cop Winston in *Cabin Fever* parties with the college kids he's supposed to be urging to behave themselves, then reluctantly leads the posse determined to kill them in order to stop the spread of the flesh-eating disease they carry. The sheriff in *Deliverance* is rightly sceptical about the story concocted by Ed and his friends, but is unable to pin anything on them. His parting words, 'Don't ever do nothin' like this again. Don't ever come back up here', are given added resonance by the fact that he is played by James Dickey. The sheriff in *Tucker and Dale vs Evil* spouts ominous warnings and finds the gore-soaked pairs claim that 'These kids are coming up here and killing themselves all over the woods' hard to swallow, but before he can untangle the snarl of misunderstanding that has entangled the well-meaning locals and the dopey college kids who mistakenly believe they are murderers, he's been accidentally killed by a falling beam. The only truly heroic law enforcement officer in any of these films is Bruce (Paul Linke) in *Motel Hell*, who saves the day by defeating his brother Vincent in a chainsaw duel. However, his bravery is considerably undermined by the fact that he's a bumbling idiot who failed to notice that his siblings were slaughtering out-of-towners and selling their flesh to tourists.

Environmental anxieties

This aspect of the Rural Gothic will be discussed in much more detail in the next chapter, but it is worth noting that ecological and environmental concerns occasionally surface in backwoods horror. The obvious precedent is found in *Deliverance*: the looming destruction of the entire region so that a dam designed to fulfil the power needs of the big city can be constructed suffuses our interpretation of the clash between middle-class interloper and working-class aggressor. Although the first film in the *Wrong Turn* franchise offers no explanation for the degeneracy of its murderous hillbillies, the 2007 sequel reveals that they are descended from mountain folk whose penchant for inbreeding and exposure to pollution from a local paper mill made them mutated freaks. *Cabin Fever*'s plot is unique in that the trouble starts when the local reservoir is contaminated by an Ebola-type virus (making the film technically a backwoods horror/pandemic narrative hybrid).

The wittiest reference to environmental concerns can be found in the final moments of *Motel Hell*. Up until this point, Vincent has prided himself on the quality and purity of his 'all natural smoked meats'. What's more, his use of human flesh even has an eco-friendly rationale, one that would have had a particular resonance at a time when bestsellers like Paul Ehrlich's *The Population Bomb* (1968) had made their impact upon the popular consciousness. He sincerely believes, 'There's too many people in the world, and not enough food. This takes care of both problems at the same time.' In his dying moments, Vincent doesn't regret any of the murders he's committed, or the monstrous wrong that has been perpetrated upon his unsuspecting customers. Instead, he confesses, 'My whole life has been a lie! I'm the biggest hypocrite of them all. My meats... I used preservatives!'

'My family's always been in meat': cannibalism

Cannibalism happens only in 'Type 2' backwoods horror movies. The cannibalism in these films is always related to a refusal or inability on the part of the antagonists to differentiate between humans and animals. Dead people are treated with exactly the same kind of utilitarian pragmatism as dead livestock. Sometimes, as in *The Texas Chain Saw Massacre*, this attitude can arguably be seen as the result of an apocalyptic, nihilistic world view.[101] More usually, however, it is a signifier of a dangerously disturbed individual (or collective) pathology. Cannibalism never features in the 'Type 1' film, although suggestions of bestiality/zoosadism do occasionally feature (the infamous 'Squeal like a pig' scene in *Deliverance*, which blurs the lines between animal and human, inevitably comes to mind). As noted earlier, the presence of cannibalism in a film always rules out the threat of sexual assault. From *Two Thousand Maniacs!* onwards, the presence of barbeque made from human flesh is another notable feature of the 'Type 2' backwoods horror narrative: like their real-life Jamestown ancestor 'Collines' (as discussed in the previous chapter), the southern cannibal not only kills humans for food, but also makes a point of turning their flesh into a well-preserved, tasty, and sellable commodity.

As Andrew Warnes (2008) establishes, the very concept of barbeque – itself an 'invented tradition' – is related to how the first European settlers saw both themselves and the 'savages' whose lands they colonised.[102] Warnes argues that

> *barbacoa* or *barbicu* or *barbeque*, however it has been spelled, not only referred to the smoked foods of American Indians, it also enacted European's deep desire to see these foods as barbarous – as the result

of a primitive kind of cookery, savage and base, akin to that which their own distant ancestors long ago performed.[103]

In addition, there exists '[...] a surprisingly long and hitherto unconsidered history of seeing barbecue as a bestial kind of cookery too close to cannibalism for comfort'.[104] Theodore De Bry's 1592 engraving 'A Tupinambán Cannibal Feast', adapted watercolours by founding Virginian colonist John White (later governor of the ill-fated Roanoke settlement) which depicted the decidedly *non-cannibalistic* cooking practices of the Algonquin Indians.[105] In Stade's picture, the Tupinambá cavort around a blazing cooking frame upon which there sits clearly recognisable human limbs, as well as a ribcage: an Indian child can be seen chewing on a hand in one corner, whilst other members of the tribe munch on severed arms and legs. De Bry's picture helped create an association between the barbeque and cannibalism that persists to this day.[106] This association features in *The Texas Chain Saw Massacre*, and its various offshoots, as well as in *Motel Hell* and *The Hills Have Eyes*. In the first two films, the cannibal is no longer the exotic native other, but the murderous rural male (barbequing is almost always represented as a male pastime in American popular culture).[107]

The roadside barbeque joint traditionally afforded rural entrepreneurs the opportunity to sell their wares to neighbours and to those just passing through: 'Across the South [...] they appealed not only to locals glad to have someone else spend long hours tending the barbeque pit but also to automobile travellers seeking the "real" America of regional traditions and customs.'[108] We find two such entrepreneurs in the person of *Motel Hell*'s Farmer Vincent and *The Texas Chain Saw Massacre*'s 'Cook' (named 'Drayton Sawyer' in the sequel). 'My family's always been in meat', the deranged 'Hitchhiker' (Edwin Neal) declares before describing how one goes about making the local delicacy known as 'headcheese'. Seeing the disgust on the faces of his audience, he exclaims, 'You'd probably like it if you didn't know what was in it.' As the youngsters are hunted down and killed by Leatherface, they die in ways that emphasise the fact that their killer doesn't see any distinction between humans and livestock. The most striking example of this comes with the first murder, that of Kurt (William Vail), who is struck on the head with a sledgehammer. Pam (Terry McMinn) is strung up by a meat hook, before being stored in the freezer; Franklin (Paul Partain) is killed by the titular chainsaw. Though she manages to escape with her life (if not perhaps her sanity), Sally (Marilyn Burns) first has to endure the feeble murder attempts made by 'Grandpa' (John Dugan), the 'best killer there ever was'. His hands are so palsied that he can't even lift the small hammer his adoring kin have presented him with so that he can relive old glories. This connection between the murderous activities of the cannibal clan and the family's prior employment in the slaughterhouse is made even more obvious in the sequel and the remake(s). Drayton Sawyer's award-winning chilli makes him a regional celebrity in *The Texas Chainsaw Massacre 2* (1986), whilst in *The Texas Chainsaw Massacre: The Beginning* (2006), we learn that Charlie Hewitt first ate human flesh as a POW in Korea, and then brought the practice home. In a line reminiscent of Scarlett O'Hara's paean to self-sufficiency in *Gone with the Wind* (1939), he even vows 'We ain't never gonna starve again!' as he and the rest of his kin tuck into the late sheriff. He refers to his victims as 'livestock', and treats them accordingly; as in the 1974 original, people are dismembered, frozen while still alive, and strung up on meat hooks before they're dead (although the remake is much more graphic). Continuing this trend, the most recent addition to the franchise, *Texas Chainsaw 3D* (2013) opens with a scene in which the lead character slices raw flesh for a supermarket meat counter. It comes as no surprise whatsoever to later find that she is, unbeknownst to herself, a descendant of the cannibal clan seen in the original.

We know already from the billboard glimpsed at the start of *Motel Hell* that 'It takes all kind of critters to make Farmer Vincent's Critters!', and it soon becomes obvious that humans fall into the 'critter' category. Vincent's captives are buried up to their necks, have their vocal cords slit, and are force-fed through funnels, like geese being fattened up to make *foie gras*.[109] As Vincent explains the ins and outs of the meat-processing business to his seriously dense new love interest, he reminisces about his roadkill-gathering grandmother, who taught him that anything and everything was fit to be eaten, if prepared in the right way. As for the rows of mutilated human captives out in his secret 'vegetable garden', well, 'There's nothing cruel in what I'm doing here. I treat most of my stock better than farmers treat their animals!' This characteristic blurring of the lines between human and animal becomes even more grotesque in the climax of the film, during which Vincent engages in a chainsaw duel with his brother, whilst wearing a pig's head. It's an inevitable precursor, of course, to being killed himself: the butcher has become livestock. Furthermore, as Blake notes, 'The image of the pig is, of course, hugely resonant in the culture of the South [...] a core component in the rituals of agricultural life, and a mainstay in the regional diet.'[110] An association between the human and the porcine frequently features in these films, and pig carcases are a frequent visual trope – see also *Southern Comfort*.

The Jupiter clan in *The Hills Have Eyes* are happy to snack upon the flesh of suburbanites silly enough to venture deep into the desert, but their *absolute* degeneracy, obvious mutations, and cave-dwelling ways arguably align them much more with the cannibalistic underground dwellers of films such as *The Descent* (2005), *C.H.U.D.* (1984), and *Death Line* (1974), all of whom lack even the vaguest social niceties, than with the backwoods cannibal. On a relative scale of culinary sophistication – in which a true gourmand such as Hannibal Lecter sits at the top while the mutant cave/subway dweller lurks at the very bottom – the barbeque-building hillbilly cannibal sits squarely in the middle: still capable of savagery and monstrous, degenerate acts, but with enough sensitivity to want to cook, season, and properly carve their prey first. They often even make a profit by selling their wares to others. Unlike as in the cases of survival cannibalism discussed in the previous chapter, this is cannibalism as lifestyle choice rather than a matter of dire necessity. Crucially, it always involves murder.

Race and the backwoods horror movie

Even though the South has for generations been the American region with the highest proportion of African Americans living there, black faces are very seldom seen in these movies, and on the rare occasion when they do feature, they are almost always peripheral or second-tier characters. Indeed, backwoods horror films often seem notably reluctant to include any plot elements that that could be interpreted as an overt commentary on racial attitudes and race relations. As a result, *Cabin Fever* is one of very few narratives to directly equate the South with racism (though it does so in a supposedly humorous fashion). When the college kids enter the local gas station, one of them sees a rifle behind the counter, and asks the owner: 'What's that gun for?' The reply shocks both visitor and the audience: 'This here gun's for niggers.' We are reminded of this exchange during the follow-up scene at the end of the film: a group of young African Americans file into the store, but instead of attracting racist insults, they are greeted as friends by the owner, who, it turns out, has been repairing the gun for one of the young men. The store owner's use of the word 'nigger' was not meant as a racial slur, but as a means of signalling his familiarity with, and appreciation of, African American street-slang.

Although the uniquely charged racial context of the South is seldom directly referenced, racial anxieties are a common undercurrent. The system of slavery was based upon the premise that African slaves were less human than their white masters, and could, therefore, justifiably be denied freedom. The slave was seen as livestock, to be bought and sold, beaten, or sexually abused, and bred in order to produce more slaves. It is perhaps significant then that scenes in which victims are treated in a dehumanising manner that emphasises the fact that the aggressor or aggressors fail to make any distinction between the human and the animal abound in southern-set backwoods horror movies. Victims are tied up, confined, and variously treated in ways that deliberately dehumanise them. In addition, as previously noted, the representatives of law enforcement tend to be either inept, absent, or complicit in this behaviour. The aggressors are, of course, always resentful poor whites, the group that often felt most threatened by African American demands for equality, because they lived in much closer physical and economic proximity to them than wealthy plantation owners.

African Americans are not the only racial group missing here, however. Asians and Hispanics are, if anything, even more uncommon, although the Creole-speaking Cajuns in *Southern Comfort* represent a very obvious stand-in for the Vietnamese. Although the Indian is often *implicitly* present in these films, Native American *characters* are entirely absent here too. The backwoods horror sub-genre is, therefore, notable for its racial homogeneity. (Although this is something that could also be said of American horror in general, as we shall see.)

The truck driver who helps Sally at the end of *The Texas Chain Saw Massacre* is black, and though his onscreen time only lasts a few seconds, we find ourselves reassured by his colour, because it means that he cannot possibly be 'one of those' crazy rednecks. Blackness here, in fact, means safety, and the hope of returning to 'civilisation' in one piece. There are no black characters at all in *Deliverance, Two Thousand Maniacs!, Wrong Turn, Motel Hell, I Spit on Your Grave, Timber Falls,* or any *The Texas Chain Saw Massacre* remakes/prequels, with the exception of the most recent, *Texas Chainsaw 3D* (typically, he is the first character to die). As previously noted, black sheriffs show up in *Straw Dogs* and *Tucker and Dale vs Evil* but both are quickly killed. The latter also has two black college students, but they're minor members of the group. Holden (Jesse Williams) in *The Cabin in the Woods* is a sympathetic and fairly well-developed character, but he also dies long before the end of the film.

As Robin R. Mears Coleman (2011) notes, on the relatively rare occasions when black characters feature as the principal protagonists of American horror movies, they are overwhelmingly associated with specifically urban settings, and with poverty, crime, and drug abuse – all issues seen to be, albeit inaccurately, problems of the urban underclass.[111] Referring to 1980s horror cinema, she argues: 'While Blacks played a central imagistic role in inciting racial, spatial, and underclass fears in 1980s horror films the actual participation of Blacks was fairly fleeting or nonexistent [...] Most notably, Blacks were nowhere to be found in popular horror films set outside of the urban.'[112] The same can certainly be said of the backwoods horror film: the assumption seems to be that little to no Black people either live in or, for whatever reason, journey through the rural South. Of course, as Coleman observes, '[...] a film need not have a black character to have something to say for or against Blackness'.[113] As I have already argued, the backwoods horror move tells us a great deal about how the poor and disenfranchised working-class rural white is often seen in American popular culture: it is equally the case, I would suggest, that these films also illustrate the extent to which the nation still struggles to come to terms with slavery.

Economic anxieties

Clover convincingly argues that class and economic disenfranchisement are central to the city/country horror film, and points out that rural dwellers in these movies are always poor, or at least, obviously poorer than those that they are tormenting.[114] As a result, economic transactions in the backwoods horror movie are usually fraught with tension. The hero of *Two Thousand Maniacs!* is, as he repeatedly reminds us, on the way to a *very* important teaching conference, a fact that leaves his middle-class credentials in little doubt. In *The Texas Chain Saw Massacre,* we are told that Sally and Franklin's grandfather reared cattle for the slaughterhouse – and presumably reaped the profits – whilst employees like the cannibal clan did the dirty work of killing the animals. (In the 2003 remake, Leatherface's first murder is that of his boss, which reinforces from the outset the idea that economic resentment is a factor in his behaviour.) The financial, intellectual, and educational superiority which the Jennifer Hills character inadvertently displays at the beginning of *I Spit on Your Grave* (2010) exacerbates the desire of her working-class attackers to 'take her down a peg or two'. David Sumner in *Straw Dogs* (2011) continuously shows off his economic superiority in ways that underline his naiveté and arrogance. (The film has a running joke in which he keeps, unsuccessfully, trying to pay for items in local businesses with his credit card). In *Southern Comfort,* the disrespect that the National Guard unit show towards the Cajuns is highlighted when they steal a poacher's boat, an essential for economic survival in this environment, and gloss over it by suggesting that they can always 'leave a note'. Similarly, Lewis's arrogance when negotiating with the men he hires to drive his group's cars to the end of the river in *Deliverance* gives us the first real jolt of urban/rural hostility in the film. The outsiders, it is clear, have all of the money, and often appear to believe that this makes them superior to the often visibly deprived locals – a misconception that usually has deadly consequences.

The car graveyard

The one-liner 'You might be a redneck if you mow your lawn and find your car' is a staple of stand-up comedian Jeff Foxworthy's well-known 'You might be a redneck… ' routine. It is therefore fitting to finish this chapter by noting that one of the prime visual signifiers of the backwoods horror movie is the car graveyard. The protagonists of 'Type 2' films are forever accidentally stumbling across rusting vehicles belonging to previous victims. These car graveyards are often located next to the home of the villains, who clearly like to keep a trophy of their nefarious crimes at close quarters. The presence of the car graveyard helps establish two things: first, that the killings have been going on for some time; and second, that this setting represents the ultimate triumph of those who remain stuck in one place at the expense of the dead car owners who were 'just passing through'. The vehicles we see immobilised in these scenes all belonged to people whose travel plans were violently disrupted by murderous degenerates happy to stagnate once they can take out their violent urges on outsiders. Just like their owners, these cars are meant to be on the road, but will never complete their journey.

The trope can first be seen enacted in the original *The Texas Chain Saw Massacre*, which features cars hidden by netting. The 2006 prequel has a scene which documents the *beginnings* of a car graveyard. *Tucker and Dale vs Evil* also features cars hidden in the woods by a killer. Whilst attempting to reach safety, *Wrong Turn*'s protagonists find themselves surrounded by old cars and trucks which still contain photographs and other items belonging to the murdered owners. The obvious question here, as elsewhere, is why the killers would choose to keep such obvious evidence of their crimes in their own backyard. The answer may lie in the fact that the car graveyard also serves a certain totemic function. It is a monument to the fixity and arrested development which in itself represents one of the most important characteristics of the backwoods horror movie (and the Rural Gothic in general). Although they serve no ritualistic function, abandoned cars are also frequently glimpsed in the 2012 film *The Tall Man*. Although it is not a backwoods horror film, the story is set in a deeply run-down and deprived former mining town in which the people are as depressed as the jobs market. Broken-down old cars are, therefore tellingly, a frequent feature of the mise en scène – these are people that are, quite literarily, going nowhere. As we shall see in Chapter 5, stalled and rusting cars are also a motif of post-apocalyptic narratives, often as a sign that 'Manifest Destiny' itself has come to a dead stop.

The post-2000 backwoods horror film

In the current era, it is rare to see an American horror film in which those who live in rural poverty are depicted with any degree of sensitivity or complexity (*The Tall Man* makes some attempt at this, but although set in the US, it is worth noting that it was written and directed by a Frenchman). What makes many of the more recent American backwoods horror movies more problematic in this regard than their 1970s antecedents is that they tend to be second-generation copies (sometimes, as in the various remakes discussed here, in a very literal sense) written and directed by film-makers who seem to have forgotten that places like rural Georgia and the Appalachian backwoods are in fact real, as are the people that live there. In post-2000 movies such as *Wrong Turn* and the various *The Texas Chain Saw Massacre* spin-offs, the rural antagonists sometimes even become so far removed from humanity as to be rendered *entirely* other. As Blake notes of *Wrong Turn* (one of the most egregious offenders in this regard), 'In its formulaic predictability, an its utterly stereotypical dehumanising of the backwoodsman as inbred and savage mutant, *Wrong Turn* is not only a highly-intersexual work, but a knowing illustration as to how the monstrous other may be deployed to serve dominant ideologies of class and nationhood).'[115]

Both *Deliverance* (book and film) and the original version of *The Texas Chain Saw Massacre* are linked to American history, past and present, in a manner that any engaged viewer is likely to be able to pick up upon. Dickey's novel, a lyrical, elegiac thriller, displays a real respect for the wilderness, and for the people who eke out their lives there. Although many of these paeans to self-sufficiency and nature come from Lewis, a narcissistic survivalist, Ed, the sympathetic narrator, also expresses admiration for those who have the skills to survive in the backwoods. He and Lewis even see self-sufficient rural folks as being superior to complacent middle-class suburbanites like themselves. It is partially for this reason that Dickey presents the terrible experience undergone by the men as an ultimately regenerative process (Richard Slotkin would approve).[116] They have been tested by the worst that mankind and nature can throw at them, and he and Lewis have survived relatively unscathed.

Although much of the complexity of this relationship between the outsiders and the locals found in the source novel are glossed over in the film (in which, importantly, the events of that weekend are not presented to us as in any way regenerative), there still remains a relative sensitivity to both people and place. This is, perhaps, best expressed in the famous 'duelling banjo' sequence, and in the scene in which Ed cries when he is overcome by the simple generosity and kindliness of the country folk who open up their home to him at the end of the film. These kinds of nuances are entirely missing from many of the films that imitate the basic plot set-up of Boorman's film, though not, it must be said, from *Southern Comfort*, which goes to some pains to make it clear that the Guardsmen have brought trouble upon themselves, and that not all the Cajuns want to kill them.

Similarly, whilst the monstrous family in *The Texas Chain Saw Massacre* are certainly depicted as hideous, disfigured Others, their deviance isn't presented to us as a direct consequence of their status as deprived backwoods inhabitants. Certainly, this aspect of their situation is important – they have been left behind by the modern world, and the jobs in which they clearly once took pride in have now been overtaken by a sanitised and mechanised slaughterhouse – but as the horoscopes read out by Pam at the start of the film make clear, the terrible fate she and her friends will soon suffer is also a manifestation of disaster on a cosmic, and not just a regional scale. In contrast, *Wrong Turn* unthinkingly depicts its backwoods antagonists as monstrous Others who lack even basic human attributes, and barely even look human. In *The Texas Chain Saw Massacre*, even Leatherface is imbued with a certain degree of psychological complexity (the viewer is even put in the disconcerting position of sympathising with him when he is violently berated by the cook), but no such nuance exists here.

Whilst the *Straw Dogs* and *I Spit on Your Grave* remakes make some token gestures towards establishing a cultural context for their city/country clashes (the former attempts to essay a rather ham-fisted 'Red State alpha male versus Blue State wealthy nerd' conflict between David and his nemesis Charlie), it is obvious that the decision to move the action of the original films to the region wasn't rooted in any desire to explore the relationship between the southern small town and the outsider, but was made rather because these days, audiences *expect* that stories like this will take place in an explicitly southern locale.

Tellingly, one of the few films of recent years to dramatise this all too familiar plot dynamic with any degree of originality or insight is *Tucker and Dale vs Evil*, which is a well-observed satire, and as such, like *The Cabin in the Woods* (another comedy film which deconstructs many of the tropes of the backwoods horror movie), is more of a movie *about* backwoods horror movies than a straightforward backwoods horror movie itself. The recent appearance of both films is a sign, perhaps, that the resurgence experienced by the sub-genre during the mid- to late 2000s has completely run out of steam, just as the release of Wes Craven's 1997 movie *Scream* sounded the temporary death knell for the slasher sub-genre.

There has, however, been one non-satirical backwoods-set film that depicts the rural poor with a striking degree of sympathy and sensitivity. Debra Granik's *Winter's Bone* (2010), based on the novel by Daniel Woodrell, is set in an impoverished, ruggedly bleak community in the Ozark Mountains of southern Missouri. Tellingly, there are hardly any outsiders at all in the film. The story is about a resourceful 16-year-old girl named Ree Dolly (Jennifer Lawrence) who must find her meth-dealing, no-good father Jessup in order to save the family home from repossession by bailiffs. Although it isn't without Gothic elements (a superbly eerie scene which takes place on a lake at night comes to mind), *Winter's Bone* certainly isn't a backwoods horror film, and nor does it aspire to be, despite containing characters who, in a slightly different context, certainly would fit in. Here, the brutal pragmatism so often twisted into callousness and cruelty in backwoods horror becomes a signifier of the stoicism and resilience necessary to survive in an environment in which both the family and nature have little nourishment to offer. (The film potentially serves as an interesting companion piece to *The Tall Man*, which has a similar setting, and is also a Gothic thriller, but which ultimately treats its rural inhabitants very differently.)

Following her acclaimed turn in *Winter's Bone*, Lawrence would be cast as Katniss Everdeen, the resourceful protagonist of the best-selling young-adult trilogy *The Hunger Games* (Suzanne Collins, 2008–10). What is interesting about *The Hunger Games* (2012) is that it explicitly presents its backwoods inhabitants as sympathetic, heroic figures opposed to a decadent, degenerate, and corrupt urban elite. Katniss and her family live in 'District 12', a sorely deprived region whose sole purpose is to mine coal for the rest of the country of Panem (formerly North America). District 12 was formerly Appalachian West Virginia, a region which, as we have seen, is more usually depicted in American popular culture as a breeding ground for murderous degenerates. In the film, District 12 and its inhabitants are shot in a way that emphasises both their innate decency and their poverty. Everyone lives in run-down shacks, the men trudge off to work in disaster-prone mines, the women wear faded print dresses, and coal dust is ingrained in every surface. In fact, apart from the electric fence meant to keep people away from the dangerous freedom of the forests beyond the settlement, and the presence of jack-booted 'Peacekeepers', it looks like nothing so much as a knowing recreation of Dorothea Lange's depression-era photographs of impoverished sharecroppers.

Like all of the other districts in Panem (there are 12 in total), which 75 years earlier took part in an ill-fated rebellion against the centralised authority of 'The Capitol', the children and teenagers of District 12 must participate in a grotesque ritual known as 'The Hunger Games', in which a boy and a girl are randomly selected as 'tributes', then sent to the city to fight to the death in a gladiatorial contest broadcast live on television. Having volunteered to participate in place of her younger sister, Katniss finds that the skills she learned whilst eking out a painful living for herself and her family provide the means to survive in the horrific 'game' that she and her fellow District 12 tribute, a boy named Peeta, will now be forced to take part in.

The antagonists here are tyrannical urban elite (lead by the sinister President Snow) whose garishly made-up faces, luridly coloured hair, and penchant for outlandish plastic surgery highlights their arrogance and materialism. *Winter's Bone* and *The Hunger Games*, therefore, represent something of a rare exception in American popular film in that they essay entirely sympathetic portraits of deprived rural protagonists. As noted, however, neither of them are backwoods horror films (rather, what we have here is a gritty thriller with Gothic elements and a sci-fi dystopia, respectively).

As well as reflecting the sense that the South is the problematic, backwards 'Other' to the rest of the US, the backwoods horror sub-genre, as we have seen, draws upon the powerful strain of eugenic thinking that flourished during the early twentieth century, and in particular, the belief that the fecund, 'feeble-minded', and 'regressive' rural family (or rogue rural male) are a threat to the racial and genetic purity of the US. According to this rationale, the rural poor are dangerous not just because they resent their betters, but because on some kind of fundamental genetic level, they truly *are* inferior. According to this logic, the stagnation and decrepitude of their surroundings and the proximity of the wilderness has bred in them a dangerous primitivism that can erupt into violence at any time. It is interesting, then, that as we shall see in my final chapter, popular narratives dealing with the apocalypse so frequently feature middle-class non-rural protagonists who find that 'civilisation' has been swept aside in an instant, and that survival in this new 'New World' necessitates becoming more 'savage' and less 'civilised'.

5

'Why Wouldn't the Wilderness Fight Us?' American Eco-Horror and the Apocalypse

Rachel Carson's 1962 book *The Silent Spring*, perhaps the most influential work of environmental advocacy ever written, opens with a 'Fable for Tomorrow'.[1] She depicts a town completely at one with its pastoral surroundings:

> Even in winter the roadsides were places of beauty, where countless birds came to feed on the berries and on the seed heads of the dried weeds rising above the snow. The countryside was, in fact, famous for the abundance and variety of wildlife, and when the flood of migrants was pouring through in spring and autumn people travelled from great distances to observe them.[2]

It's all too good to last. Soon, 'a strange blight crept over the area and everything began to change'.[3] It's a development that she casts in distinctly Gothic terms: 'Some evil spell had settled on the community: mysterious maladies swept the flocks of chickens; the cattle and sheep sickened and died. Everywhere was a shadow of death.'[4] One of the most eerie developments is the fact that there are no birds anymore: 'It was a spring without voices.' However, there is nothing supernatural about this ecological devastation: 'No witchcraft, no enemy action had silenced the rebirth of new life in this stricken world.' The awful truth is: 'The people had done it themselves.'[5] Carson made it clear that every disaster described in her 'fable' had already happened somewhere.[6] Ecological catastrophe was no longer an alarmist fantasy, but a stark reality of late twentieth-century life. Her book '[...] helped spark a tsunami of catastrophic rhetoric in environmental science and literature'.[7] It is partially due to the immense impact made by *The Silent Spring* that '[...] our society is haunted by nightmares of an ecological apocalypse':[8]

> We live under the constant threat that the world of life will be irrevocably undermined by a society gone mad in its need to grow – replacing the organic by inorganic, soil by concrete, forest by barren earth, and the diversity of life forms by simplified ecosystems; in short a turning back of the evolutionary clock to an earlier, more inorganic, mineralised world that was incapable of supporting complex life forms of any kind, including human species.[9]

Bookchin's rhetoric evokes Susan Sontag's 1963 contention, 'Modern historical reality has greatly enlarged the imagination of disaster.'[10] Sontag argued that fantasy both distracted people from their likely fate (nuclear annihilation) and helped normalise what was psychologically unbearable. During the 1950s and 1960s, American audiences and readers certainly had plenty of material to help them get used to the idea of the nuclear holocaust, in part because, as Sacvan Bercovitch has noted, the popular culture of the time embraced what 'higher' culture tended to treat evasively.[11]

A similar pattern can be observed in American popular culture from the late 1960s onwards regarding the threat of environmental catastrophe. In 1971, Thomas M. Disch opened his collection *The Ruins of Earth* by 'remarking that, while 1950s concerns about nuclear holocaust had been successfully "black-boxed" ('one had learned to live with the bombs largely by looking the other way'), environmental crisis was different because "[...] now, in 1971, it isn't possible to look the other way" '.[12] Frederick Buell describes how this urgent sense of looming eco-catastrophe was quickly diffused by political, industrial, and business interests for whom the danger of increased environmental regulation was a threat. 'Something happened to strip environmental crisis of what seemed in the 1970s to be its self-evident inevitability. Something happened to allow environmentalism's antagonists to stigmatise its erstwhile stewards as unstable alarmists and bad-faith prophets – and to call their warnings at best hysterical, and at worst crafted lies.'[13] For him, as for other commentators (such as Bill McKibben) a 'Politics of Denial' came to dominate the way in which environmental concerns were perceived in the US. In recent eco-horror films such as *The Last Winter* (2006), *The Happening* (2008), and *Take Shelter* (2011), we shall see the ways in which this perception – that an absolutely catastrophic ecological disaster looms not in the distant future, but is in fact *already unfolding* – has been assimilated into contemporary popular culture. As Lisa Garforth puts it:

> At the beginning of the Twenty-First century the threat of ecological breakdown is deeply imbedded in our social consciousness. Although the intensity of announcements of the 'environmental crisis' of the 1970s has faded and even been absorbed and normalised by the institutions of capitalist modernity, through the lens of environmentalism the future can seem an unthinkable or utterly miserable prospect. Whether framed in terms of the risk of catastrophic disasters associated with nuclear accidents like Chernobyl, or the steady decline implied by current scenarios of global climate change, it appears that things can only get worse.[14]

This sense of powerful foreboding – reinforced, of course, by the fact that the impact which global warming is beginning to have upon this planet is fast becoming obvious to all but the most entrenched sceptics – is also, I will argue, reflected in the post-2000 release of a number of strikingly similar genre movies, novels, and TV shows in which the collapse of the US means that the protagonists have to embark upon perilous road trips through a ravaged, depopulated American landscape. These narratives not only have much to say about the way in which a nation currently beset by all manner of economic, political, and environmental woes sees itself. They also imagine a future in which the American landscape is transformed once more into an inhospitable 'wilderness' straight out of Puritan nightmare. As such, it is my contention that these post-apocalyptic fantasies represent the 'final frontier' for the Rural Gothic.

I will begin this chapter by discussing the wave of eco-horror films which emerged during the 1970s, and served as precursors to the even despairing visions of environmental catastrophe seen in recent narratives of this type. Although ecocriticism has become an increasingly prominent facet of literary studies, not much has yet been written from this perspective about the relationship between the natural world and horror in literature and popular culture. As Tom J. Hillard (2009) notes, 'Throughout its relatively short life, ecocriticism has largely overlooked representations of nature inflected with fear, horror, loathing or disgust [...] Examining this darker side of nature writing, with its emphasis on fear, inevitably intersects with an examination of Gothic fiction and literature.'[15] He goes on to mention the likes of William Bradford, Cotton Mather, Charles Brockden Brown, and Edgar Allan Poe as being examples of American authors whose work often reflected this 'darker side of writing about nature', and might, therefore, be profitably looked at from this perspective. Hillard's starting point here is Simon Estok's term 'ecophobia':

> Ecophobia is an irrational and groundless hatred of the natural world, as present and subtle in our daily lives and literature as homophobia and racism and sexism. It plays out in many spheres; it sustains the personal hygiene and cosmetics industries (which cite nature's 'flaws' and 'blemishes' as objects of their work); it supports city sanitation boards that issue fines seeking to keep out 'pests' and 'vermin' associated in municipal mentalities with long grass; it keeps beauticians and barbers in business; it is behind landscaped gardens and trimmed poodles in women's handbags on the Seoul subway system; it is about power and control; it is what makes looting and plundering of animal and non animal resources possible.[16]

Estok further suggests that 'Human history is a history of controlling the natural environment', and argues, 'Ecophobia is one of the hallmarks of human progress.'[17] However, whilst the 'nature strikes back' horror films of the 1970s are obviously linked to the sense of ecological crisis that become a part of American life following the publication of *The Silent Spring*, they also belong to the much longer tradition of American narratives in which the natural world and the landscape itself are seen as actively hostile. Referring to the initial colonisation of North America, Francis Jennings notes, 'To the European who lacked woodcraft, knew not the native trails, and imagined gothic horrors in every copse, the familiar hunting parks of the Indians were lethal wilderness.'[18] If 'ecophobia', as Estok defines it, is related to the human drive to control and exploit the natural world, then it stands to reason that American popular culture would frequently encompass narratives in which this kind of hatred of the natural world is dramatised. Eco-horror films are most commonly found in the US and Australia, both nations established by the descendants of white settlers who set out to create a 'new world' in the midst of a vast, unfamiliar, and often physically treacherous landscape already occupied by resentful native inhabitants. Catherine Simpson has recently observed (in relation to Australian eco-horror) that films in which the natural world 'strikes back' serve as a means of dealing with environmental topics and issues of trespass, as well as of extending 'post colonial anxieties over settler Australian issues of belonging'.[19] I will argue here that American eco-horror serves much the same function, combining an urgent sense of present-day crisis with a much older awareness of the fraught relationship between the white colonist and the unfamiliar landscape inhabited by potentially hostile plants, animals, and humans.

As we have seen, the project of transforming what they perceived to be a 'howling' wilderness into a settled, 'productive' landscape was one of the main objectives of the colonists. The presence of the Indians was certainly one of the most disquieting elements, but the animal population was also a source of anxiety:

> Wild animals added to the danger of the American wilderness, and here too the element of the unknown intensified feelings. Reporting in 1630 on the 'discommodities' of New England, Francis Higginson wrote that 'this Countrey being verie full of Woods and Wilderneses, doth also much abound with Snakes and Serpents of strange colours and huge greatnesse'. There were some, he added, 'that haue [have] Rattles in their Tayles that will not Flye from a Man... but will flye upon him and sting him so mortally, that he will dye within a quarter of an houre after'. Clearly there was some truth here and in the stories that echo through frontier literature of men whom 'the savage Beasts devoured... in the Wilderness,' but often fear led to exaggeration. Cotton Mather, for instance, warned in 1707 of 'the *Evening Wolves*, the rabid and howling *Wolves* of the *Wilderness* [which] would make... Havock among you *and not leave the Bones* till the morning.'[20]

It is, perhaps, hardly surprising that narratives in which animals, insects, bird life, and amphibians 'strike back' at humanity should recur so frequently in the American horror movie. As Nash observes, it was midst the unfamiliar territory of the 'New World' that the settlers re-experienced afresh their old, insecure relationships with the wilderness and the beasts that dwelled there.[21] What is particularly interesting about 1970s eco-horror films is that whilst there are certainly attacks by animals that humans have long feared for good reason – sharks, bears, dogs – aggression in these films is also exhibited by creatures whose potential for menace is much less immediately obvious (such as ants, earth worms, and rabbits). The 'ecophobia' which Estok cites as enabling the commercial and industrial exploitation of the natural world is, in these films, violently turned back upon the humans whose explicit or implicit disrespect for the natural world has precipitated a *wholesale* revolt of nature. As in the real-life examples cited by Carson in *The Silent Spring*, the desire to actively control and/or profit from nature results, instead, in chaos and disorder. Ironically, therefore, the fear of the natural world that facilitated these doomed attempts at control is retrospectively vindicated.

American eco-horror movies made between the 1960s and 1970s tend to conform to the same basic formula, summarised as follows:

- Setting: a small town within a distinctly rural setting. This is already a place in which humans live in close proximity to the natural world.
- Protagonist: almost always an out-of-towner who foolishly seeks peace and quiet in the countryside. They must work with local allies (often a local love interest) in order to defeat or, at least, escape the natural menace.
- Starting point: some kind of violent disruption of the natural world – often the result of foolish human interference in or indifference towards nature (occasionally no definite explanation is given, however).
- Antagonist: usually one specific animal or species.
- Anti-humanism: there is often a distinct sense in these films that, whilst the revenge of nature may be disproportionate and indiscriminate, humanity has nevertheless brought the horror upon itself by disrespecting the environment.
- The role of authority: local authority figures ignore or disastrously downplay the threat, refuse to believe the warnings of the main protagonist and his/her allies, and only act when they really must. Their greed has often contributed to the problem in the first place. Their behaviour strongly resembles that of the corrupt mayor in Ibsen's *An Enemy of the People* (1882).
- The ending: although the protagonist and their allies usually escape the immediate threat, and sometimes defeat it entirely, there is almost always a moment just before the closing credits when it is made clear that the threat has yet to be completely defused – in fact, the true horror may only just be beginning.

Alfred Hitchcock's *The Birds* (1963) did more than any other film to establish the formula cited above, in part because it had a very timely release date. Although there is no direct connection between *The Silent Spring* and *The Birds* (the film was well into production when Carson's first articles appeared in *The New Yorker* in 1962), in one of those striking coincidences that popular culture so often provides, the book and film appeared within months of each other. If Carson's book can indeed be considered the Ur-text of modern environmentalism, then Hitchcock's claustrophobic, eerie film is the foundational narrative of post-Carson eco-horror.[22] In *The Silent Spring*, the loss of birdsong 'comes to function as a synecdoche for a more general environmental apocalypse'.[23] One of the things that had most impressed the early European visitors to New England was the birdlife, and in particular, the flocks of passenger pigeons so large that they briefly blocked out the sun.[24] The passenger pigeon, of course, had been hunted to extinction by the early twentieth century. It is appropriate that Carson would choose the absence of birds as the key symbol of a fable which presents us with an idealised small town in which agriculturally based prosperity and natural abundance exist alongside each other, until disrupted by human interference. There is also the fact that 'Small towns have featured so prominently in American culture that they have become a deeply rooted symbol in the country's collective consciousness.'[25] The small town is, therefore, the most common setting for 1970s eco-horror because it also often serves as a stand-in for the nation.

Although *The Birds* begins with a long, establishing scene set amidst the bustling streets of San Francisco, once spoiled-but-vulnerable socialite Melanie Daniels (Tippi Hedren) impulsively heads for the coastal town of Bodega Bay she, like the viewer, spends the rest of the film trapped there. As is the case in many of the other films discussed here, there is no immediately obvious cause for the events that transpire. Various theories have been mooted by critics, with many noting that the bird attacks seem to revolve around Melanie herself.[26] However, the fact remains that the narrative itself, like Du Maurier's original story, gestures towards a much more ominous explanation: an apocalyptic revolt of nature.

The various strains of public opinion regarding the reason for the bird attacks is best represented during the film's masterful restaurant scene, which, as Paglia notes, is '[...] like a play within a play'.[27] Having just witnessed a flock of crows attack children from the local school, Melanie telephones her father. Gradually, the other patrons in the restaurant join in a heated discussion about what has happened. Amongst them there is an Irish drunk who declares it as sign of 'the end of the world', a cynical travelling salesman who opines, 'If you ask me, we should wipe them all out. World would be better off without them', a mother travelling with her two children who becomes increasingly hysterical, and Mrs Bundy, the local bird expert.[28] Mrs Bundy is quick to correct Melanie and the others when they display their dangerous ignorance of the natural world. 'Why, if we believe that birds are attacking, why... why next we'll believe that grasshoppers and cockroaches are capable of [...].'

If, as Melanie claims, birds of a father are flocking together in order to wage war against humanity, 'We wouldn't have a chance. How could we possibly hope to fight them?' As the following scenes make clear, Mrs Bundy is indeed correct: humanity would have little or no way of defending itself. *The Birds* ends not with a triumphant fight-back but with a retreat, as Melanie (who has been rendered catatonic by a bird attack) and the Brenner family slowly drive away. They're heading out of town, and hopefully towards safety, but as the absence of any other noise on the soundtrack save the cry of birds and the flapping of wings makes clear, the world may well belong to their avian foes now.

As *The Birds* demonstrated, even the smallest creatures could be imbued with menace. Further evidence of this came in the *The Hellstrom Chronicle*, which won the 1971 Academy Award for best documentary.[29] What brings the film firmly into my purview is the fact that its real footage of insect life is interspersed with sequences scripted by David Seltzer (who also wrote *The Omen* (1976) and *Prophecy* (1979) which will be discussed later) in which the movie's narrator, 'Dr Nils Hellstrom, MD, PhD' (Lawrence Pressman), urgently expands upon his theory that humankind's dominion over the earth will soon be over. The film's melancholy tone is established in the opening sequence, which indicates that from the outset, the struggle for survival has been a bitter one. 'Masked beneath the beauty of nature's world is one single and ugly truth. Life must take life, in the interests of life itself. It is a mistake of arrogance to mistake size with significance. For the less visible one's enemy, the more powerful its strength.' Hellstrom, in standard maverick scientist tradition, is privy to truths those in positions of authority would prefer to ignore. He has, he says, 'learned something that no one wants to hear. But unless someone does hear – unless someone is at least exposed to it – we as a species might pass from existence without knowing why.'

The Hellstrom Chronicle anticipates the most recent (post-2000) cycle of American eco-horror in that, unlike the other films of this kind from the 1970s, the threat here poses a danger to the future of humanity rather than just one small town. Inevitably, the use of DDT to control the insect population and safeguard agriculture is mentioned. In a conclusion that echoes Carson, we are told, 'In fighting the insect, we have killed ourselves.' The insect is 'waiting patiently beside our death bed'.[30] Like *The Birds*, the film is very obviously a product of a post-Carson world. It reminds the viewer, 'Extinction is the ultimate fate of every species.'[31] *The Hellstrom Chronicle* was succeeded by a number of other insect-attack films. Amongst them were the atmospheric

1973 Saul Bass-directed oddity *Phase IV* (in which desert ants affected by cosmic radiation battle the scientists who have been investigating their strange behaviour); *Bug* (1975) (in which fire-starting cockroaches invade a small town); *Empire of the Ants* (1977) (tag line: 'They shall inherit the earth – sooner than you think'); *Kingdom of the Spiders* (1977) (in which a small-town veterinarian played by William Shatner battles giant tarantulas mutated by crop-dusting spray); and in 1978, two 'bee attack' flicks – *The Bees* and *The Swarm.*

It wasn't only the insects you had to keep an eye on during the 1970s. Even the most harmless-seeming mammal – the rabbit – becomes a deadly threat in William F. Claxton's *Night of the Lepus* (1972). The plot revolves around the consequences of an ill-advised scheme to come up with a 'safe' alternative to DDT. An Arizona cattle rancher faces ruin because his land is being overrun by voracious bunnies. His plea for help reaches the husband-and-wife team of scientists based at the local university, who come up with a cunning plan: they'll inject a breeding pair with hormones that disrupt their reproductive cycle. Inevitably, tinkering with nature has dire effects once a modified rabbit is accidentally released by the couple's meddling little girl Amanda, who otherwise exists merely so that she can ask questions such as, 'Mommy, what's a control group?' In no time at all, the region has been overrun by giant rabbits that roar like lions and sound like stampeding horses. The local authorities, as is invariably the case, refuse at first to believe in the threat: 'Rabbits as big and ferocious as wolves? It just isn't conceivable!' During the deliriously silly climax, the rabbits are herded into traps made from downed power lines.

Night of the Lepus further dramatises the very fear that even the most well-meaning attempts to control the development of plants and animals can go awry, and that the most innocuous creatures may evolve in ways that cannot be predicted or controlled. In other words, 'Chaos reigns' when humans interfere with natural processes that should be left alone. An odd real-life corollary to *Night of the Lepus* appeared to occur in August 1979, when *The Washington Post* ran a story headed 'President Attacked by Rabbit'. However, the truth of Jimmy Carter's odd encounter with the frantically swimming animal (he was in a boat) was rather less exciting than initial reports suggested.[32]

The most famous eco-horror movie of the decade, *Jaws* (1975), differs substantially from many other 'revenge of nature' films cited here in that the Great White's attacks are never at any point explicitly blamed on the humans themselves. The shark hasn't been affected by poisonous chemicals or meddling scientists, even if it is larger than usual, and inhabiting waters unusually close to shore. The shark also acts alone. In fact, it actually serves as an effective stand-in for any random, unpleasant, and unpredictable eruption of disorder into an otherwise orderly environment. (It is for this reason that the shark is often compared to Michael Meyers in *Halloween* [1978].)[33] As such, the film evokes a paradigm which we have also seen enacted in Rural Gothic texts such as *Wieland*, *Ravenous*, and *The Village*, in which a close-knit and seemingly contented community is disrupted by the intrusion of a mysterious outsider. *Jaws*, like *Moby Dick* (1851), also reminds viewers that there is a whole other world around them that contains forces that we can never fully understand. 'Beyond human control, the sea takes on all the aspects of wilderness that the virgin forest or desert might possess. And it is as archetypal and immediately recognisable as any other wilderness.'[34] Even though it doesn't contain the same resoundingly obvious environmental message hammered home by many of the films discussed here, *Jaws* shares with them the paranoid suspicion that the natural world is a chaotic, pitiless place populated by resentful 'lesser' creatures waiting for an excuse to get their own back.

Rather less obviously terrifying than a Great White are the flesh-eating worms that slither amuck in writer/director Jeff Lieberman's 1976 film *Squirm*. The revolt of nature's slimiest denizens is caused by a downed power line that transforms them into human-chomping menaces that like to pop up at unexpected moments (such as in the middle of an egg-cream soda being enjoyed by the film's hero). As in *Night of the Lepus*, the director gamely tries to make a resolutely unterrifying creature frightening by providing us with lots of extreme close-ups and dubbing the soundtrack with unlikely noises (these worms screech). There's a tentative feint early on towards some kind of overtly eco-conscious angle, when it is noted that tourists pollute the local bay, but this is never directly connected to the activities of the worms, even if it does help explain some of the hostility directed towards the hero, who is an out-of-towner. The most memorable thing about *Squirm* is the immortal line, 'The worms are coming up the stairs!', and the closing shots, which oddly resemble the final moments of *Halloween* (1978) – a slow pan through the by now worm-free house which ends on an ominous close-up of the ground outside. *Squirm*, therefore, leaves us with the feeling that further worm-related disorder can happen again at any time. As noted earlier, it is rare for eco-horror films to end with a definitive defeat of the threat concerned (exploding sharks aside). How can one escape nature, after all?

The most painfully earnest eco-horror film of the 1970s was John Frankenheimer's *Prophecy* (1979). The film attempts to tackle a number of pressing contemporary issues – contemporary debates about Indian land rights and concern about the polluting ways of big business; and mixes it all up with a story which exploits one of the most characteristic preoccupations of 1970s horror: reproductive anxiety.[35] Robert Verne (Robert Foxworth) is a crusading public health doctor working for the Environmental Protection Agency (EPA). When we first see him (after a prologue in which a team of illegal loggers are violently dispatched by an unseen, but massive creature), he's been called out to a decrepit apartment building because a baby has been gnawed on by rats. In an early acknowledgement of the complex relationship between humans and the animal world, one of the building's residents shrugs and says, 'The rats got to have room to live too.' The building is owned by an absentee landlord who refuses to do anything to improve the lot of his tenants, just as the paper mill central to the narrative is owned by a company that cares nothing for the environment. Sensing that Verne is burnt-out, his supervisor suggests that he take on an assignment in the backwoods of Maine, which involves managing a conflict between restive local Indians and the paper company that has purchased a tract of forest the tribe considers its own. Verne is, however, merely the latest in a long line of city dwellers who find that the wilderness is a lot less relaxing that they have anticipated. He also brings along his wife Maggie (Talia Shire). Unbeknownst to him, Maggie is pregnant, but has yet to break the news, because Robert is so disgusted by the state of the world that he doesn't want to bring a child into it. Later events will make Robert's reluctance to reproduce seem entirely reasonable.

Initially, it seems as if exposure to the wilderness will be just the thing to help patch up the couple's relationship. This positive view of wilderness as a restorative and regenerative site is, of course, one that first emerged during the nineteenth century, when it increasingly came to represent '[...] a highly attractive natural alternative to the ugly artificiality of modern civilisation'.[36] As they fly over the forest, Robert marvels, 'I forgot the world could look like this.' In a reminder, however, of the reason why they are there in the first place, we also see the paper mill sitting on the edge of the river like a carbuncle – a reminder that even in the wilderness, commercial interests have established themselves. The sense of unease is compounded when plant manager Isley (Richard Dysart), greets them with the warning, 'This particular forest isn't too safe right now.' An Indian protest group, led by activist John Hawks (Armand Assante), has blocked access to local logging trails. Isley is dismissive of their claims that the forest is inhabited by a mythological creature known as the 'Ka Tha Din' [sic]. It is worth noting that 'Kathadin' was the Maine peak climbed by Thoreau in 1846, his account of which formed a key chapter of *In the Maine Woods* (1864). The experience was a profoundly unsettling one for him, because it was where:

> Thoreau for the first time encountered nature in its most primitive and forbidding state, where it was devoid of organic life [...] The validity of Thoreau's quest was founded on the pantheistic belief that the universe was congenial to human life and that human meaning could therefore be found in nature. The stark, inhuman nature Thoreau experienced at Katahdin thus threatened his most basic premise.[37]

The association of the creature which causes so much destruction in *Prophecy* with a feature of the Maine landscape which had proved famously inhospitable to Thoreau is one that further emphasises the ways in which the American landscape had long resisted white understanding and control. Further emphasising the Thoreau connection is the fact that Rob and Maggie are given a lakeside cabin in the woods to stay in – accommodation, which, as we have seen, seldom bodes well (in stark contrast to Thoreau's time on the shores of Walden Pond). Rob catches a giant salmon in the lake, which he and Maggie eat. Later that same night, they are attacked by a raccoon which appears to be suffering from brain damage. In what may be an early indication of the films reproductive anxieties, the first thing the racoon does upon breaking into the cabin is launch itself at Rob's crotch.

When he and Maggie visit the local Indian village, the tribe's elder expresses his belief that 'Ka Tha Din' has awakened to protect his people – a misconception that will later prove fatal. Rob notices that the trees that surround the village have become twisted and malformed, and upon finding a giant tadpole (and hearing about the high rate of birth defects in the tribe) he realises that the water has been contaminated. Isley gives the couple a tour of the paper mill, during which Rob notices a distinctive silver residue clinging to Maggie's shoe. After analysing it, he discovers that the mill has been discharging methyl mercury into the river, and as a result, 'This whole place has been contaminated.' The compound acts on the nervous system and destroys the brain, but it is also a powerful mutagenic which can corrupt the chromosomes of a developing foetus. Rob's discovery reflects an infamous incident which took place in Japan in 1956. A hundred people died and thousands were paralysed after eating contaminated fish from Minamata Bay. The cause was methyl mercury poisoning caused by pollution.[38] Although the Minamata incident obviously took place outside of the US, there were also plenty of home-grown eco-disasters of this sort: '[...] events like the 1969 Santa Barbara oil spill alerted middle-class Americans to the dangers of environmental disaster, and many mainstream organisations worried about pollution, toxic waste, and development of wilderness lands'.[39] As W. Scott Poole (2011) notes, one of the most infamous instances of industrial pollution involved the upstate New York city of Love Canal. During the 1960s and 1970s, children born to residents suffered an unusually high number of birth defects. These defects were later attributed to the fact that the working-class community had been erected on an industrial waste dump.[40]

Whilst Rob and Maggie are visiting the scene of a vicious attack by the creature, they discover a deformed bear cub trapped in a poacher's net and decide that they must bring it back as evidence. As Rob says to John, '[...] it could save your people, and this forest'. In a by now familiar turn of events, the film treats the Indians and the forest as synonymous. Rob is now seized with an almost messianic sense of mission, but he fails to notice the hollow-eyed desperation of his wife, who is forced to care for the grotesque cub whilst the group shelter from a storm. It is during this scene that Maggie cracks and reveals that she is expecting a child which may have been affected by the contaminated fish they ate earlier. She punctures her husband's belief that all will be well when the truth is exposed. 'It's not a nightmare that's going to end. It's just beginning, because it's inside me!'

Isley finally admits that he knew all along that the mill was polluting local waterways. He plays a steep price for his transgressions: the creature emerges from the forest and rips off his legs. 'Kah Ta Din' is no mythical figure (it even kills the old man who believes it to be such), but a mutant grizzly driven insane by mercury poisoning. Although Rob eventually manages to kill it with an arrow (in yet another example of the white man in the hostile wilderness surviving by adopting Indian ways), it is obvious that all will not be well. Maggie is still carrying a baby that will probably be as deformed as the animals in the forest, and in the final shot, we see another mutant grizzly emerge from the forest. The damage has been done. Even middle-class white folks will now suffer in the same way that the Indians have for years. The 'prophecy' here, as the film's poster art makes clear (it shows a mutant bear foetus), is that the reckless disregard for the natural world that characterises the present has irrevocably damaged future generations.

It is notable that Foxworth's character works for the EPA, because this organisation had only been established nine years previously. It is only when Verne sees with his own eyes evidence of the effect that the mill's rampant pollution has had that he takes definitive action – and even then, he has already exposed his wife and unborn child. Verne's haplessness reflects the fact that, in real life, the ecological agenda of the EPA was and is often secondary to the interests of big business.

> Over and over again, Nixon ensured that environmental regulations would remain subordinate to economic growth and that they would rely much more heavily on market mechanisms and less on established bureaucratic and judicial controls [...] He established the EPA rather than the broad-based, more powerful agency that the environmental groups favoured.[41]

The conclusion of the film, which suggests that governmental failure to protect the environment will have a terrible impact upon Verne's family, vividly highlights the cost of putting profits before the natural world. As in *The Hellstrom Chronicle*, it is once more made obvious that in poisoning the earth, Americans have poisoned themselves.

Less well-known eco-horror films from the decades dramatised similar concerns. They included the likes of *Frogs* (1970) (in which the amphibious inhabitants of a Louisiana swamp besiege an isolated mansion in order to take revenge upon the arrogant patriarch, who has been exterminating them with pesticide), *Dogs* (1976), *Grizzly* (1976) *Day of the Animals* (1977), and cult classics such as *Piranha* (1978) and *Alligator* (1981) (which teaches the viewer that they should never flush an unwanted pet down the toilet lest it return after a 20-year growth spurt with vengeance on its mind).

Despite the relative frequency with which eco-horror and its sci-fi counterpart, the eco-dystopia (films of this kind released during the period included *Soylent Green* [1973] and *Silent Running* [1971]) surfaced in American popular culture during the 1970s, the sub-genre had a low profile during the 1980s and 1990s. It was not until the post-2000 era that eco-horror resurfaced as a significant element of American popular culture. Buell suggests that the eco-dystopianism often found in 1970s sci-fi continued in the new wave of cyberpunk narratives which emerged during the 1980s, but with one important difference: 'Environmental apocalypse was depicted not as the end of everything, but as a milieu people dwelt in as they moved out beyond the limits of nature.'[42] He argues that these texts were characterised by the perverse sense of possibility found amidst the ravaged landscapes they presented. 'Environmental apocalypse was depicted as a source of excitement, not dismay, a stimulus to thrilling new adventures and a path to hitherto undreamt of new modes of being, not an account of doom and destruction.'[43] It is this sense that the threat of environmental catastrophe had, in fact, come to pass, and had as a result been normalised that perhaps helps explain just why it is that eco-horror had such a low profile from the early 1980s up until the mid-2000s. It had become clear that the changes predicted by commentators such as Carson had already come to pass, and, in particular, that global warming, a preoccupation that only really came to the public consciousness during the mid- to late 1980s, was well underway.

This awareness means that the most recent expressions of ecological anxiety in the horror genre differ in some significant ways from their 1970s predecessors. Aside from the likes of the cult bad movie *Birdemic* (2008) and the many self-consciously terrible films of this kind made by the SyFy Channel, modern eco-horror films that adhere to the 1970s formula are rare.[44] A notable recent exception to this rule, however, is Barry Levinson's *The Bay* (2012) which, apart from its canny use of the currently ubiquitous 'found footage' format, closely adheres to the 'classic' eco-horror paradigm (even down to its use of a small-town setting and the presence of short-sighted local officials). The threat here comes from waterborne parasites which have been mutated by pollution, and eat people from the inside out (often in glorious close-up). As in *Prophecy*, the events depicted are partially inspired by real-life incidents (albeit ones that are greatly exaggerated in the film). Levinson initially wanted to make a documentary about the despoliation of Chesapeake Bay, but decided that a horror film would be a more effective means of drawing public attention to the issue.[45]

A storm is coming: eco-horror in the post-2000 era

In *The End of Nature: Humanity, Climate Change and the Natural World*, Bill McKibben writes about what he characterises as a 'new nature' most notable for its very unpredictability:[46]

> Our comforting sense of the permanence of our natural world, our confidence that it will change gradually and imperceptibly, if at all, is, then, the result of a subtly warped perspective. Changes that can

> affect us can happen in our lifetime in our world – not just changes like wars but bigger and more sweeping events. I believe that without recognising it we have already stepped over the threshold of such a change: that we are at the end of nature. By the end of nature, I do not mean the end of the world. The rain will still fall and the sun will shine, though differently than before. When I say 'nature', I mean a certain set of human ideas about the world and our place in it. But the death of these ideas begins with concrete changes in the reality around us – changes that scientists can measure and enumerate. More and more frequently, these changes will clash with our perceptions, until, finally, our sense of nature as eternal and separate is washed away, and we will see all too clearly what we have done.[47]

William Cronon challenges this argument by arguing that this perspective '[...] is only possible if we accept the wilderness premise that nature, to be natural, must also be pristine'.[48] Nevertheless, this sense of being confronted by violent changes in the normal patterns of nature which are the result of human arrogance finds its fullest and most despairing expression in eco-horror narratives from the past decade. Whereas in the 1970s films, the terror is always a localised one, usually focused on a small town (with the exception of events in *The Hellstrom Chronicle*, and, possibly, *The Birds*); in the films I shall discuss next, the revolt of nature is ultimately on a global scale, rather than a regional one. Whereas 1970s eco-horror generally focused upon a specific animal, insect, or sea creature as the threat to an otherwise orderly environment, in post-2000 American eco-horror, there no longer *is* such a thing as natural order. As a result, the 'revolt of nature' is much more nebulous, and indeed, downright apocalyptic.

In their essay on Al Gore's *An Inconvenient Truth: A Global Warning* (2006), Thomas Rosteck and Thomas Frentz note that:[49]

> Americans have always had a complicated relationship with the environment. From the colonial Puritans, to the birth of the environmental movement at the turn of the twentieth century, and through annual Earth Day celebrations, we have remained preoccupied with the Earth. However, this preoccupation is curiously double-sided. On one side, the environment is revered as an awe-inspiring sublime, a synecdoche of our relation to the cosmos – and on the other, it is the resilient source of raw materials, a wilderness to be mastered, the site of our manifest destiny. Our bifurcated attitude towards nature is

> thus both spiritual and political, with the dominant trend in any era being a kind of barometer of cultural attitudes.[50]

This 'bifurcated' attitude is perhaps best expressed in modern eco-horror by writer/director Larry Fessenden's *The Last Winter* (2006). Here, the conflict between those who see the Alaskan wilderness as a resource ripe for exploitation and those who view it as a place of sacred significance informs a plot which concludes, like the other films I will discuss here, with the (possible) end of the world. In fact, *The Last Winter* and *An Inconvenient Truth* were released in the same year, and even serve as unintentional companion pieces. Gore's impassioned call to arms accessibly outlined the case for global warming and encouraged the viewer to take action in their own lives to help reverse, or at least, mitigate these effects. As such, though his lecture was sobering, it held out the possibility that if the will to change was there, disaster could perhaps be averted. *The Last Winter* takes place in a world in which the devastating effects predicted by Gore are not only underway, but unstoppable.

As well as being of immense ecological significance, Alaska has an important symbolic charge – it is, essentially, the 'last' American wilderness. Writing about Jimmy Carter's signing of the Alaska National Interest Lands Conservation Act (which granted Federal protection to land totalling 28 per cent of the state) in 1980, Nash notes that the favourable public response to this then unprecedented move tapped into the sense that Alaska was '[...] America's last frontier', a place where,

> [...] Americans could visit their past both in person and as an idea.[51] Indeed, though many Alaskans were wary of the rules and restrictions that accompanied wilderness preservation, 'Armchair' tourists, intellectual importers of Alaska's wilderness, were amongst the most vocal in defending land that they never expected to see. They said that Alaska represented the nation's last chance to do things right the first time.[52]

Carter's signing of the act was preceded by the 1960 establishment of the Arctic National Wildlife Refuge (ANWR), an 8 million acre tract of wilderness granted Federal protection for the purposes of '[...] preserving unique wildlife, wilderness and recreational values'.[53]

Over the past two decades, there has been increasing pressure for the government to remove the ban on drilling in the ANWR. It amplified with findings of a 1998 US Geological Survey report which concluded that the coastal plain of the refuge likely contained at least 20 billion barrels of oil.[54] The question then became, 'To drill or not to drill?'[55] Fessenden's film, therefore, dramatises a specifically *American* environmental conundrum – whether or not to prioritise the nation's ever-growing energy needs, or preserve the last relatively unpolluted natural landscape. In the film, the former consideration triumphs over the latter, with catastrophic results.

The 'triumph' of big business is highlighted even in the opening moments, which feature a promo made by 'North Industries'. It's a slick piece of corporate propaganda which characterises Alaska as 'The Land of Black Gold', and neatly sets up the rest of the film. In 1986, the company drilled a test well in the ANWR (the 'K.I.K.' [sic] well). Following a vote in Congress authorising further development, North is now determining future drill sites in the expectation that full-on drilling will be authorised 'within the decade'. The promo is being watched from a company camp in the far north by a young employee named Maxwell. Maxwell's interest in the K.I.K. well is more than just professional curiosity: the test site will soon reveal itself as the focal point of all a manner of eerie, mysterious occurrences – in fact, it is Ground Zero for the eco-apocalypse.

The main action of the film begins with the return to camp of blustering team leader Ed Pollack (Ron Perlman) who agrees entirely with the business-first attitude of his employers. Ed is put out on both a personal and professional level when he discovers that the bed of his romantic interest Abby (Connie Britton) is now occupied by environmentalist James Hoffman (James LeGros). Hoffman has spent years as an environmental activist and climate-change researcher but has now, along with his colleague Eliot Jenkins (Jamie Harrold), been brought in to perform the impact study needed before drilling to be authorised. Hoffman is burnt out by years of dealing with disasters like the Exxon Valdez oil spill, and the trip to the ANWR is, for him, 'A chance to come to the last place with pristine, untouched wilderness before we fuck it up.' The trouble is, the 'wilderness' has already been 'fucked up' – the data that he and Eliot collect proves that global warming is accelerating exponentially, and nature, as McKibben predicted, is reacting in ways that confound conventional assumptions.

In the film, as in real life, the permafrost beneath the tundra has begun to melt. Despite the fact that it is winter, the temperature is freakishly warm. More disturbing is the sense that an immensely powerful (and hostile) natural intelligence has begun to assert itself. Fessenden includes repeated shots of the camp and the people that inhabit it as though seen from above, to reinforce the sense that they are being watched by an all-seeing higher intelligence. The technique evokes Hitchcock's use of a similar trick in *The Birds* (which featured shots from the avian perspective which emphasised the vulnerability of the townsfolk) and the opening scenes of *The Shining* (1981). These shots also bring home the fact that *The Last Winter* is engaging with the 'Gaia Hypothesis' first popularised by James Lovelock. Lovelock's suggestion was that '[...] the Earth could be described as a self-regulating mechanism, analogous to a living organism'.[56] Fessenden combines this sense of the earth as a sentient, self-regulating organism with elements of the Windigo mythology discussed in Chapter 3. *The Last Winter* is a thematic companion piece to his 2001 film *Wendigo* (2001). Like *The Last Winter, Wendigo* focuses on a small group of individuals isolated in an ultimately unknowable natural landscape. Further aligning it with *The Last Winter* is the sense that the wilderness is imbued with an intelligence that may not be sympathetic to humankind, and the overt referencing of Windigo belief. In both films, it is also the youngest character – a little boy named Miles in *Wendigo,* and Maxwell in *The Last Winter* – who is the first to be influenced by this intelligence. *The Last Winter* also resembles *Ravenous* in that it has Indian characters who are the first to bring up the Windigo mythos. In *The Last Winter,* camp cook and mother-figure Dawn mentions her tribe's belief that 'familiar friends' can be replaced by a 'stranger'. However, the fact that Dawn and fellow Indian Lee are full members of the North Industries crew highlights the fact that, as the opening promo tells us, the company is a partnership between both business and Native Alaskan interests. No one here has clean hands.

As the thaw accelerates, relations between the camp's inhabitants grow more strained. Ed believes that the need for energy should outweigh all other considerations. Hoffman disagrees, and his opposition is reinforced by his sense that nature's delicate balance has fallen desperately out of kilter. There are repeated shots of the K.I.K. well, an off-white steel box that sits monolith-like in the snow, which seems to emit an eerie hum. Maxwell goes missing after being mysteriously drawn to it, only to return when the rest of the crew have given him up for dead. He's incoherent and unable to provide an explanation for his absence. His pragmatic colleagues dismiss it as claustrophobia, but he's not the only one affected. Hoffman seems like one of the more reasonable members of the team, but when Eliot leafs through his colleagues' note books, he finds not just graphs and figures, but also a rambling stream-of-consciousness-style rant that becomes increasingly apocalyptic in tone (a similar scene occurs in *Antichrist*, when the extent of 'the woman's' madness is revealed by her journal entries). According to Hoffman, 'The biosphere has turned – become indifferent to us.' He asks, 'Why wouldn't the wilderness fight us? Like any organism would fend off a virus?' Hoffman tries to convince Ed that 'something's out there, and it's trying to drive us out of here'.

Abby initially seems to have some sympathy with Hoffman's position, but as their relationship deteriorates, she increasingly aligns herself with Ed. The sense of crisis accelerates when Maxwell is found frozen to death, naked, in front of the well. His eyes have been pecked out by the ravens that show themselves increasingly often, and remind the audience of the film's connection to Native American folklore. Maxwell's body is also surrounded by reindeer tracks, and the video footage he shot in order to convince the others that 'There's something out there in the snow' is inconclusive. Hoffman tries to convince the team they have all been poisoned by 'Sour Gas' – a toxic by-product of natural gas and oil – 'This ground's been frozen for at least ten thousand years. Who knows what's coming out of it?' After Eliot dies from a nose bleed, Ed finally decides that they should all head to the nearest town for medical examinations. The plan is that they will travel back on the plane due to arrive the next day with the company boss, Foster, on board. Catastrophe strikes when the plane crashes into the camp, killing all of the passengers, severing the electrical supply, and destroying all but one of the snowmobiles. Whilst Ed and Hoffman team up to seek help (Hoffman wants to go to the local Indian village, which is nearer, whilst Ed, typically, insists they head towards the company's ice road construction site), Abby and the others are left behind. The ice road site is devoid of a crew, and the men discover that their snowmobile no longer works. They make a camp so that Ed, who has fallen through the ice, can dry off. In a sentiment that would sound familiar to former Alaska governor and vice-presidential candidate Sarah Palin, who encouraged chants of 'Drill, baby drill!' at her campaign rallies during the 2008 presidential campaign, as the men rest, Ed argues, 'What's needed out here is a pipeline [...] that's what God wants.'[57]

Back at the camp, things deteriorate even further when Dawn suddenly goes insane and suffocates Motor, an injured member of the crew. Abby accidentally kills the other woman during the ensuing struggle, leaving her as the camp's only remaining survivor. The increasing dominance of the elemental forces of nature is signalled by the intrusion of ravens into the camp interior. Hoffman, whose boots have been stolen by Ed, knows that he will not survive, but contacts Abby via walkie-talkie, and urges her, to 'tell the whole world' about what has happened. In an ironic echo of Gore, he predicts, 'They're gonna rise up, make a change', but there is a strong sense that they both know that any such effort would be futile. Ultimately, Hoffman is carried off by the phantom reindeer that here epitomise the presence of an actively defensive natural world. Whilst Ed is trampled to death by the spectres, Hoffman is granted a comforting vision of home in his dying moments. The concluding moments depict Abby waking up in a deserted hospital in town. The corridors are eerily quiet, beds are empty, and one of the doctors has hanged himself. Abby slowly walks outside, finding herself ankle deep in water. Sirens and alarms ring in the air, and emergency vehicles and cars lie abandoned in the street. She almost seems to be the only person left. As the wind picks up around her, we hear the sound of hooves, as she turns to stare at something that remains unseen by us, the film ends. A comment made by Maxwell on the night of his death hangs in the air – 'I just hope this isn't happening everywhere else.'

A film which has much in common with *The Last Winter* – most particularly this sense that the natural world will justifiably rise up against humanity – is M. Night Shyamalan's *The Happening* (2008). It begins in the style of any number of other horror films in which previously normal individuals suddenly begin to act in irrational and violent ways, such as *28 Days Later* (2002), *The Crazies* (1972, 2010), and *Impulse* (1984). We see two women conversing on a park bench, when suddenly a scream pierces the air. All of a sudden, people walking past stop, as though frozen by some unseen force. One of the women on the bench begins to repeat the same phrase over and over (always a precursor to homicidal insanity) and then stabs herself in the neck. As police cars tear down the street in response to what is clearly a citywide emergency, construction workers plummet from the scaffolding of a nearby sky rise. In an early clue as to who the culprit is, there is a shot of nearby trees gently waving in the breeze. The 'happening' has begun.

The film's hero is Eliot Moore (Mark Wahlberg), a Philadelphian high-school science teacher. His role is mainly to serve as a mouthpiece for the film's clunky pseudo science. In his opening lines, he addresses his students, 'Look, I don't know if you guys read this article in *The New York Times* about honeybees vanishing [...].' Where as in 1970s eco-horror, the presence of (killer) bees was the problem, here it is their absence. Although he allows the kids to brainstorm a few possible explanations, Moore concludes his lesson by (inaccurately) declaring that it is 'An act of nature, something we'll never fully understand' – an attitude the film ultimately takes towards the 'happening'. Moore's class is interrupted by the principal, who announces that something very bad indeed is happening in New York. As the situation escalates, and it becomes obvious that the 'attacks' are also happening in other cities on the East Coast, and that they involve a toxin that overrides the brain's natural self-defence mechanisms, Moore, along with his wife Alma (Zooey Deschanel), their friend Julian (John Leguizamo), and his little girl Jess (Ashlyn Sanchez), decide to travel to the supposed safety of the countryside by train. The train comes to a halt in the middle of nowhere when the driver loses communication with the outside world. Having clearly never seen a horror movie, Moore reassures the child that, 'We're in a small town, Jess. Nothing bad can happen to us here.' He and Alma, who have been having marital problems, are left to look after Jess when Julian leaves try and find his wife (he dies shortly thereafter). The couple decide to leave the town and walk to safety through the countryside.

In a moment of epiphany which occurs when they rest in a plant nursery, Moore realises, 'It's the plants. They can release chemicals.' The decision to seek shelter in rural Pennsylvania may not have been so smart after all. They join up with a group of fellow refugees under the 'command' of a terrified young soldier. As they make their way across a field in two separate groups, an exaggeratedly sinister rustling noise (indicating the presence of the tress around them) indicates the spread of the toxin. Everyone in the other cohort kills themselves. The remaining refugees for some reason look to Moore for an answer, and he reasons that if they can 'stay ahead of the wind', they'll escape exposure to the toxin triggered as they traipse across the field. As they flee, we see a billboard which helps explain why nature has acted to eradicate humanity: the site is the spot where 'Clear Hill Community Development' will soon be building a new housing estate.

The realisation that plants respond to human stimuli leads to a scene in which Walberg speaks to a houseplant as though it were a gun-toting homeowner: 'We're just here to use the bathroom. Then we're going to leave. Is that ok?' The house concerned is a show home promoting the future estate. The relationship between the human destruction of the natural landscape and the 'happening' is further emphasised when two groups of refugees spotted in the distance converge and end up killing themselves. In the film's only moment of wit, the camera pans to a nearby billboard that cheerily reads, 'You deserve this!'

Eventually, Alma, Eliot, and Jess hide out in the isolated home of Mrs Jones, a dangerously eccentric old woman (Betty Buckley), and, after a close call during which the couple prove their love for one another by meeting outside just as the phenomenon crests, they make it to the end of the 'happening'. However, as is usually the case, the end of the initial revolt of nature doesn't mean that order has indefinitely been restored. In a coda set three months later, we see the couple happily bustling around their apartment. Talking heads on the television blame the 'happening' on a rapidly evolving plant defence mechanism, and conclude, 'This was an act of nature. And we'll never fully understand it', whilst noting, 'We have become a threat to this planet.' The shot cuts to a park in France, and we see two men walk down a pretty, tree-lined street – one of who suddenly stops dead and begins to repeat himself. The horror has returned, but this time, the phenomenon is obviously of global, rather than regional extent. As in *The Last Winter*, we are presented with a scenario in which the natural world violently rejects humanity in a manner that begins in one specific location but which in the closing moments is shown to be a worldwide phenomenon. In both films, the character who realises what is happening before everyone else is a male scientist whose profession has tuned him in to the vicissitudes of the natural world, and in both cases, this knowledge proves useless in the long term, because the damage has been done.

Take Shelter (2011), is an even more recent narrative in which, as in *The Happening*, an apocalyptic revolt of nature is counterpointed with a relationship crisis for a married couple. The film is about a blue-collar everyman named Curtis La Forche (Michael Shannon) who suddenly begins to experience what are either psychotic delusions or prophetic visions of eco-catastrophe. *Take Shelter* is set in 2010, less than two years after the beginning of the fiscal catastrophe that rapidly took a heavy toll on the American middle-classes. It is all the more fitting then that one of the first portents of impending doom glimpsed by Curtis – who, in an echo of *The Last Winter*, works on a drill site owned by a local sand company – is a rain of oil. The rise in oil and gas prices which took place in the summer of 2008 was one of the most notable harbingers of the economic calamity to come. It was also another painful reminder of the fact that the modern American way of life is predicated upon the availability of cheap oil. This awareness underpins the thinking of those who believe that the nation will only achieve true energy independence by opening up protected sites such as the ANWR.

In a scene that evokes Carson and Hitchcock, one of Curtis's most notable visions involves a flock of birds that flies above him in eerily structured patterns. Curtis also has exceptionally vivid dreams that bleed their way into his waking life, including one in which the beloved family dog, 'Red', violently attacks him. Convinced that the dream is some kind of portent, he gives Red away. Curtis is an exceptionally self-contained man who, nevertheless, has a close relationship with his wife Sam (Jessica Chastain), and their young daughter Hannah (Tova Stewart), who is deaf. Horrified by a news report about a local family killed by a chemical spill, Curtis is seized by the conviction that he needs to 'protect' them. Although he is painfully aware that his 'visions' are most likely signs of the mental illness that struck his now institutionalised mother at the same age (many of the film's most affecting scenes involve his attempt to seek medical help without alerting those around him), Curtis is simply unable to stop himself from taking direct action. He does so by expanding the storm shelter in their backyard. Things reach crisis point for the family when Curtis loses his job as a result of his obsession, which means the cochlear implant Hannah was scheduled to have fitted will not be paid for by the insurance company. He takes out a large loan to help refurbish the shelter without telling Sam.

When Curtis has a seizure, he for the first time reveals to her something of his troubled inner life. It always starts, he says, '[...] with a kind of storm. A real powerful storm. Dark, thick rain, like thick motor oil. People go crazy and attack me.' His delusions become public knowledge when he is attacked by the workmate who was disciplined for helping facilitate his unauthorised use of company equipment. Curtis's fragile self-control snaps, and he rages like an Old Testament prophet in full view of friends and neighbours. 'There is a storm coming, like nothing you have ever seen, and not a one of you is prepared for it!' Throughout the film, the implication is that Curtis's fear is most likely a manifestation of inherited mental disorder. However, when a real storm happens, he finally gets the chance to protect his family, by ushering them into the shelter. When the storm subsides, he refuses to let them leave. It seems for a moment as if he may even harm Sam and Hannah in order to further 'protect' them. Forced by Sam to choose between obeying his compulsion and losing his family, Curtis finally unlocks the doors. There's been some damage, but the sun is still shining – indeed, 'It's fine.'

If the film had ended there, it would have served as a vivid portrait of blue-collar masculinity during a time of crippling economic and psychological crisis. What brings *Take Shelter* firmly into the eco-horror category, however, are its closing minutes, which are set in a beach house where the family has gone to relax before Curtis starts a new treatment regimen. As he plays in the sand with Hannah, the wind picks up, and the little girl looks out over the ocean. We see reflected in the screen doors of the house a giant waterspout, and a black storm cloud. Sam nods at Curtis, as if in anguished confirmation of something, and he nods back. She has clearly seen whatever it is that's out there too. As rain that is thick and black like oil begins to fall, we hear a crack of thunder, and there is one final, ambiguous snatch of dialogue before the end credits. It isn't really clear whether the events we see here are actually happening, or are merely another of Curtis's dreams. As in 'Young Goodman Brown', it doesn't really matter. The apocalyptic conclusion ties in perfectly with the sense of impending doom that pervades the film. The sense of environmental crisis is still profound, as is the suggestion that the patterns of living and consumption innate in twenty-first-century American life are to blame.

Indeed, it is this implication that makes the visions of eco-horror depicted in *The Last Winter, Take Shelter,* and even *The Happening* so compelling. Although the sense of urgency and genuine desperation evoked in these films has, as we have seen, much to do with the entirely reasonable sense of environmental crisis that pervades modern American life, it is also the latest manifestation of a paradigm that originated in the earliest encounters between European settlers and the North American landscape. 'On every frontier in the nation's past, man's economic interest had been pitted against wilderness in an either-or relationship. And wilderness, in general, fared poorly.'[58] The uncompromisingly materialist perspective which many settlers and colonists expressed towards the plants, trees, and animals of the 'New World' soon manifested itself in the effort to ship back to the Old World every exploitable natural resource that they could get their hands on. 'Most of the early explorers sought to discover what Richard Hakluyt called "merchandisable commodities" [...] These were the natural products which could be shipped to Europe and sold at a profit in order to provide a steady income for colonial settlements.'[59] Although the characterisation of the Indians as nomadic savages fits neatly into the Puritans' pre-existing theological world view, it also allowed the likes of the Reverend Samuel Purchas to justify the seizure of their land. He argued that Christian Englishmen might rightfully seize Indian lands because God had intended his land to be cultivated and not to be left in the condition of 'that unmanned wild Countrey, which they [the savages] range rather than inhabite' [sic].[60] The land was there to be cleared and settled; trees existed so that they could be chopped down; and animals were for taming, eating, or hunting for sport.

Yet, as seen in Chapter 1, if the 'New World' was a place laden with promise and opportunity, for the Puritans, in particular, it was also a territory inhabited by wild beasts and wild men. As such, until it was neatly mapped and bounded, and made to resemble, as much as was possible, the English landscape, it was a threat. This perception of the wilderness was irrevocably linked to the theological imperatives that had brought Puritans across the Atlantic in the first place.[61] In post-2000 American eco-horror narratives, the natural world, and the creatures that inhabit it, are once more perceived as threatening – so much so, in fact, that they threaten the very future of humanity itself. But the threat this time is largely free of the theological and practical considerations that fuelled early colonial anxieties about the wilderness. Few Americans these days believe that the forests are home to the servants of Satan; and just as few have good reason to fear being eaten by wild animals. As a result, the revolts of nature that we have seen so far in this chapter are extreme but understandable payback for the irrevocable damage that humanity has inflicted upon the natural world. If there is a devil in the modern eco-horror film, it is humanity itself.

The return to wilderness in post-apocalyptic narratives

'Forest preceded man, desert follows him', stated graffiti scrawled in Paris in May 1968.[62] Such is certainly the case in the narratives which will be briefly discussed in this concluding section, which focuses on texts which do not conform to the 'eco-horror' formula just outlined. For a start, they are all *post*- rather than *pre*-apocalyptic stories, and the various catastrophes which bring about the end of the US here include pandemics (the most common trigger for the collapse of civilisation), nuclear warfare, and the sudden disappearance of electricity. There is, as we shall see, only the occasional environmental catastrophe, and even when there is, these texts deal not so much with a 'revolt of nature' as with a 'return to wilderness' (which is not quite always the same thing). What brings these narratives under the purview of this study is the fact that they are all set in ruined American landscapes populated by survivors who tend to find themselves sliding towards chaos and savagery – the ultimate nightmare in the Rural Gothic.

Perhaps the most significant early example of this post-apocalyptic loss of 'civilised' impulses in American popular fiction can be found in the 1889 novel *The Last American* by John Ames Mitchell, which is presented to the reader as the journal of a Persian explorer from the thirtieth-century, who travels to a backwards, desolate America long since devastated by climate change. The basic premise has much in common with that of J.G. Ballard's satirical novel *Hello America* (1981) in which a motley crew of scientists and sailors travel through the US several generations after an ecological catastrophe caused by attempts to find new energy sources. Ballard makes it clear that their journey is a blackly comic re-enactment of the initial European settlement of North America. The explorers have left behind a grey, austere Europe, departed from Plymouth (where else), and for a moment mistake the glint of the bright yellow sand dunes that have swallowed up lower Manhattan for gold. Although they are meant to remain on the East Coast, they find themselves gradually drifting ever westward, towards the gaudy remains of Las Vegas, and they encounter eccentric 'native' tribes and all manner of iconic and bitterly humorous ruined Americana.

Jack London's 'The Scarlet Plague' (originally published in 1912) is like many of the texts discussed here, in that a deadly virus is responsible for the death of the US. The main character is a contrary old man who is the last survivor of the pre-apocalyptic era, and who becomes a founding member of a new 'tribe' of savage but resilient youngsters. The story begins with the kind of detail that arises again and again in these kinds of narratives, as the old man and his grandson walk on an overgrown track that had once been part of a railway line. Now, it has been 'swallowed up' by the forest, and is no more than 'A wild animal runway' (the same image appears repeatedly during the opening episodes of the television show *Revolution* [ABC 2013 –] which will be discussed later).[63] In 2013, the old man was a youthful professor of English literature named James Howard Smith. Then the 'Scarlet Plague' killed off most of the population – though not before an accompanying epidemic of murder, robbery, and drunkenness. As he puts it, 'Ten thousand years of culture and civilisation passed in the twinkling of an eye.'[64] San Francisco is set alight once more, and the streets are clogged with thousands of 'stalled motor cars' (a recurrent motif of the Rural Gothic). Howard spends several years journeying through a 'deserted land', noting that before long, horses and dogs have begun to degenerate into more hardy, less refined versions of themselves. At the same time, 'a sea of rank vegetation' has smothered California's farmland. The 'reversion' undergone by both animals and the landscape is replicated in the newfound primitivism of the few humans to survive. When Howard (an inveterate snob) finally encounters other people, he is horrified to find that a crude, uneducated former chauffer – 'the most abhorrent man I have ever known' – is now married to a women who was once 'the most perfect flower of generations of the highest culture this planet has ever produced'.[65]

Although he loathes the chauffer, Howard is too cowardly to challenge his authority, and joins his growing 'tribe'. We see in the frame narrative that surrounds his account of the plague and its aftermath that in the years since 2013, the few 'Americans' that remain have embraced a way of life that resembles greatly that practised by the Indians before colonisation. Howard and his grandson are clad in goatskin, and the boy, like his peers, has brown skin, 'prehistoric weapons', and 'lean muscles'. Their language is '[...] an English that had gone through a bath of corrupt usage'.[66] Although Howard has stowed away books and a key to the alphabet in the hope that they will one day spark a new age of enlightenment, the story ends with a line that emphasises how far they have fallen: 'And old man and boy, skin-clad and barbaric, turned and went along the right-of-way into the forest in the wake of the goats.'[67] It's a narrative that has a great deal in common with another tale of a US similarly depopulated by pandemic: George R. Stewart's *Earth Abides* (1949).

Once more, the protagonist is a male academic, this time, a graduate student named 'Ish' who is in the woods working on his thesis when he's bitten by a snake (as throughout this study, efforts to enjoy the 'peace and quiet' of the wilderness always fail). He feverishly stumbles back to his cabin, and wakes up to discover that during his illness, 'Super-measles' has killed off what seems like every other human being in the world. The frequency with which epidemics depopulate the US in these kinds of stories owes much to the fact that the European invasion of the Americas was greatly facilitated by the rapid spread of disease amongst the native population. North America has already seen one civilisation seriously undermined by infectious disease, so it is not all that surprising that pandemics so often manifest themselves in popular literature and culture as a means of facilitating rapid depopulation.

Although shocked and saddened, Ish-the-scientist isn't really all that surprised: 'Biologically, man has for too long a time been rolling an uninterrupted run of sevens.'[68] The plague has taken hold without too much of the chaos that London associates with the collapse of civilisation: 'Mankind seemed to have been removed rather neatly, with a minimum of disturbance.'[69] It is a conclusion which echoes the sentiment expressed in the novel's title, which emphasises the permanence of the natural world. The main action of the story, also as in London, takes place in and around San Francisco. Perhaps because San Francisco is a city established on the Pacific Ocean, like Alaska, it represents a logical end point for American 'civilisation'.

Ish, always a loner, soon adjusts to his solitary new life, and takes a view of events which consciously draws upon the beginnings of 'America'. 'The world of those Indians passed away', he thought. 'And now our world that followed theirs has passed too.' Armed with food, guns, and a canine companion, he embarks on a lengthy road trip, finding solace in the very act of movement. As he travels east, he realises that '[...] in twenty-five or fifty years some kind of moderately stable situation would result and that the land would steadily get to look more and more like what it had been before the white men came'.[70] His journey ultimately brings him to New York, which is slowly but inexorably disintegrating. After a brief stay with a pair of friendly but hapless survivors (they can't even drive – the ultimate sign of urban dependence), Ish heads home, all the time looking for '[...] the small things that showed how the wilderness was moving in to take charge – the tiny sprout of a poplar tree standing up in the shaggy grass of a lawn, a telephone wire dangling on the road [...]'.[71] Resurgent native grasses begin to crowd out the wheat planted by white farmers, hordes of insects invade his home, and domesticated dogs go wild. The reassertion of native plant species means that *Earth Abides* dramatises a reversal of the process of 'ecological imperialism' known as the 'Columbian Exchange', during which plants, micro-organisms, and animals brought over by Europeans quickly overwhelmed many native species.[72] Although he douses troublesome insects with DDT, Ish can't help but ponder, in a precursor to *The Hellstrom Chronicle*, if 'With the removal of man were they now destined to inherit the earth?'[73]

After he returns home, Ish finds love with a fellow survivor named Emma, who, in another indication of the erosion of pre-catastrophe social mores, reveals that she is of mixed-race descent. Together with a number of other family groups, the couple establish a new community in the suburbs of San Francisco, and for as long as the electricity supply lasts (several years), they are able to live a life that roughly approximates existence before the plague. As children are born, and a generation that has never known anything other than this way of life begins to grow up, Ish and the rest of the adults jokingly begin to refer to themselves as 'The Tribe'. His attempts to educate the younger generation in the old manner fail, but Ish's one hope for the continuity of 'civilisation' lies in his precocious son Joey. When the boy dies, he realises that he must let go of his 'hope for the future'.[74]

As time passes, the community becomes ever more superstitious and ritualistic, and certain artefacts from the 'time before' – such as Ish's old rock hammer – take on a totemic significance (in fact, it becomes more and more like the small towns discussed in Chapter 2). When the tribe's youngest children remark 'Why, the *Americans* made everything!', Ish inspires awe by proclaiming, 'I am an American.'[75] Having relinquished his hopes for the re-establishment of 'civilisation' as he knew it, Ish realises that ritual will help maintain a sense of cohesion for the community. He also teaches the children how to make bows and arrows so that when the last of the ammunition runs out, they will be able to hunt and protect themselves. Ish is, 'The Last American' as he puts it, and in his final years he can only observe as the generational divide widens ever further. His descendants will, he knows, gradually establish their own civilisation, which will inevitably collapse and then be succeeded by another.[76] After all, 'Men come and go, but Earth abides'.[77]

As we have already seen, a more pessimistic perspective on life after catastrophe comes in Cormac McCarthy's *The Road*. The novel is set in a US devastated by an unspecified apocalyptic event – which may or may not have been ecological in nature – that has killed off all forms of plant and animal life. Birds no longer sing; the only food left comes in cans, and cannibal bands hunt other humans. 'The Man' and 'The Boy' shuffle ceaselessly down empty roads and through dead forests, heading to the 'country to the South' in the hope that once they arrive, things will be just a little better. John Hillcoat's 2009 film version also features scene after scene in which the protagonists trudge through a landscape littered with ruined houses and abandoned cars. Lending the visuals an extra air of melancholy verisimilitude is the fact that the settings included real-life sites of environmental and natural disaster such as post–hurricane Katrina New Orleans and the industrial ash-piles of Pittsburgh. As in London and Stewart, father–son relationships are key here: for the protagonist, his boy is for keeping 'the fire' alive.

The Book of Eli (2010) also features interminable scenes of the hero walking through an ecologically devastated and depopulated American landscape, though with added gun play and an extra dose of mawkish religiosity. The event which brought it all crashing down here is 'The Flash', a massive nuclear detonation which tore a hole in the ozone layer (a sudden flash also marks the onset of disaster in McCarthy). The few humans who survived sheltered underground until the worst had passed. Denzel Washington stars as Eli, a man with a mission from God. Once again, the collapse of centralised authority results in cannibalism, looting, and disorder. Unlike as in *The Road*, there are still a few functioning cars left, but they're all in the hands of the villains, which means that Eli spends almost the entire film on foot. At one point he passes by the ruins of a collapsed highway, a melancholy reminder of the freedom of movement that he and his fellow Americans once took for granted.

Rueben Fleischer's road-trip horror-comedy *Zombieland* (2009), opens with a shot of the American flag and a voice-over from the youthful lead, Columbus (Jesse Eisenberg). 'I wish I could tell you this is still America. But I've come to realise that you can't just have a country without any people. And there are no people here.' This is now 'The United States of Zombieland'. The quartet of misfits who become the main characters are known to each other not by their given names, but by those of their respective hometowns. Who they were before the disaster no longer matters, but in their new names there is still some connection to the US that was. In spite of the fact that they face the constant threat of zombie attack, the survivors here actually have a pretty good time. For instance, Columbus, who was a phobia-ridden shut-in before the outbreak, discovers that his obsessive fixation upon rules is now a lifesaver. Although he soon realises that there is no point in going home to Ohio because his parents are already dead, his companions have Quixotic quests of their own in mind. 'Tallahassee' (Woody Harrelson) wants to eat the last Twinkie on earth before the expiration date runs out, whilst sisters 'Wichita' (Emma Stone) and 'Little Rock' (Abigail Breslin) are bound for an LA amusement park they visited as children. On their way to LA, the group take great pleasure in smashing up a gloriously phoney gift shop on an Indian reservation, and, in the comic highlight of the film, even take a breather in actor Bill Murray's Hollywood mansion. Ultimately, the four realise, 'Without other people, you might as well be a zombie', and create a loving, ad hoc family amidst the ruins.

Carriers (2009) is essentially *Zombieland* without the laughs (or the zombies). It too features a quartet of young people travelling by car across a US strewn with dead bodies, empty houses, and abandoned cars. The plague this time is a highly infections kind of Super-SARS. We also once more have siblings, although this time, brothers – one a reckless slacker with a mean streak, and the other a cautious, Ivy League-bound neurotic, who like Columbus, believes that sticking to a strict set of rules will ensure survival. This group also revels in aspects of the freedom that catastrophe has granted – they can speed down the highway, loot stores, and smash windows at the Country Club – but tellingly, this lack of behavioural restriction is ultimately depicted as unsatisfying and dangerous. In the end, it is the two survivors who have restrained their appetites, played by the rules, and been willing to put them into practice no matter the cost, who make it to their final destination (a beach the brothers played together on as children). The closing shot plays like a melancholic reprise of the start of *Zombieland.* We see a flashback to the brothers as little boys, trying, but failing to touch a tattered Stars and Stripes waving in the breeze. The implication – that the US is dead and gone, and the survivors will not be far behind – is obvious.

Zombies also feature in the remorselessly grim TV show *The Walking Dead* (AMC 2010–), based on Robert Kirkman's long-running comic book series of the same name. The living dead, here known as 'walkers' (like the cannibals in *The Book of Eli*), are condemned by their ceaseless appetites to mindlessly keep moving. So too are the small band of perpetually bickering survivors forever moving from one site of temporary safety to another (a farm, a prison), because to stay put is to die. A visual trope often seen in the show – the sight of roads filled with rusting, corpse-filled cars – it is as grim and suggestive a metaphor for twenty-first-century American life as one can possibly imagine. The vast network of highways built during the apex of the nation's economic, political, and technological power has simply ground to a halt. Certainly, there is a kind of freedom in the terrible new world depicted in these narratives, but, *Zombieland* aside, it is a freedom most fully exploited by the devious, the crazy, and the immoral. The absence of external authority, as in many of the novels and films already discussed in this study, leads to degeneration and chaos.

Such is also the case in another, even more recent TV show, *Revolution*, which is set ten years after a mysterious blackout during which the electricity that powers almost every aspect of modern life is switched off, seemingly permanently. Although those who survived the chaos and disorder that quickly swept the nation have not yet resorted to cannibalism, the US is no more (even the Stars and Stripes have been outlawed), cities lie in vegetation-strewn ruins clearly inspired by the speculations contained in Alan Wiseman's *The World without Us* (2007), and survivors live in feudal villages beset by the fascistic 'Monroe Militia'. The main character is a teenage girl named Charlie whose ability with a crossbow highlights her suitability for taking part in the nomadic rescue mission (her brother has been kidnapped) that drives the plot of the first season. The bow and arrow has, in fact, featured rather prominently in American popular culture in recent years, usually as signifier of a dystopian reversion to the use of primitive weaponry. Katniss Everdeen's skill with a longbow is a key element of *The Hunger Games*; whilst Saba, the heroine of Moira Young's 2011 novel *Blood Red Road* (set in a post-apocalyptic North America that has become largely desert) wields a crossbow. Whereas in some of the texts discussed in previous chapters, scenes in which the protagonists adopt weaponry associated with the Indians signify a regression to primitive behaviour (as in *Edgar Huntly*), here, crucially, as in *Earth Abides* and 'The Scarlet Plague', the bow is used by young protagonists whose penchant for archery signifies *adaptation* rather than *degeneration*. This may be because they are citizens of a *new* 'New World' in which there is no longer any 'civilisation' (at least in the old sense of the word), left to fight for, even if they themselves often seem to embody nobility. This is particularly the case in the narratives just mentioned, all of which feature capable and adaptable young women who represent the hope for a better future.

In *The Walking Dead*, as in *The Road*, *The Book of Eli*, and *Zombieland*, those who manage to survive the initial disaster are robbed of a home of their own. As such, one of the things that most bothered the first European settlers about the Indians – their nomadic lifestyle – becomes associated with whites of European descent (and these characters are indeed overwhelmingly white). Along with the recurrent archery motif, it furthers the sense that one of the most notable effects of the end of the world is that it turns white Americans of European descent into Indian, or rather, *Indian-like* figures – sometimes almost literally, as in London and Stewart, sometimes obliquely, as in McCarthy, Collins, and Young. In all of the narratives discussed in this concluding section, there are scenes in which the reader, or the viewer, is confronted with images of a depopulated US in which centralised authority has collapsed, and the wilderness has begun to reclaim the urban, suburban, and even rural landscapes. It is a development which often parallels the reversion to primitivism or outright savagery of the few citizens that remain alive. This sense that the physical trappings of 'civilisation' are much more tenuous than we like to think informs non-fiction works such as *The World without Us*, which discusses what would become of a world from which humans were suddenly 'extracted'. 'Wipe us out, and see what's left. How would the rest of nature respond if it were suddenly relieved of the relentless pressures we heap on it and our fellow organisms?'[78] Wiseman explains why 'The time it would take nature to rid itself of what urbanity has wrought may be less than we might suspect', and illustrates his contention with scientifically grounded case studies. New York is the subject of a chapter entitled, 'The City without Us', which charts the surprisingly rapid collapse of the city in a scenario in which humans are no longer present to perform maintenance, kill weeds, and pump water from the storm drains.

Wiseman also discusses the so-called 'Mannahatta Project', 'an attempt to recreate, virtually, Manhattan Island as it was when Henry

Hudson's crew first saw it in 1609: a pre-urban vision that tempts speculation about how a posthuman future might look'.[79] The result is a remarkable interactive map which superimposes the New York-that-is over the New York-that-was, and includes detailed descriptions of the kind of landscape, animals, and flora that would have been there when European exploration first began.[80] We see a panoramic image of the modern city that is haunted by the 'ghost forest'. I would argue that American literature and popular culture in general is similarly haunted by this idea of the 'wilderness-that-was', and that this legacy finds its fullest expression in the narratives which I have identified in this study as examples of the 'Rural Gothic'. The cities and suburbs that define the US in the twenty-first century are very far removed indeed from the forests and small settlements that dotted the coasts of Virginia and New England 400 years ago, and a nation that was, until just over a century ago, still predominately rural, certainly isn't anymore. Yet, a significant strand within American literature, film, and popular culture still returns repeatedly to anxieties and the tensions that, as we have seen, have their beginnings in early European responses to the American landscape.

Whilst my definition of the 'Rural Gothic' is obviously drawn from a specifically American set of historical and cultural contexts, it is, finally, important to note that some of the more general characteristics of the sub-genre can be found in horror and Gothic narratives from other nations, and, in particular, those which, like America, were colonised by white settlers who displaced an existing native population. For instance, as I noted earlier, the only nation to have an eco-horror tradition as significant as that found in the US is Australia. In Australian cinema we also find a 'backwoods horror' tradition that strongly resembles that seen in the US. Greg McLean's *Wolf Creek* (2005), one of the most disturbing films of the past decade, is particularly interesting. It is certainly distinctively Australian – indeed, it initially evokes the eeriness of home-grown films from the 1970s 'New Wave' such as *Picnic at Hanging Rock* (1975) and *Long Weekend* (1978), both of which inspire unease by suggesting that the natural landscape is possessed of an intelligence that may not see white Australians in a particularly welcoming light. The horror that McLean's film inspires also owes much to the fact that it was inspired by a number of real-life serial killings which took place in the Outback during the 1980s and 1990s. Nevertheless, *Wolf Creek* soon evolves into a story very clearly influenced by classic American backwoods horror tropes, as its likeable young backpackers are captured, tortured, and murdered by a bushman who initially seems like an exemplar of rural friendliness and practicality (the car graveyard surrounding his lair should have been a dead giveaway). *Storm Warning* (2007), a much more by-the-numbers kind of film, also deploys the familiar 'city folks versus evil rural clan' formula within a specifically Australian setting. Indeed, as far back as 1974, in Peter Weir's *The Cars that Ate Paris*, Australian film-makers were dramatising the conflict between urban outsiders 'just passing through' and rural aggressors in distinctively Australian films that, nevertheless, also have much in common with their American equivalents.

The past decade has also seen the release of a series of intense European backwoods horror films, many of which also owe a major debt to the American variety of the Rural Gothic. They include the genuinely bizarre 2005 Belgian/French film *Calvaire* (*The Ordeal*), *Frontiers* (France, 2007), *The Cottage* (UK, 2008), *Small Town Folk* (UK, 2007), *Severance* (UK, 2006), and the Spanish thriller *King of the Mountain* (*El rey de la montaña*, 2007).

In European-set backwoods horror, national and continental history is often evoked as a background factor in the terrible scenes that are unfolding, just as the American Rural Gothic draws upon that nation's past. *Frontiers* begins in a near-future Paris riven by racial dissent and riots, and dispatches its mixed-race heroine to the supposed safety of the countryside, where she is tortured by an inbred, insane clan of neo-Nazi farmers who want her to participate in a hellish 'breeding programme' that evokes fascist eugenics. In *Severance*, British and American office workers employed by military defence contractors named 'Palisade Defences' embark on a team-building trip to Eastern Europe but accidentally stumble into the Former Yugoslavia (they've taken a wrong turn, of course) and are picked off one-by-one by vengeful paramilitaries. We later discover that the paramilitaries were actually armed by Palisade Defences. The final confrontation of the film takes place in an abandoned death camp that evokes the Holocaust but also resembles those established by Serbian forces operating in Bosnia during the mid-1990s. Although it is obviously an American film, *Hostel*, as mentioned earlier, is set in Slovakia and draws heavily on the perceived anti-Americanism that existed in Europe in the aftermath of the American-led invasions of Iraq and Afghanistan.

As observed in Chapter 4, the recent remakes of two of the most famous non-American-set Rural Gothic films of the 1970s – *The Wicker Man* and *Straw Dogs* – move the action to the US. Both remakes serve as cautionary tales which demonstrate that moving the Rural Gothic text away from its original context is usually a bad idea. Neil LaBute's version of *The Wicker Man* attempts to substitute Washington State for the Scottish islands, and new-age matriarchal religion for the cod-Celtic mysticism of the original, but amongst the film's *many* other problems, when robbed of the conflict between High Church Presbyterianism and opportunistic paganism, which powered the original, the film becomes merely an insubstantial shadow of a classic. The same could be said of the *Straw Dogs* remake. In the original, David Sumner's status as the only American in an insular Cornish town highlighted his naiveté and outsider status: he was very literally on unfamiliar territory (in every sense). Although the remake attempts to echo this conceit by making the new version of David an urban outsider in God-fearing, football-loving, small-town Mississippi, the transplant is once again unsuccessful, because the story lacks the historical and cultural contexts of the original, and botches the job of establishing a satisfactory American substitute.

The Rural Gothic in its very *broadest* outlines is, therefore, by no means necessarily a specifically American phenomenon. As Carol J. Clover has pointed out, 'An enormous proportion of horror takes as its starting point the visit or move of (sub) urban people to the country', and this scenario rests on 'what may be a universal archetype'. It is only to be expected, therefore, that elements of the sub-genre as I have outlined it here would be found elsewhere. As we have seen, however, no other nation has a Rural Gothic tradition as rich, or as influential, as that found in the US.

In his famous preface to *Edgar Huntly* (1799), Charles Brockden Brown urged American writers to look to their own history, and to write about their own wilderness, rather than slavishly imitate the 'gothic castles and chimeras' of the European Gothic tradition.[81] He need not have worried. Long before *Edgar Huntly*'s publication, as we have seen, many of American literature's most interesting and most evocative narratives were doing just that. The many twentieth- and twenty-first-century texts discussed here would indicate that they still do.

The primal struggle between the forces of order and chaos, 'savagery' and 'civilisation', which so fascinated and troubled the Puritans, in particular, surfaces time and time again in American horror and Gothic narratives. Despite the fact that hundreds of years have passed since Europeans first encountered the North American wilderness, first impressions (and subsequent adaptations) had an impact that lingers still. The Rural Gothic endures, and will continue to do so, for one simple reason: the US is not out of the woods yet.

Notes

Introduction

1. *The Blair Witch Project* is essentially 'Young Goodman Brown' meets *Cannibal Holocaust* (Dir: Ruggero Deodato, 1980).
2. N. Hawthorne (1835) 'Young Goodman Brown' in (ed.) B. Harding, *Young Goodman Brown and Other Tales* (Oxford: Oxford University Press, 1987), 119.
3. M. Rockman and J. Steele (2003) *Colonisation of Unfamiliar Landscapes: The Archaeology of Adaptation* (London: Routledge, 2003), 26.
4. W. Cronon (1983) *Changes in the Land: Indians, Colonists and the Ecology of New England* (New York: Hill and Wang), 10.
5. W.C. Williams (1925) *In the American Grain* (New York: New Directions), 174.
6. D. Varma (1985) *The Gothic Flame* (London and New Jersey: Scarecrow Press), 11.
7. G. Byron and D. Punter (2004) *The Gothic* (Oxford: Wiley Blackwell), 7.
8. D. Punter (1981) *The Literature of Terror: Vol. 1* (London: Longman), 5.
9. R. Davenport-Hines (1998) *Gothic: 400 Years of Excess, Horror, Evil and Ruin* (London: Fourth Estate), 266.
10. Davenport-Hines, 266.
11. T. Goddu (1997) *Gothic America: Narrative, History and Nation* (New York: Columbia University Press), 4.
12. A.G. Lloyd Smith (2000) 'Nineteenth-Century American Gothic' in D. Punter (ed.) *A Companion to the Gothic* (Oxford: Blackwell), 109.
13. W.C. Cronon (1996) 'The Trouble With Wilderness, or, Getting Back to the Wrong Nature', *Environmental History*, Vol. 1, No.1 (Jan. 1996), 7.
14. M. Lewis (ed.) *American Wilderness: A New History* (Oxford: Oxford University Press, 2007), 4–5.
15. Cronon, 9.
16. S. Stoll, 'Farm against Forest' in M. Lewis (ed.), *American Wilderness: A New History*, 4.
17. Cronon, 8.
18. Ibid., 8.
19. R. Nash (1967) *Wilderness and the American Mind* (New Haven: Yale University Press), 18.
20. Lewis, Introduction, 6.
21. T.G. Jordan and M. Kaups (1992) *The American Backwoods Frontier: An Ethical and Ecological Interpretation* (The Johns Hopkins University Press, 1992).
22. Jordan and Kaups, 3–4.
23. Ibid., 6.
24. D.T. Lichter and D.L. Brown (2011) 'Rural America in an Urban Society: Changing Spatial and Social Boundaries', *Annual Review of Sociology*, Vol. 37, No. 566.

25. P. Carr and M. Kefalas (2010) *Hollowing out the Middle: The Rural Brain Drain and What It Means for America*; R.E. Woods *Survival of Rural America: Small Victories and Bitter Harvests*; D.L. Brown (2004) *Challenges for Rural America in the Twenty First Century*; T.A. Lyson and W.W. Falk (1993) *Forgotten Places: Uneven Development and the Loss of Opportunity in Rural America*; and O.G. Davidson (1996) *Broken Heartland: The Rise of America's Rural Ghetto*.
26. D.L. Brown and K. A. Schafft (2011) *Rural People and Communities in the 21st Century: Resilience and Transformation* (Cambridge: Polity, 2011), 9.
27. C.J. Clover (1992) *Men, Women and Chain Saws: Gender and the Modern Horror Film* (London: BFI Publishing), 124.
28. Cronon, 53.
29. Ibid., 53.
30. M. Perrault (2007) 'American Wilderness and First Contact', *American Wilderness: A New History*, 15.
31. T. Goddu (1997) *Gothic America: Narrative, History, Nation* (New York: Columbia University Press).
32. E. Savoy (2002) 'The Rise of American Gothic' in J.E. Hogle (ed.) *The Cambridge Companion to Gothic Fiction* (Cambridge: Cambridge University Press), 187.

1 The Cabin in the Woods: Order versus Chaos in the 'New World'

1. J.H. St John Crévecœur (1782, 2009) *Letters from an American Farmer* (Oxford: Oxford World's Classics), 51.
2. The film aroused more than its fair share of negative critical attention. Writing in *The Guardian*, Peter Bradshaw summarised the film as 'a technically accomplished hoax of ineffable nastiness', whilst *The Daily Mail* asked, 'What DOES it take for a film to get banned these days?'.
3. See, for instance, B.M.S. Thomsen (2009) '*Antichrist* – Chaos Reigns: The Event of Violence and the Haptic Image in Lars von Trier's Film', *Journal of Aesthetics & Culture*, Vol. 1.
4. 'Lars Von Trier Interview', 28 June 2005, *TimeOut London*, http://www.timeout.com/film/news/553/ (accessed 19 August 2010).
5. A.O. Scott, 'It Fakes a Village: Lars von Trier's America', *New York Times*, 21 March 2004.
6. R. Nash (1967) *Wilderness and the American Mind* (New Haven: Yale University Press), 128.
7. See also: S. Fender, (1981) *Plotting the Golden West: American Literature and the Rhetoric of the California Trail* (Cambridge: Cambridge University Press) and R. Nash on the 'Wilderness Cult', 148–160.
8. See K. Janisse's *House of Psychotic Women: An Autobiographical Topography of Female Neurosis in Horror and Exploitation Films* (FAB Press, 2012) for a convincing reading of the woman's continual attempts to shift responsibility for the child's death, 165.
9. F. Ringel (1995) *New England's Gothic Literature* (Edward Mellen Press), 54–55.
10. For example, *Antichrist* is dedicated to Andrei Tarkovsky.

11. M. Bradbury and R. Ruland (1991) *From Puritanism to Postmodernism: A History of American Literature* (New York: Viking), 3.
12. A dynamic described by Robert Frost in his 1935 poem 'The Gift Outright' (which he recited at J.F. Kennedy's inauguration), which has the resonant opening line: 'The land was ours before we were the land's.'
13. Nash, XI.
14. Ibid., XI.
15. Ibid., XI.
16. Ibid., 2.
17. Y. Tuan (1979) *Landscapes of Fear* (Oxford: Basil Blackwell), 81.
18. Nash, 2.
19. Ibid., 8.
20. Ibid., 8.
21. See also R. Abrams, *Language and Ideology in American Renaissance Literature* (2004).
22. W. Mignolo (2003) *The Darker Side of the Renaissance* (Chicago: University of Michigan), 259.
23. Bradbury and Ruland, 4.
24. A. Taylor (2001) *American Colonies: The Penguin History of the United States* (New York: Penguin), 24.
25. Taylor, 24.
26. D.B. Quinn (1998) *European Approaches to America 1450–1640* (London: Ashgate), 93.
27. Quinn, 94.
28. Ibid., 94.
29. M. Rockman and J. Steele (2003) *Colonisation of Unfamiliar Landscapes: The Archaeology of Adaptation* (London: Routledge), xix.
30. Quinn, 95.
31. Ibid., 55.
32. Mignolo, 309.
33. Bradbury and Ruland, 3.
34. Abrams, 3.
35. F. Jennings (1975) *The Invasion of America: Indians, Colonialism, and the Cant of Conquest* (New York: W.W. Norton and Company), 15.
36. Taylor, 40.
37. Nash, 7.
38. Ibid., 8.
39. Nash, XI.
40. Jennings, 10.
41. Taylor, 24.
42. W. Cronon (1983) *Changes in the Land: Indians, Colonists and the Ecology of New England* (New York: Hill and Wang), 19.
43. M. Perreault (2007) 'American Wilderness and First Contact' in M. Lewis (ed.) *American Wilderness: A New History* (Oxford: Oxford University Press), 22.
44. Cronon, 19.
45. Ibid., 20.
46. Ibid., 6.
47. Ibid., 6.

48. Ibid., 3.
49. Ibid., 33.
50. Ibid., 33.
51. Ibid., 33.
52. Cronon, 53.
53. Ibid., 53.
54. Ibid., 25.
55. Ibid., 14.
56. Taylor, 25.
57. Cronon, 156.
58. Ibid., 24.
59. Ibid., 24.
60. Ibid., 130.
61. Ibid., 130.
62. P. Seed (1965) *Ceremonies of Possession in Europe's Conquest of the New World* (Cambridge: Cambridge University Press), 39.
63. This originating event is reflected in the significant part that plague narratives play in American imaginings of apocalypse (discussed in Chapter 5).
64. Taylor, 39.
65. Cronon, 85.
66. Ibid., 86.
67. Ibid., 86.
68. Ibid., 86.
69. Ibid., 86.
70. Taylor, 39.
71. Cronon, 39.
72. Ibid., 86.
73. Ibid., 40.
74. For more on this, see A.W. Crosby (1972–2003) *The Columbian Exchange: Biological and Cultural Consequences of 1492* (Westport: Praeger).
75. Cronon, 90.
76. Ibid., 90.
77. Taylor, 44.
78. Cronon, 90.
79. Ibid., 90.
80. Taylor, 49.
81. Ibid., 49.
82. Bradbury and Ruland, 8.
83. Ibid., 5.
84. J. Smith, *A Description of New England* (1616), online electronic text edition, ed. Paul Royster (accessed 28 February 2013), http://digitalcommons.unl.edu/cgi/viewcontent.cgi?article=1003&context=etas.
85. Perreault, 20.
86. Taylor, 188.
87. J. Gatta (2004) *Making Nature Sacred: Literature, Religion and the Environment in America from the Puritans to the Present* (Oxford: Oxford University Press), 18.
88. Philbrick, 3.
89. Bradford, 4.

90. Ibid., 4.
91. Ibid., 4.
92. Gatta, 19.
93. Ibid, 19.
94. Nash, 43.
95. Tuan, 81.
96. Ibid., 5.
97. F. Turner (1980) *Beyond Geography: The Western Spirit against the Wilderness* (New York: Viking Press), 195.
98. L. Miller (2000) *Roanoke: Solving the Mystery of the Lost Colony* (New York: Arcade Publishing), 14.
99. 'The Fifth Voyage of M. John White, 1590', in Henry S. Burrage, ed., *Early English and French Voyages, Chiefly from Hakluyt, 1534–1608* (New York: Charles Scribner's Sons, 1906), 315–320.
100. Turner, 198.
101. Ibid., 199.
102. S.W. Poole (2011) *Monsters in America: Our Hideous Obsession with the Hideous and the Haunting* (Baylor: Baylor University Press), 34.
103. A. Taylor (2002) *American Colonies: The Settling of North America* (New York: Penguin), 130.
104. Taylor (2002), 130.
105. Ibid., 130.
106. Ibid., 131.
107. D. Leach (1963) *The Northern Colonial Frontier, 1607–1763* (Vanderbilt University: Holt, Rhinehart, and Wilson), 30.
108. Taylor (2002), 159.
109. Ibid., 159.
110. Bradford, 17–24.
111. Nash, 31.
112. Ibid., 35.
113. Ibid.,16.
114. P. Johnston (1997) 'A Puritan in the Wilderness: Natty Bumppo's Language and America's Nature Today', *James Fenimore Cooper: His Country and His Art (No. 11)*, Papers from the 1997 Cooper Seminar (No. 11), (The State University of New York College at Oneonta: Oneonta, New York), 60–63.
115. Ibid., 62.
116. R. Abrams (2004) *Language and Ideology in American Renaissance Literature* (Cambridge: Cambridge University Press), 7.
117. R. Vanderbeets (1991) 'The Indian Captivity Narrative: An American Genre' in E. Eliot (ed.) *The Columbia History of the American Novel* (New York: Columbia University Press), 32.
118. Quoted in Ringel, 8.
119. Gatta, 19.
120. S.W. Poole (2009) *Satan in America: The Devil We Know* (New York: Rowman and Littlefield), 15.
121. Ibid., 16.
122. Taylor, 188.
123. Perreault, 15.

124. J.D. Hartman (1999) *Providence Tales and the Birth of American Literature* (Baltimore: Johns Hopkins University Press), 169.
125. Bradbury and Ruland, 27.
126. K.Z. Derounian-Stodola (1998) *Women's Indian Captivity Narratives* (London: Penguin Classics), xi.
127. S. Faludi (2007) *The Terror Dream: What 9/11 Revealed about America* (London: Henry Holt), 213.
128. Vanderbeet, 32.
129. D. Reynolds (2011) *Beneath the American Renaissance: The Subversive Imagination in the Age of Emerson and Melville* (Oxford: Oxford University Press), 191–193.
130. R. Bauer (2003) *The Cultural Geography of Colonial American Literature* (Cambridge: Cambridge University Press), 120.
131. Ringel, 8.
132. Nash, 36.
133. Bradbury and Ruland, 28.
134. K.Z. Derounian-Stodola (1988) 'The Publication, Promotion, and Distribution of Mary Rowlandson's Indian Captivity Narrative in the Seventeenth Century', *Early American Literature*, Vol. 23, No. 3, 239–261.
135. Nash, 36.
136. Quoted in Nash, 28.
137. Hartman, 16.
138. Ibid., 16.
139. Ibid., 17.
140. C.J. Clover (1992) *Men, Women and Chainsaws: Gender in the Modern Horror Film*, (London: British Film Institute), 35.
141. 'She heartened the *Nurse* and the *Youth* to assist her in this Enterprise; and all furnishing themselves with *Hatchets* for the purpose, they struck home Blows upon the Heads of their *Sleeping Oppressors*, that e'er they could any of them struggle into an effectual resistance, *at the Feet* of those Poor Prisoners, *they bow'd, they fell, they lay down* [...]' (Derounian-Stodola, *Women's Indian Captivity Narratives*, 60).
142. Bauer, 139.
143. Rowlandson, (in Philbrick), 167.
144. Ibid., 168.
145. Ibid., 167.
146. Ibid., 168.
147. Ibid., 169.
148. Ibid., 169.
149. Bauer, 146.
150. Rowlandson, 169.
151. Perreault, 28.
152. Perreault, 173.
153. Vanderbeets, 32.
154. Rowlandson, 173.
155. Bauer, 140.
156. Rowlandson, 175.
157. Ibid., 179.
158. Ibid., 180.

159. Ibid., 180.
160. Ibid., 184.
161. Proverbs, 27:7.
162. Willem Dafoe's character in *Antichrist* gets his first inkling that his trip to the woods will not be an altogether uneventful one when he comes across a deer giving birth to a stillborn fawn.
163. K. Biggs (1967) *The Fairies in English Tradition and Literature* (London: Taylor and Francis), 143.
164. Ibid., 209.
165. See Deroundian-Stodola (*Women's Indian Captivity Narratives*, xvi).
166. Bergland (2000) *The National Uncanny: Indian Ghosts and American Subjects* (Hanover and London: University Press of New England), 32.
167. Rowlandson, 211.
168. R. Slotkin (1977) *Regeneration through Violence: The Mythology of the American Frontier, 1600–1860* (Normal: University of Oklahoma Press, 1973), 91.

2 'We Are But a Little Way in the Forest Yet': The Community in the Wilderness

1. This account of the final hours of life in Jonestown is taken from T. Reiterman (1982, 2008) *Raven: The Untold Story of the Reverend Jim Jones and his People* (New York: Penguin), 487–569.
2. Reiterman, X.
3. J.E. Hall (2004) *Gone from the Promised Land: Jonestown in American Cultural History* (New York: Transaction Publishers), 191.
4. Ibid., 207.
5. Ibid., 207.
6. S. Bercovitch (1996) *The Cambridge History of American Literature* (London: Cambridge University Press), 32.
7. A. Bradstreet, 'To My Dear Children' cited in D. Anderson (1999) *A House Divided: Domesticity and Community in American Literature* (Cambridge: Cambridge University Press), 9.
8. Anderson, 9.
9. Anderson, 9.
10. J. Stockwell (1998) *The Encyclopaedia of American Communes, 1663–1963* (North Carolina: McFarland), 3.
11. Stockwell, 3.
12. C. Berryman (1979) *From Wilderness to Wasteland: The Trials of the Puritan God in the American Imagination* (New York: National University Publications, Kennikat Press), 21.
13. P. Miller (1996) *Errand into the Wilderness* (Cambridge: Harvard University Press), 15.
14. Miller, 15.
15. Berryman, 22.
16. Miller, 15.
17. Berryman, 22.
18. Berryman, 22.
19. Berryman, 30.

20. P. Boyer and S. Nissenbaum (1974) *Salem Possessed* (Cambridge: Harvard University Press), XIII.
21. These theories are outlined in more detail in P. Bartel (2000) *Spellcasters: Witches and Witchcraft in History* (Lanham: Taylor), 130–155.
22. Rosenthal, 3.
23. P. Kafer (2005) *Charles Brockden Brown's Revolution and the Birth of American Gothic* (Pennsylvania: Pennsylvania University Press), 115. Kafer also rightly notes that *Wieland* has much in common with Stephen King's *The Shining* (1977).
24. J.G. Frank (1950) 'The Wieland Family in Charles Brockden Brown's Wieland', *Monatshefte*, Vol. 42, No. 7 (Nov.), 347–353.
25. Details cited in H. Brogan (2001) *The Penguin History of the USA* (London: Penguin), 93–94.
26. Brown, *Wieland*, 8.
27. Ibid., 7.
28. Ibid., 8.
29. Ibid., 9.
30. Kafer, 114.
31. Mettingen is a municipality in North Rhine-Westphalia.
32. Brown, 11.
33. Ibid., 16.
34. Ibid., 18.
35. Kafer, 124.
36. J. Tompkins (1986) *Sensational Designs: The Cultural Work of American Fiction, 1790–1860* (Oxford: Oxford University Press). Tompkins' very persuasive reading of *Wieland* has considerably influenced my own.
37. Kafer, 44.
38. A.G. Lloyd-Smith (2000) 'Nineteenth-Century American Gothic' in D. Punter (ed.) *A Companion to the Gothic* (London: Blackwell), 111.
39. Tompkins, 50.
40. Brown, *Wieland*, 19.
41. Ibid., 23.
42. Ibid., 19.
43. Ibid., 24.
44. Lloyd-Smith, 111.
45. Rather like Heath Ledger's Joker in *The Dark Knight Returns* (whose origin story changes every time he tells it).
46. Brown, *Wieland*, 47.
47. Ibid., 49.
48. Ibid., 49.
49. Ibid., 51.
50. Ibid., 56.
51. Shirley Jackson's 1959 novel *The Sundial* owes much to *Wieland*.
52. Brown, *Wieland*, 56.
53. Ibid., 121.
54. A.G. Lloyd-Smith (1989) *Uncanny American Fiction: Medusa's Face* (Basingstoke: Macmillan Press), 24.
55. Ibid., 24.
56. Brown, *Wieland*, 93.

57. Tompkins, 52.
58. Brown, *Wieland*, 91.
59. Tompkins, 52.
60. Ibid., 53.
61. Ibid., 54.
62. Brown, *Wieland*, 172.
63. Ibid., 172.
64. Ibid., 217.
65. Ibid., 214.
66. We are never told where, exactly, Pearl ends up, but it is said that Hester was, in her later years 'the object of love and interest with some inhabitant of another land', and that 'letters came with armorial seals upon them, though of bearings unknown to English heraldry'. Hawthorne (1992) *The Scarlet Letter* (Hertfordshire: Wordsworth Classics), 314.
67. Brown, *Wieland*, 224.
68. Tompkins, 55.
69. Nash, 39.
70. N. Hawthorne (1835, 2008) 'Roger Malvin's Burial' in *Young Goodman Brown and Other Tales* (Oxford: Oxford World's Classics), 59.
71. Hawthorne, 'Malvin', 62.
72. Ibid., 63.
73. Ibid., 63.
74. Ibid., 66.
75. Ibid., 66.
76. H. Levin (1958, 1980) *The Power of Blackness: Hawthorne, Poe, Melville* (Ohio University Press), 184.
77. Ibid., 70.
78. Hawthorne, 'Malvin', 72.
79. Ibid., 73.
80. Ibid., 73.
81. N. Hawthorne (1850) *The Scarlet Letter* (Hertfordshire: Wordsworth), 22.
82. R. Miller (2009) *American Literary History*, 21 (3): 464–491.
83. C. Ryskamp (1959) 'The New England Sources of *The Scarlet Letter*', *American Literature*, Vol. 31, No. 3 (Nov.), 257–272.
84. Nash, 39.
85. J. Stockwell (1998) *The Encyclopaedia of American Communes, 1663–1963* (North Carolina: McFarland), 40.
86. Stockwell, 41.
87. N. Hawthorne (1852, 2009) *The Blithedale Romance* (Oxford: Oxford University Press).
88. Stockwell, 87.
89. Hawthorne, 'Gentle', 31.
90. Ibid., 9.
91. Ibid., 13.
92. Ibid., 16.
93. Ibid., 18.
94. Ibid., 25–6.
95. Ibid., 36.

96. M. Zuckerman (1977) 'Pilgrims in the Wilderness: Community, Modernity and the Maypole at Merry Mount', *The New England Quarterly*, Vol. 50, No. 2, 255.
97. Hawthorne, 'Merrymount', 133.
98. Ibid., 134.
99. Ibid., 135.
100. Ibid., 138.
101. See Zuckerman 261–262 for more on Morton's relationship to the natural landscape.
102. Hawthorne, 'Merrymount', 139.
103. Ibid., 141.
104. Ibid., 141.
105. Ibid., 141.
106. Zuckerman, 263.
107. Ibid., 263.
108. Ibid., 274–277.
109. Ibid., 274.
110. Levin, 54.
111. N. Hawthorne (1835) 'Young Goodman Brown', *Young Goodman Brown and Other Tales* (Oxford: Oxford World's Classics), 350.
112. Hawthorne, 'Goodman', 112.
113. Ibid., 112.
114. M. Rowlandson (1676) 'The Sovereignty and Goodness of God' in N. Philbrick and T. Philbrick (eds) *The Mayflower Papers: Selected Writing of Colonial New England* (New York: Penguin, 2007), 179.
115. Hawthorne, 'Brown', 112.
116. Ibid., 113.
117. Ibid., 113.
118. Ibid., 117.
119. Ibid., 118.
120. Ibid., 119.
121. Ibid., 119.
122. Ibid., 119.
123. Ibid., 119.
124. Ibid., 121.
125. Ibid., 121.
126. Ibid., 120.
127. Ibid., 122.
128. Ibid., 122.
129. Ibid., 123.
130. Ibid., 122.
131. Tuan, 8.
132. Ibid., 151.
133. Ringel, 201 and 205.
134. S. Jackson (1956, 1996) *The Witchcraft of Salem Village* (New York, Random House).
135. Jackson lived in New England from 1945 until her death in 1965. See 'The People of the Village Have always Hated Us: Shirley Jackson's New England

Gothic' in B.M. Murphy, (ed.) *Shirley Jackson: Essays on the Literary Legacy* (North Carolina: McFarland), 104–126.
136. H.E. Nebeker (1974) 'The Lottery as Symbolic Tour de Force', *American Literature*, Vol. 46, No. 1 (Mar.), 100–108.
137. S. Jackson (2010) 'The Lottery' in *Shirley Jackson: Novels and Stories* (New York: The Library of America), 227.
138. Jackson, 'Lottery', 228.
139. Ibid., 231.
140. One wonders if it was the same item of furniture mentioned in 'The Custom House': 'In the way of furniture, there is a stove with a voluminous funnel; an old pine desk, *with a three-legged stool beside* it [...]' (my italics).
141. T. Tryon (1974) *Harvest Home* (New York: Hodder Stoughton), 33.
142. Ibid., 60.
143. S.T. Joshi (2001) *The Modern Weird Tale* (North Carolina: McFarland), 195.
144. Ibid., 60.
145. Ibid., 60.
146. Joshi, 106.
147. T.E.D. Klein (1984) *The Ceremonies* (London: Pan), 63.
148. Klein, 152.
149. King, 'Children of the Corn' (1976, 1979) in *Night Shift* (London: NEL), 206.
150. Ibid., 205.
151. Ibid., 206.
152. The same 'children turning violently against adults' plot device is used much more effectively in the neglected Spanish horror classic *Who Could Kill A Child?* (1976).
153. King, 'Children', 207.
154. R.C. Wood, Ralph (2005) *Flannery O'Connor and the Christ-haunted South* (Alban), 13.
155. A. Cooke (1996) *Fun and Games with Alistair Cooke: On Sport and Other Amusements* (New York: Arcade Publishing), 40.
156. Hawthorne, 'Merrymount', 138.
157. J.C. Oates (2011) *The Corn Maiden and Other Nightmares* (New York: The Mysterious Press).
158. F. Oehlschlaeger (1988) 'The Stoning of Mistress Hutchinson: Meaning and Context in "The Lottery"', *Essays in Literature,* Vol. XV, No. 2 (Fall), 259–265.
159. Nebecker, 104.
160. Ibid., 107.
161. More information on each of these films can be found on the *Science Fiction, Horror and Fantasy Film Review* site (http://moria.co.nz/ accessed 23 June 2011).
162. See Ira Levin's *The Stepford Wives* (1971) and Bentley Little's *The Association* for suburban-set variations on the 'flawed utopian community' plot. Edgar Wright's *Hot Fuzz* is a deeply affectionate and very English horror/comedy take on this trope (2007).
163. My nomination for most ridiculous euphemism in the film is 'the old shed that is not to be used'.
164. L. Coats, M. Cohen, J.D. Miles, K. Nishikawa, and R. Walsh (2008) 'Those We Don't Speak Of: Indians in the Village', *PMLA,* Vol. 123, No. 2, 358–374.

This article discusses the film in relation to the Puritan creation of an American sense of self, and the ways in which it 'offers an opportunity to interrogate the ways stories about early America continue to shape the United States'.

165. 'Despite Shyamalan's professed efforts to make it "period-accurate," the film is likely to be gratingly off-key from the start to those expecting historical accuracy' (L. Coats, M. Cohen, J.D. Miles, K. Nishikawa, and R. Walsh, 360).
166. J. Baudrillard (1989) *America* (London: Verso), 98.
167. Ibid., 90.
168. Berryman, 21.
169. As Patrick C. Collier observes, this scene takes on a very different meaning when viewed with knowledge of the revelations to come. 'Our Silly Lies: Ideological Fictions in M. Night Shyamalan's *The Village*', *Journal of Narrative Theory*, Vol. 38, No. 2 (Summer), 276.
170. Collier, 288.

3 'Going Windigo': 'Civilisation' and 'Savagery' on the New Frontier

1. F.J. Turner (1920, 2008) *The Significance of the Frontier in American History* (London: Penguin, 1920; 2008), 48. See also K. Clark and L. Tiller (1966) *Terrible Trail: The Meek Cutoff, 1845* (Bend, OR: Maverick Publications Inc.) for more on the film's source story.
2. Reichardt's film ends on an ambiguous note: having placed their trust in a captured Indian, who they hope will lead them to water, the pioneers anxiously watch him stride off into the distance, unsure as to whether he is leading them to salvation or death at the hands of his fellow braves. In real life, Meek's pioneers eventually made it to safety, though with many fatalities along the way.
3. S. Lindenbaum (2004) 'Thinking About Cannibalism', *Annual Review of Anthropology*, Vol. 33, 477.
4. J. Berglund (2006) *Cannibal Fictions: American Explorations of Colonialism, Race, Gender and Sexuality* (Wisconsin: University of Minnesota Press), 3. See also M. Kilgour (1990) *From Communion to Cannibalism: An Anatomy of Metaphors of Incorporation* (Princeton University Press).
5. Berglund, 8.
6. R.H. Pearce (1953, 1956) *The Savages of America: A Study of the Indian and the Idea of Civilisation* (Baltimore: The Johns Hopkins Press), 5.
7. http://nationalhumanitiescenter.org/pds/amerbegin/settlement/text2/JamestownPercyRelation.pdf (accessed 24 October 2011).
8. R.B. Hermann (2011) 'The "Tragicall Historie": Cannibalism and Abundance in Colonial Jamestown', *The William and Mary Quarterly*, Vol. 61, No. 1 (Jan.), 56. See: http://news.nationalgeographic.com/news/2013/13/130501-jamestown-cannibalism-archeology-science/ for details on recent archaeological discoveries confirming the occurance of cannibalism at Jamestown during this period (accessed June 18th 2013).
9. http://nationalhumanitiescenter.org/pds/amerbegin/settlement/text2/JamestownPercyRelation.pdf.

10. Ibid. This account is highly reminiscent, as we shall see, of the opening scene of *Ravenous*.
11. Ibid. Percy also tells of a colonist named Hugh Pryse [sic] who, 'being pinched with extreme famine, in a furious distracted mood did come openly into the market place blaspheming, exclaiming, and crying out that there was no God, alleging that if there were a god he would not suffer his creatures whom he had made and framed to endure those miseries and to perish for want of foods and sustenance'. The next day, God's displeasure, says Percy, is made clear when Pryse, having wandered into the woods, is killed by Indians: to add insult to injury, his corpse is savaged by wild beasts.
12. R. Appelbaum (2005) 'Hunger in Early Virginia: Indians and English facing off over excess, want and need' in. R. Appelbaum and J. Wood Sweet (eds) *Envisioning an English Empire: Jamestown and the Making of the North Atlantic World* (Philadelphia: University of Pennsylvania Press), 214.
13. Appelbaum, 214.
14. Ibid., 49.
15. Ibid., 68.
16. Berglund, 10.
17. Ibid., 10.
18. N. Grabo, 'Introduction' in C. Brockden Brown, *Edgar Huntly: Or, Memoirs of a Sleepwalker* (Harmondsworth: Penguin Classics), XI.
19. Brown, *Huntly*, 23. Maze references also occur at 95 and 122.
20. Ibid., 92.
21. Ibid., 96.
22. Ibid., 100.
23. S. Matterson (1996) 'Indian Hating in the Confidence Man', *Arizona Quarterly*, Vol. 52, No. 2 (Summer), 21–24, 28.
24. Matterson, 28.
25. Grabo, XIII. See also Brown, *Huntly*, 118.
26. Brown, *Huntly*, 118.
27. The terms 'cougar' and 'panther' are used interchangeably in the novel. The 'Eastern' Cougar/Panther of the kind described by Brown is now classified as extinct. Source: 'Department of Environmental Conservation': Eastern Cougar Fact Sheet, http://www.dec.ny.gov/animals/6974.html (accessed 14 February 2013).
28. Brown, *Huntly*, 156.
29. Berglund, 8. Perhaps the most memorable fictional representation of auto-cannibalism is found in Stephen King's stomach-churning story 'Survivor Type' (1982).
30. There has long been an association between cave dwelling and cannibalism in American and British popular culture – something which owes much to the notoriety of the infamous (and most likely, entirely fictional) case of Scottish serial murderer and cannibal Sawney Beane. Cave-dwelling mutants feature in British horror film *The Descent*, whilst subway-set horror films such as *Death Line* (1972) and, more recently, *Creep* (2004) feature them as well (after all, a subway really is just an urban cave).
31. As we shall see further in Chapters 4 and 5, when white Americans start using weapons associated with the Indians in the backwoods horror and

the Rural Gothic, it is usually a sign that they have become dangerously detached from 'civilisation' and are in danger of 'going native'.

32. Brown, *Huntly*, 160.
33. Ibid., 164.
34. Ibid., 160.
35. Ibid., 170.
36. Ibid., 175.
37. Ibid., 189.
38. Ibid., 190.
39. Ibid., 191.
40. Ibid., 192.
41. Ibid., 191.
42. Ibid., 191.
43. G. Toles (1981) 'Charting the Hidden Landscape: *Edgar Huntly*', *Early American Literature*, Vol. XVI, 133–53, 150.
44. Ibid., 150.
45. Grabo, XIII.
46. Ibid.
47. Ibid.
48. Brown, *Huntly*, 227.
49. Grabo, XVII.
50. Pearce, 224–225.
51. Ibid., 222.
52. R. Hine, and J.M. Faragher (2007) *Frontiers: A Short History of the American West* (New Haven: Yale University Press), 29.
53. J.H. Merrell (1999) *Into the American Woods: Negotiations on the Pennsylvania Frontier* (New York: W.W. Norton), 23.
54. Ibid., 24.
55. The original title for the Pennsylvania-set film *The Village* was *The Woods*, and the insular villagers continually refer to the forested territory beyond their small settlement as such.
56. Merrell, 25.
57. Ibid., 26.
58. Ibid., 29.
59. Ibid., 27.
60. Faragher and Hine, 29.
61. Ibid., 29.
62. Ibid., 29.
63. Ibid., 29.
64. Ibid., 29.
65. A. Taylor (2001) *American Colonies: The Penguin History of the United States* (New York: Penguin), 196.
66. Ibid., 196.
67. Ibid., 196.
68. Ibid., 199–200.
69. Ibid., 200.
70. W.S. Poole (2009) *Satan in America: The Devil We Know* (New York: Rowman and Littlefield), 15.
71. Taylor, 200.

72. Ibid., 200.
73. Ibid., 200.
74. S.F. Cook (1973) 'Interracial Warfare and Population Decline among the New England Indians', *Ethnohistory* 20/1 (Winter 1973), 1–24, 4.
75. R. Slotkin (1977) *Regeneration through Violence: The Mythology of the American Frontier, 1600–1860* (Normal: University of Oklahoma Press), 156.
76. Slotkin, 156.
77. Ibid., 161.
78. Ibid., 267.
79. Turner, 3.
80. Taylor, 200.
81. Ibid., 33.
82. Ibid., 33.
83. Ibid., 34.
84. Ibid., 40.
85. Ibid., 42.
86. Ibid., 42.
87. Ibid., 42. For more on this process, see A. Linklater (2002) *Measuring America: How the United States Was Shaped by the Greatest Land Sale in History* (London: Harper Collins).
88. Slotkin, 179.
89. Turner, 4.
90. Pearce, 226.
91. Turner, 3.
92. H.L. Kushner (1992) 'The Persistence of the "Frontier Thesis" in America: Gender, Myth and Self-Destruction', *Canadian Review of American Studies*, Special Issue 1, Vol. 23, 53–83.
93. Kushner, 84.
94. Ibid., 84.
95. Hine and Faragher, 62.
96. Ibid., 62.
97. Ibid., 62.
98. M.S. Joy (2003) *American Expansionism, 1783–1860: A Manifest Destiny?* (London: Pearson Longman), 100–101.
99. Joy, 102.
100. Ibid., 102.
101. E. Rarick (2008) *Desperate Passage: The Donner Party's Perilous Passage West* (New York: Oxford University Press), 14.
102. G.R. Stewart (1936, 1988) *Ordeal by Hunger: The Story of the Donner Party* (New York: Houghton Mifflin), 13.
103. S.A. McCurdy (1994) 'Epidemiology of Disaster: The Donner Party (1846–7)', *WJM* (April 1994), Vol. 160, No. 4, 338.
104. Rarick, 46–57.
105. Ibid., 105.
106. Ibid., 110.
107. McCurdy, 339.
108. Rarick, 192. The fact that they still have blood on their faces reinforces a motif present in Rowlandson and Brown also.

109. Rarick, 241.
110. Ibid., 241.
111. Ibid., 242.
112. Ibid., 143.
113. Ibid., 244.
114. Stewart, 298.
115. D. Di Stefano (2006) 'Alfred Packer's World: Risk, Responsibility and the Place of Experience in Mountain Culture, 1873–1907', *Journal of Social History* (Fall 2006), 181–204.
116. M. Brottman (1997) *Meat is Murder! An Illustrated Guide to Cannibal Culture* (London: Creation), 15.
117. Brottman, 182.
118. Joy, 78.
119. Ibid., 176.
120. Di Marco (2011) 'Going Wendigo: The Emergence of the Iconic Monster in Margaret Atwood's *Oryx and Crake* and Antonia Bird's *Ravenous*', *College Literature* 38.4 (Fall 2011), 142.
121. Di Marco, 142.
122. D. Gilmore (2003) *Monsters: Evil Beings, Mythical Beasts, and All Manner of Imaginary Terrors* (Philadelphia: University of Pennsylvania Press), 75.
123. Ibid., 79.
124. Cited in Di Marco, 136.
125. T.H. Hay (1971) 'The Windigo Psychosis: Psychodynamic, Cultural and Social Factors in Aberrant Behaviour', *American Anthropologist*, 73, 1–19.
126. Di Marco, 143.
127. Hay, 1.
128. R.A. Brightman (1988) 'The Windigo in the Material World', *Ethnohistory* 35:4 (Fall 1988), 338–379, 376.
129. C. Podruchny (2004) 'Werewolves and Windigos: Narratives of Cannibal Monsters in French-Canadian Voyageur Oral Tradition', *Ethnohistory*, Vol. 51, No. 4 (Fall 2004), 677–700, 686. The 'creatures' who are said to populate the woods in *The Village* share much the same purpose, and must also be appeased with offerings of fresh meat (not human flesh, however).
130. Di Marco, 144.
131. D. Duclos (1988) *The Werewolf Complex: America's Fascination with Violence* (Oxford: Berg), 28–29.
132. Di Marco, 151.
133. Faragher and Hine, 102.
134. As the recent documentary *Room 237* (2012) illustrates, Kubrick's film has inspired numerous conspiracy theories.
135. S. King (1977, 2007) *The Shining* (London: Hodder Headline), 205.
136. Ibid., 38.
137. Ibid., 106.
138. Ibid., 66.
139. Ibid., 67.
140. Ibid., 80.
141. Ibid., 99.
142. Ibid., 219.

143. Ibid., 225.
144. Ibid., 10.
145. Ibid., 151.
146. My thanks to Dr Dara Downey for this observation.
147. King, *Shining*, 27.
148. Ibid., 118.
149. Gilmore, 83.
150. Hay, 8.
151. Ibid., 17.
152. Nolan, 188.
153. King, *Shining*, 173.
154. Gilmore, 79.
155. King, *Shining*, 473.
156. T. Magistrale (2003) *Hollywood's Stephen King* (Basingstoke: Palgrave Macmillan), 90.
157. A. Nolan (2011) 'Seeing is Digesting: Labyrinths of Historical Ruin in Stanley Kubrick's *The Shining*', *Cultural Critique*, Vol. 77 (Winter 2011), 182.
158. See S. Jackson, *The Haunting of Hill House* (1959).
159. *The Shining* (Shooting Script) by Diane Johnson and Stanley Kubrick (July 1980).
160. Nolan, 153.
161. Magistrale, 96.
162. B. Blakemore, 'The Family of Man', *The San Francisco Chronicle Syndicate*, 29 July 1987.
163. Ibid.
164. Magistrale, 170. See also F. Jameson (1981) 'The Shining', *Social Text*, No. 4 (Autumn 1981), 115–125, 120.
165. The less said about the 1997 made-for-TV version of the novel written by King, the better.
166. C. McCarthy (2006) *The Road* (London: Picador), 16.
167. Ibid., 43.
168. Ibid., 18.
169. Ibid., 57.
170. Ibid., 213.
171. Ibid., 22.
172. Ibid., 146.
173. Ibid., 146.
174. Ibid., 58.
175. Ibid., 94.
176. Ibid., 116.
177. Ibid., 304.
178. Ibid., 307.

4 Backwoods Nightmares: The Rural Poor as Monstrous Other

1. L. Blake (2008) *The Wounds of Nations: Horror Cinema, Historical Trauma and National Identity* (Manchester: Manchester University Press), 131.

2. Or, as Kim Newman puts it, 'The South had to wait for Tobe Hooper before it had a good ole boy horror director it could take pride in' (1988) *Nightmare Movies: A Critical Guide to Horror Films* (London, Titan), 52.
3. D. Bell (1997) 'Anti-idyll: Rural Horror' in *Contested Countryside Cultures: Otherness, Marginalization and Rurality* (London and New York: Routledge), 94–108.
4. Blake, 128.
5. C.J. Clover (1992) *Men, Women and Chainsaws: Gender in the Modern Horror Film* (London: British Film Institute), 124. Clover's seminal consideration of the urban/rural divide in backwoods horror has influenced aspects of my own reading of these films.
6. M. Stoll (2007) 'Religion Irradiates the Wilderness' in M. Lewis (2007) *American Wilderness: A New History* (Oxford: Oxford University Press), 58.
7. T.G. Jordan and M. Kaups (1992) *The American Backwoods Frontier: An Ethical and Ecological Interpretation* (Baltimore: Johns Hopkins University Press), 1.
8. Jordan and Kaups, 3–4.
9. Ibid., 4.
10. K.E. Ledford (2004) '"Singularly Placed in Scenes so Cultivated": The Frontier, the Myth of Westward Progress, and a Backwoods in the Mountain South', *American Transcendental Quarterly*, Vol. 18, No. 3, 217.
11. Blake, 129.
12. See B.M. Murphy, 'The People of the Village Have always Hated Us: Shirley Jackson's New England Gothic' in *Shirley Jackson: Essays on the Literary Legacy* (McFarland, 2005).
13. H.P. Lovecraft (1924) 'The Picture in the House', (in) *H.P. Lovecraft: Omnibus 3: The Haunter in the Dark* (London: Harper Collins), 272–282.
14. J. Ketchum (1980, 1995) *Off Season* (London: Headline).
15. A. Graham (2007) 'The South in Popular Culture' in R. Gray and A. Robinson (eds) *A Companion to the Literature and Culture of the American South* (London: Blackwell Publishing), 335.
16. M. Allain (1986) 'Glamour and Squalor: Louisiana on Film', *Louisiana History: The Journal of the Louisiana Historical Association*, Vol. 27, No. 3 (Summer 1986), 229–237, 231.
17. A. Taylor (2001) *American Colonies: The Settling of North America* (New York: Penguin), 118.
18. Taylor, 142.
19. Ibid., 153.
20. H. Brogan (2001) *The Penguin History of the USA* (London: Penguin), 104.
21. Taylor, 154.
22. Brogan, 101.
23. Ibid., 103.
24. Ibid., 280.
25. D.B. Danbom (2006) *Born to the Country: A History of Rural America* (Baltimore: The Johns Hopkins University Press), 53.
26. Danbom, 53.
27. R. Gray (2001) 'Writing Southern Cultures' in *A Companion to the Literature and Culture of the American South*, 4.
28. Danbom, 50.
29. Ibid., 28.

30. Taylor, 157.
31. Ibid., 157.
32. Brogan, 187.
33. K.E. Ledford (2004) '"Singularly Placed in Scenes so Cultivated": The Frontier, the Myth of Westward Progress, and a Backwoods in the Mountain South', *American Transcendental Quarterly*, Vol. 18, No. 3. 211.
34. Danbom, 107.
35. Ibid., 109.
36. Brogan, 357.
37. Ibid., 365.
38. Ibid., 366.
39. S. Kidd (2001) 'Visualising the Poor White' in *The Literature of the American Culture and South*, 110.
40. Ibid., 110.
41. Danbom, 129.
42. Kidd, 110.
43. Ibid., 110.
44. Ibid., 111.
45. Ibid., 115.
46. Danbom, 129.
47. Ibid., 129.
48. A. Newitz and M. Wray (1996) *White Trash: Race and Class in America* (London: Routledge), 1.
49. D. Smith (1987) 'Cultural Studies' Misfit: White Trash Studies', *Mississippi Quarterly*, 385.
50. Smith, 370.
51. J.Z. Wilson (2002) 'Invisible Racism: The Language and Ontology of "White Trash"', *Critique of Anthropology*, Vol. 22, 387, 389.
52. Newitz and Ray, 2.
53. Ibid., 2.
54. S.C. Reed (1979) 'A Short History of Human Genetics in the USA', *American Journal of Medical Genetics*, 3(3): 282–295, 283.
55. F.H. Danielson, and C.B. Davenport (1912) 'The Hill Folk: Report on a Rural Community of Hereditary Defectives', *Eugenics Record Office – Memoir No. 1*, Cold Spring Harbour, NY, 1 August 1912.
56. Ibid., 2.
57. Ibid., 'Preface', V.
58. P. Lombardo (2012) '"The Return of the Jukes"': Eugenics Mythologies and Internet Evangelism', *The Journal of Legal Medicine*, 33, 207–233.
59. M.L. Wehmeyer (2003) 'Eugenics and Sterilization in the Heartland', *Mental Retardation* (February 2003) Vol. 41, No. 1, 57–60, 57.
60. E. Black (2003) *War against the Weak: Eugenics and America's Campaign to Create a Master Race* (New York: Four Walls Eight Windows), 4.
61. Newitz and Ray, 2. Black's book exhaustively details the massive influence that the American eugenics movement had upon the 'racial purity' movement in Germany.
62. Newitz and Ray, 2–3.
63. C.D. Shirley (2010) '"You Might be a Redneck if...": Boundary Work among Rural, Southern Whites', *Social Forces*, Vol. 89, No. 1, 35–62, 371.

64. J.W. Williamson (1995) *Hillbillyland: What the Movies Did to the Mountains and What the Mountains Did to the Movies* (Chapel Hill: University of North Carolina Press), 1.
65. Williamson, 1.
66. Ibid., 37.
67. Ibid., 37.
68. Ibid., 37.
69. Ibid., 37.
70. A. Harkins (2005) *Hillbilly: A Cultural History of an American Icon* (Oxford: Oxford University Press), 6–7.
71. E. Churchill Semple (1910) 'The Anglo-Saxons of the Kentucky Mountains: A Study in Anthropogeography', *Bulletin of the American Geographical Society*, Vol. XLII (August 1910), 561–594.
72. Semple, 561.
73. Ibid., 566.
74. Clover, 126.
75. Ibid., 263.
76. J. Brown (2012) *Cannibals in Literature and Film* (Basingstoke: Palgrave Macmillan), 91.
77. C. Vatnsdal (2004) *They Came from within: A History of Canadian Horror Cinema* (Winnipeg: Arbeiter Ring Publishing), 115.
78. H.D. Thoreau (1854, 1995) *Walden: Or, Life in the Woods* (London: Wordsworth), 26.
79. J. Brown, 118.
80. R. Wood (1984) 'An Introduction to the American Horror Film' in B.K. Grant (ed.) *Planks of Reason* (New Jersey: Scarecrow Press), 107–141.
81. Ibid., 130.
82. For tips on dispatching a corpse to a watery grave, see P. Barber (1988) *Vampires, Burial and Death: Folklore and Reality* (New Haven: Yale University Press).
83. Clover similarly notes that city visitors are 'laden with expensive gear' (126).
84. W. Cronon (1996) 'The Trouble with Wilderness: Or, Getting Back to the Wrong Nature', *Environmental History*, Vol. 1. No.,1, 7–28, 21.
85. Jordan and Kaups, 3.
86. Clover, 125.
87. J. Dickey (1970, 2005) *Deliverance* (London: Bloomsbury), 48.
88. V.P. Sydenstricker (1948) 'The History of Pellagra, Its recognition as a Disorder of Nutrition and Its Conquest', *The American Journal of Clinical Nutrition* (July–August 1948), 409–414, 410.
89. J. Winders (2003) 'White in All the Wrong Places: White Rural Poverty in the Postbellum US South', *Cultural Geographies*, 10, 45–63.
90. S.J. Kunitz (1988) 'Hookworm and Pellagra: Exemplary Diseases in the New South', *Journal of Health and Social Behaviour*, Vol. 29 (June) 139–148, 142.
91. P.H. Buck (1925) 'The Poor Whites of the Ante-Bellum South', *The American Historical Review*, Vol. 31, No. 1, 41–54.
92. Clover, 125.
93. Ibid., 125.
94. Ibid.,127–128.

95. Indeed, *Timber Falls* is unique, in that its villains are defined by their deranged Christian fundamentalism: religion is almost never directly mentioned in these films.
96. Clover, 135–136.
97. See Blake 136–138, and J. Muir (2007) *Horror Films of the 1980s* (North Carolina: McFarland), 205.
98. K. Newman, 'Empire Essay: *The Texas Chainsaw Massacre*', http://www.empireonline.com/reviews/reviewcomplete.asp?FID=132656 (accessed 22 March 2012).
99. Clover, 126.
100. Ibid., 131.
101. See C. Sharrett, 'The Idea of Apocalypse in *The Texas Chainsaw Massacre*' in *Planks of Reason: Essays on the Horror Film*, 300–320.
102. A. Warnes (2008) *Savage Barbecue: Race, Culture, and America's First Fast Food* (Athens: University of Georgia Press), 3–4.
103. Warnes, 4.
104. Ibid., 7.
105. Ibid., 44.
106. Ibid., 46.
107. See 'How to barbeque like a real man' (http://www.cracked.com/funny-2271-how-to-bbq-like-real-man/ (accessed 28 March 2012).
108. Warnes, 96.
109. Michel Faber's 2001 novel *Under the Skin* has a fascinating take on this idea from a science-fiction perspective.
110. Blake, 140 (n. 9).
111. R.R. Means Coleman (2011) *Horror Noire: Blacks in American Horror Film from the 1890s to the Present* (London: Routledge), 145.
112. Ibid., 145.
113. Ibid., 145.
114. Clover, 126–132.
115. Blake, 143.
116. R. Slotkin (1973) *Regeneration through Violence: The Mythology of the American Frontier, 1600–1860* (Normal: University of Oklahoma Press).

5 'Why Wouldn't the Wilderness Fight Us?' American Eco-Horror and the Apocalypse

1. As Frederick Buell (2004) observes, it '[...] led the way in making concern about environmental crisis a national issue'. *From Apocalypse to Way of Life: Environmental Crisis in the American Century* (London: Routledge), XII.
2. R. Carson (1962, 2000) *The Silent Spring* (New York: Penguin Classics), 21.
3. Carson, 21.
4. Ibid., 21.
5. Ibid., 21.
6. Ibid., 21.
7. Buell, XII.
8. J.M. Killingsworth and J.S. Palmer (1996) 'Millennial Ecology: The Apocalyptic Narrative Form from *The Silent Spring* to Global Narrative' in C. Hendl,

C. George, and S.C. Brown (eds) *Green Culture: Environmental Rhetoric in Contemporary America* (University of Wisconsin Press).
9. Murray Bookchin, quoted in Killingsworth and Palmer, 22.
10. S. Sontag (1976) *Against Interpretation and Other Essays* (London: Octopus), 213.
11. S. Bercovitch (1996) *The Cambridge History of American Literature* (London: Cambridge University Press), 224.
12. Buell, XIV and XV. See also T.M. Disch (1975) *The Ruins of Earth* (London: Arrow Books).
13. Buell, 3.
14. L. Garforth (2005) 'Green Utopias: Beyond Apocalypse, Progress and Pastoral', *Utopian Studies*, Vol. 16, No. 3 (Winter 2005), 393–427.
15. T.J. Hillard (2009) 'Deep into that Darkness Peering: An Essay on Gothic Nature', *Interdisciplinary Studies in Literature and Environment*, Vol. 16, No. 4 (Autumn 2009), 691.
16. S.C. Estok (2009) 'Theorising in a Space of Ambivalent Openness: Ecocriticism and Ecophobia', *Interdisciplinary Studies in Literature and the Environment*, Vol. 16, No. 2, 203–225.
17. Estok, 225.
18. F. Jennings (1975) *The Invasion of America: Indians, Colonialism, and the Cant of Conquest* (New York: W.W. Norton and Company), 33.
19. C. Simpson (2010) 'Australian Eco-horror and Gaia's Revenge: Animals, Eco-nationalism and the "New Nature"', *Studies in Australasian Cinema*, Vol. 4, No. 1, 43–54.
20. R. Nash (1967) *Wilderness and the American Mind* (New Haven: Yale University Press, 1967; 1982), 28–9.
21. Ibid., 7.
22. *The Silent Spring* was published in book form in September 1962: *The Birds* was released in the US in March 1963.
23. G. Garrard (2004) *Ecocriticism* (London: Routledge), 2.
24. Cronon, *Changes in the Land*, 23.
25. E. Levy (1991) *Small Town America in Film: The Decline and Fall of Community* (New York, Continuum), 15.
26. C. Paglia (1991) *The Birds* (BFI Film Classics, London: BFI Publishing), 74.
27. Ibid., 69.
28. All excerpts from *The Birds*, Final Shooting Script, March 1962, by Evan Hunter, http://www.horrorlair.com/scripts/TheBirds.pdf.
29. It also inspired Frank Herbert's sci-fi novel *Hellstrom's Hive* (1973).
30. It's an ending which lacks only the perspective of *The Simpsons'* Kent Brockman, who declares, 'I, for one, welcome our new insect overlords' when he believes giant space ants have invaded earth ('Deep Space Homer', 24 February 1994). The line originally appeared in *Empire of the Ants*.
31. F. Browswimmer (2001) *Ecocide: A Short History of the Mass Extinction of Species* (London: Pluto Press), 3.
32. http://politicalticker.blogs.cnn.com/2010/11/21/jimmy-carter-explains-rabbit-attack/ (accessed 26 February 2013).
33. See J. Muir (2002) *Horror Films of the 1970s* (North Carolina: McFarland).
34. J. Lemkin (1984) 'Archetypal Landscapes and *Jaws*' in B.K. Grant (ed.) *Planks of Reason* (New Jersey: Scarecrow Press), 279.

35. See D.J. Skal's (1993) discussion of the trend in *The Monster Show: A Cultural History of Horror* (London: Plexus).
36. W. Cronon (1996) 'The Trouble with Wilderness: Or, Getting Back to the Wrong Nature', *Environmental History*, Vol. 1. No. 1, 15.
37. J.G. Blair and A. Trowbridge (1960) 'Thoreau on Katahdin', *American Quarterly*, Vol. 12, No. 4 (Winter 1960), 508–517.
38. A. Kudo, Y. Fujikawa, S. Miyahara, J. Zhen, H. Takigami, and M. Sugahara Muramatsu 'Lessons from Minamata Mercury Pollution, Japan – After a Continuous 22 Years of Observation', *Water Science and Technology*, Vol. 38, No. 7, 187–193.
39. B. Schulman (2002) *The Seventies: The Great Shift in American Culture, Society and Politics* (Boston: Da Capo Press), 30.
40. W.S. Poole (2011) *Monsters in America: Our Historical Obsession with the Hideous and the Haunting* (Waco: Baylor University Press), 117.
41. Schulman, 31.
42. Buell, 248.
43. Ibid., 248.
44. Titles include: *Piranhaconda* (2012), *Swamp Shark* (2011), *Megashark vs Crocasaurus* (2010), and *Arachnoquake* (2012).
45. http://www.shocktillyoudrop.com/news/170731-shock-interview-the-bay-director-barry-levinson (accessed 27 February 2013).
46. B. McKibben (2006) *The End of Nature: Humanity, Climate Change and the Natural World* (New York: Random House), 105.
47. Ibid., 7.
48. Cronon, 'The Trouble', 19.
49. M. Lindstrom (2011) (ed.) *Encyclopaedia of the U.S. Government and the Environment: History, Policy and Politics, Vol. 1: Essays and Entries A–I* (Santa Barbara: ABC Clio).
50. T. Frentz and T. Rosteck (2009) 'Myth and Multiple Readings in Environmental Rhetoric: The Case of *An Inconvenient Truth*', *Quarterly Journal of Speech*, 95: 7, 1–19.
51. Nash, 273.
52. Ibid., 273.
53. Public Land Order 2214, 6 December 1960. [F.R. Doc. 60–11510].
54. J.M. Conrad and K. Kotani (2005) 'When to Drill? Trigger Prices for the Arctic National Wildlife Refuge', *Resource and Energy Economics*, Vol. 27, No. 4, 273–286.
55. M. Kotchen, M.J. Burger, and E. Nicholas (2007) 'Should We Drill in the Arctic National Wildlife Refuge? An Economic Perspective', *Energy Policy*, Vol. 35, No. 9 (September), 4720–4729.
56. Garrard, 173.
57. http://thehill.com/blogs/e2-wire/e2-wire/95963-senior-senate-republicans-distance-themselves-from-drill-baby-drill. The catchphrase was not coined by Palin, but was repeatedly referenced by her during the 2008 campaign, most notably during her VP debate with Joe Biden.
58. Nash, 290.
59. W. Cronon, *Changes*, 20.
60. Jennings, 80.

61. P.N. Carroll (1969) *Puritanism and the Wilderness: The Intellectual Significance of the New England Frontier, 1629–1700* (New York: Columbia University Press), 11.
62. C. Carlsson (2002) 'La forét précède l'homme, le désert le suit', *Critical Mass: Bicycling's Defiant Celebration* (San Francisco: AK Press), 23.
63. J. London (1912) 'The Scarlet Plague' in *The Scarlet Plague and Other Stories* (Dover: N.H. Pocket Classics), 1.
64. Ibid., 22.
65. Ibid., 30.
66. Ibid., 4.
67. Ibid., 40.
68. G.R. Stewart (1949, 1999) *Earth Abides* (London: Gollancz), 8.
69. Ibid., 8.
70. Ibid., 50.
71. Ibid., 72.
72. For more on this process, see A. Crosby, *The Columbian Exchange: Biological and Cultural Consequences of 1492*, and W. Cronon, *Changes in the Land: Indians, Colonists and the Ecology of New England.*
73. Stewart, 83.
74. Ibid., 207.
75. Ibid., 213.
76. The conclusion anticipates that of Walter M. Miller's post-apocalyptic classic, *A Canticle for Liebowitz* (1960).
77. Stewart, 302.
78. A. Wiseman (2007) *The World without Us* (London: Virgin), 4.
79. Ibid., 22.
80. The map and project description can be found at http://welikia.org/explore/mannahatta-map/ (accessed 22 August 2012).
81. C.B. Brown (1799, 1998) 'To the Public' in *Edgar Huntly: Or, Memoirs of a Sleepwalker* (London: Penguin Books), 3.

Bibliography

Abrams, R. (2004) *Language and Ideology in American Renaissance Literature* (Cambridge: Cambridge University Press).

Allain, M. (1986) 'Glamour and Squalor: Louisiana on Film', *Louisiana History: The Journal of the Louisiana Historical Association*, Vol. 27, No. 3, 229–237.

Anderson, D. (1999) *A House Divided: Domesticity and Community in American Literature* (Cambridge: Cambridge University Press).

Appelbaum, R. and J. Wood Sweet (2005) *Envisioning an English Empire: Jamestown and the Making of the North Atlantic World* (Philadelphia: University of Pennsylvania Press).

Bachelard, G. (1958, 1994) *The Poetics of Space* (Boston: Beacon Press).

Ballard, J.G. (1981, 2008) *Hello America* (London: Harper Collins).

Barber, P. (1988) *Vampires, Burial and Death: Folklore and Reality* (New Haven: Yale University Press).

Baudrillard, J. (1989) *America* (London: Verso).

Bauer, R. (2003) *The Cultural Geography of Colonial American Literatures: Empire, Travel, Modernity* (Cambridge: Cambridge University Press, 2003).

Bell, D. (1997) 'Anti-idyll: Rural Horror' in P. Cloke and J. Little (eds) *Contested Countryside Cultures: Otherness, Marginalization and Rurality* (London and New York: Routledge).

Bercovitch, S. (1993) *The Rites of Assent: Transformations in the Symbolic Construction of America* (New York: Routledge).

Bercovitch, S. (1996) *The Cambridge History of American Literature* (London: Cambridge University Press).

Bergland, R. (2000) *The National Uncanny: Indian Ghosts and American Subjects* (Hanover and London: University Press of New England).

Berglund, J. (2006) *Cannibal Fictions: American Explorations of Colonialism, Race, Gender and Sexuality* (Madison: University of Minnesota Press).

Berryman, C. (1979) *From Wilderness to Wasteland: The Trials of the Puritan God in the American Imagination* (New York: Kennikat Press).

Biggs,K. (1967) *The Fairies in English Tradition and Literature* (London: Taylor and Francis).

Black, E. (2003) *War against the Weak: Eugenics and America's Campaign to Create a Master Race* (New York: Four Walls Eight Windows).

Blake, L. (2008) *The Wounds of Nations: Horror Cinema, Historical Trauma and National Identity* (Manchester: Manchester University Press).

Blair, J.G. and A. Trowbridge (1960) 'Thoreau on Katahdin', *American Quarterly*, Vol. 12, No. 4, 508–517.

Boyer, P. and S. Nissenbaum (1974) *Salem Possessed* (Cambridge: Harvard University Press).

Bradford, W. (1630–1651, 2007) 'Of Plymouth Plantation' in N. Philbrick and T. Philbrick (eds) *The Mayflower Papers: Selected Writings of Colonial New England* (New York, Penguin Classics).

Bradbury, M. and R. Ruland (1991) *From Puritanism to Postmodernism: A History of American Literature* (New York: Viking).
Brightman, R.A. 'The Windigo in the Material World', *Ethnohistory*, Vol. 35, No. 4 (Fall 1988), 338–379.
Brogan, H. (2001) *The Penguin History of the USA* (London: Penguin).
Brottman, M. (2001) *Meat is Murder! An Illustrated Guide to Cannibal Culture* (London: Creation).
Brown, C.B. (1798, 1998) *Wieland; Or the Transformation* (Oxford: Oxford University Press).
Brown, C.B. (1799, 1998) *Edgar Huntly: Or, Memoirs of a Sleepwalker* (London: Penguin Books).
Brown, D.L. and K. Schafft (2011) *Rural People and Communities in the 21st Century: Resilience and Transformation* (Cambridge: Polity).
Brown, J. (2012) *Cannibalism in Literature and Film* (Basingstoke: Palgrave Macmillan).
Browswimmer, F. (2001) *Ecocide: A Short History of the Mass Extinction of Species* (London: Pluto Press).
Buck, P.H. 'The Poor Whites of the Ante-Bellum South', *The American Historical Review*, Vol. 31, No. 1 (Oct. 1925), 41–54.
Buell, F. (2004) *From Apocalypse to Way of Life: Environmental Crisis in the American Century* (London: Routledge).
Burger, N.E. and M. Kotchen (2007) 'Should We Drill in the Arctic National Wildlife Refuge? An Economic Perspective', *Energy Policy*, Vol. 35, No. 9, 4720–4729.
Burrage, H.S. (1906) 'The Fifth Voyage of M. John White, 1590' in *Early English and French Voyages Chiefly from Hakluyt, 1534–1608* (New York: Charles Scribner's Sons).
Byron, G. and D. Punter (2004) *The Gothic* (Oxford: Wiley Blackwell).
Carroll, P.N. (1969) *Puritanism and the Wilderness: The Intellectual Significance of the New England Frontier, 1629–1700* (New York: Columbia University Press).
Carson, R. (1962, 2000) *The Silent Spring* (New York: Penguin Classics).
Churchill Semple, E. (1910) 'The Anglo-Saxons of the Kentucky Mountains: A Study in Anthropogeography', *Bulletin of the American Geographical Society*, Vol. XLII, 588–623.
Clark, K. and L. Tiller (1966) *Terrible Trail: The Meek Cutoff, 1845* (Bend, OR: Maverick Publications).
Clover, C.J. (1992) *Men, Women and Chainsaws: Gender in the Modern Horror Film* (London: British Film Institute).
Coats, L., M. Cohen, J.D. Miles, K. Nishikawa, and R. Walsh (2008) '"Those We Don't Speak Of": "Indians in The Village"', *PMLA*, Vol. 123, No. 2, 358–374.
Collier, P.C. (2008) 'Our Silly Lies: Ideological Fictions in M. Night Shyamalan's *The Village*', *Journal of Narrative Theory*, Vol. 38, No. 2, 269–292.
Cook, S.F. (1973) 'Interracial Warfare and Population Decline among the New England Indians', *Ethnohistory* 20/1, Winter, 1–24.
Cronon, W. (1983) *Changes in the Land: Indians, Colonists and the Ecology of New England* (New York: Hill and Wang).
Cronon, W. (1996) 'The Trouble with Wilderness: Or, Getting Back to the Wrong Nature', *Environmental History*, Vol. 1, No. 1, 7–28.

Crosby, A.W. (1972, 2003) *The Columbian Exchange: Biological and Cultural Consequences of 1492* (Westport: Praeger).

Danbom, D.B. (2006) *Born to the Country: A History of Rural America* (Baltimore: The Johns Hopkins University Press).

Danielson, F.H. and C.B. Davenport (1912) 'The Hill Folk: Report on a Rural Community of Hereditary Defectives', *Eugenics Record Office – Memoir No. 1* (Cold Spring Harbour, New York).

Davenport-Hines, R. (1998) *Gothic: 400 Years of Excess, Horror, Evil and Ruin* (London: Fourth Estate).

Derounian-Stodola, K.Z. (1998) *Women's Indian Captivity Narratives* (London: Penguin Classics).

Derrida, J. (2000) 'Hospitality', *Angelaki: Journal of the Theoretical Humanities*, Vol. 5, No. 3, 3–18.

Di Marco, D. (2011) 'Going Wendigo: The Emergence of the Iconic Monster in Margaret Atwood's *Oryx and Crake* and Antonia Bird's *Ravenous*', *College Literature*, Vol. 38, No. 4, 134–155.

Disch, T.M. (1973, 1975) *The Ruins of Earth* (London: Arrow Books).

Di Stefano, D. (2006) 'Alfred Packer's World: Risk, Responsibility and the Place of Experience in Mountain Culture, 1873–1907', *Journal of Social History*, Fall, 181–204.

Duclos, D. (1988) *The Werewolf Complex: America's Fascination with Violence* (Oxford: Berg).

Eliot, E. (1991) *The Columbia History of the American Novel* (New York: Columbia University Press).

Estok, S.C. (2009) 'Theorising in a Space of Ambivalent Openness: Ecocriticism and Ecophobia', *Interdisciplinary Studies in Literature and the Environment*, Vol. 16, No. 2, 203–225.

Faludi, S. (2007) *The Terror Dream: What 9/11 Revealed about America* (London: Henry Holt).

Frank, J.G. (1950) 'The Wieland Family in Charles Brockden Brown's *Wieland*', *Monatshefte*, Vol. 42, No. 7, Nov. 1950, 347–353.

Frentz, T. and T. Rosteck (2009) 'Myth and Multiple Readings in Environmental Rhetoric: The Case of *An Inconvenient Truth*', *Quarterly Journal of Speech*, Vol. 95, No. 7, 1–19.

Garforth, L. (2005) 'Green Utopias: Beyond Apocalypse, Progress and Pastoral', *Utopian Studies*, Vol. 16, No. 3, Winter 2005, 393–427.

Garrard, G. (2004) *Ecocriticism* (London: Routledge).

Gatta, J. (2004) *Making Nature Sacred: Literature, Religion and the Environment in American from the Puritans to the Present* (Oxford: Oxford University Press).

Gilmore, D.D. (2003) *Monsters: Evil Beings, Mythical Beasts, and All Manner of Imaginary Terrors* (Philadelphia: University of Pennsylvania Press).

Goddu, T. (1997) *Gothic America: Narrative, History and Nation* (New York: Columbia University Press).

Graham, A. (2004) 'The South in Popular Culture' in R.J. Gray, Richard and O.A. Robinson (eds) *Companion to the Literature and Culture of the American South* (London: Blackwell Publishing).

Grant, B.K. (1984) *Planks of Reason* (New Jersey: Scarecrow Press).

Hall, J.E. (2004) *Gone from the Promised Land: Jonestown in American Cultural History* (New York: Transaction Publishers).

Harkins, A. (2005) *Hillbilly: A Cultural History of an American Icon* (Oxford: Oxford University Press).

Hartman, J.D. (1999) *Providence Tales and the Birth of American Literature* (Baltimore: Johns Hopkins University Press).

Hawthorne, N. (1852, 2009) *The Blithedale Romance* (Oxford: Oxford University Press).

Hawthorne, N. (2008) *Young Goodman Brown and Other Tales* (Oxford: Oxford World's Classics).

Hay, T.H. (1971) 'The Windigo Psychosis: Psychodynamic, Cultural and Social Factors in Aberrant Behaviour', *American Anthropologist*, Vol. 73, 1–19.

Hermann, R.B. (2011) 'The "Tragicall Historie": Cannibalism and Abundance in Colonial Jamestown', *The William and Mary Quarterly*, Vol. 61, No. 1, 47–74.

Hillard, T.J. (2009) 'Deep into that Darkness Peering: An Essay on Gothic Nature', *Interdisciplinary Studies in Literature and Environment*, Vol. 16, No. 4 (Autumn 2009), 685–695.

Hine, R. and J.M. Faragher (2007) *Frontiers: A Short History of the American West* (New Haven: Yale University Press).

Hoffer, C.P. (1996) *The Devil's Disciples: Makers of the Salem Witchcraft Trials* (Baltimore: Johns Hopkins University Press).

Jackson, S. (2010) *Shirley Jackson: Novels and Stories* (New York: The Library of America).

Jameson, F. (1981) 'The Shining', *Social Text*, No. 4, Autumn 1981, 115–125.

Janisse, K. (2012) *House of Psychotic Women: An Autobiographical Topography of Female Neurosis in Horror and Exploitation Films* (London: FAB Press).

Jennings, F. (1975) *The Invasion of America: Indians, Colonialism, and the Cant of Conquest* (New York: W.W. Norton and Company).

St John Crévecœur, J.H. (1782, 2009) *Letters from an American Farmer* (Oxford: Oxford World's Classics).

Jordan, T.G. and M. Kaups (1992) *The American Backwoods Frontier: An Ethical and Ecological Interpretation* (Baltimore: Johns Hopkins University Press).

Joshi, S.T. (2001) *The Modern Weird Tale* (North Carolina: McFarland).

Kafer, P. (2005) *Charles Brockden Brown's Revolution and the Birth of American Gothic* (Pennsylvania: Pennsylvania University Press).

Ketchum, J (1980, 1995) *Off Season* (London: Headline).

Killingsworth, J.M. and J.S. Palmer (1996) 'Millennial Ecology: The Apocalyptic Narrative from *The Silent Spring* to Global Warming' in C.G. Hendl and S.G. Brown (eds), *Green Culture: Environmental Rhetoric in Contemporary America* (Madison: University of Wisconsin Press).

King, S (1977, 1997) *The Shining* (London: Hodder Headline).

Klein, T.E.D. (1984) *The Ceremonies* (London: Pan), 63.

Kunitz, S.J. (1988) 'Hookworm and Pellagra: Exemplary Diseases in the New South', *Journal of Health and Social Behaviour*, Vol. 29 (June): 139–148.

Kushner, H.L. (1992) 'The Persistence of the "Frontier Thesis" in America: Gender, Myth and Self-destruction', *Canadian Review of American Studies*, Special Issue 1, Vol. 23, 53–83.

Laymon, R. (1981, 1991) *The Woods Are Dark* (London: Headline).

Leach, D. (1963) *The Northern Colonial Frontier, 1607–1763* (Vanderbilt University: Holt, Rhineheart, and Wilson).

Ledford, K.E. (2004) '"Singularly Placed in Scenes so Cultivated": The Frontier, the Myth of Westward Progress, and a Backwoods in the Mountain South', *American Transcendental Quarterly*, Vol. 18, No. 3. 205–222.
Levin, H. (1958, 1980) *The Power of Blackness: Hawthorne, Poe, Melville* (Ohio: Ohio University Press).
Levy, E. (1991) *Small Town America in Film: The Decline and Fall of Community* (New York: Continuum).
Lewis, M. (2007) *American Wilderness: A New History* (Oxford: Oxford University Press).
Lichter, D.T. and D.L. Brown (2011) 'Rural America in an Urban Society: Changing Spatial and Social Boundaries', *Annual Review of Sociology*, Vol. 37, 565–592.
Lindenbaum, S. (2004) 'Thinking about Cannibalism', *Annual Review of Anthropology*, Vol. 33, 475–498.
Lindstrom, M. (ed.) (2011) *Encyclopaedia of the U.S. Government and the Environment: History, Policy and Politics, Vol. 1: Essays and Entries A–I* (Santa Barbara: ABC Clio).
Linklater, A. (2002) *Measuring America: How the United States Was Shaped by the Greatest Land Sale in History* (London: Harper Collins).
Lloyd-Smith, A.G. (1989) *Uncanny American Fiction: Medusa's Face* (Basingstoke: Macmillan Press).
Lloyd-Smith, A.G. (2000), 'Nineteenth-century American Gothic' in D. Punter (ed.) *A Companion to the Gothic* (London: Blackwell).
London, J. (1912, 1995) *The Scarlet Plague and Other Stories* (Dover: N.H. Pocket Classics).
Lovecraft, H.P. (2000) *H.P. Lovecraft: Omnibus 3: The Haunter in the Dark* (London: Harper Collins).
Magistrale, T. (2003) *Hollywood's Stephen King* (Basingstoke: Palgrave Macmillan).
Matheson, R. (2003) *Richard Matheson: Collected Stories, Volume Two* (Colorado: Gauntlet Press).
Matterson, S. (1996) 'Indian Hating in the Confidence Man', *Arizona Quarterly*, Vol. 52, No. 2, Summer, 21–24.
McCarthy, C. (2007) *The Road* (London: Picador).
McCurdy, S.A. (1994) 'Epidemiology of Disaster: The Donner Party (1846–7)', *Western Journal of Medicine*, April 1994, Vol. 160, 338–342.
McKibben, B. (2006) *The End of Nature: Humanity, Climate Change and the Natural World* (New York: Random House).
Means Coleman, R.R. (2011) *Horror Noire: Blacks in American Horror Film from the 1890s to the Present* (London: Routledge).
Merrell, J.H. (1999) *Into the American Woods: Negotiations on the Pennsylvania Frontier* (New York: W.W. Norton and Co.).
Mignolo, W. (2003) *The Darker Side of the Renaissance* (Chicago: University of Michigan).
Miller, L. (2000) *Roanoke: Solving the Mystery of the Lost Colony* (New York: Arcade Publishing).
Miller, P. (1956, 1978) *Errand into the Wilderness* (Cambridge: Harvard University Press).
Murphy, B.M. (2005) (ed.) *Shirley Jackson: Essays on the Literary Legacy* (North Carolina: McFarland).

Murphy, B.M. (2009) *The Suburban Gothic in American Popular Literature* (Basingstoke: Palgrave Macmillan).
Nash, R. (1967) *Wilderness and the American Mind* (New Haven: Yale University Press).
Nebeker, H.E. (1974) '"The Lottery" as Symbolic Tour de Force', *American Literature*, Vol. 46, No. 1, 100–108.
Newitz, A. and M. Wray (1996) *White Trash: Race and Class in America* (London: Routledge).
Newman, K. (1988) *Nightmare Movies: A Critical Guide to Horror Films* (London: Titan).
Nolan, A. (2011) 'Seeing is Digesting: Labyrinths of Historical Ruin in Stanley Kubrick's *The Shining*', *Cultural Critique*, Vol. 77, Winter, 180–204.
Oehlschlaeger, F. (1988) 'The Stoning of Mistress Hutchinson: Meaning and Context in "The Lottery"', *Essays in Literature*, Vol. XV, No. 2, Fall, 259–265.
Paglia, C. (1991) *The Birds* (London: BFI Publishing).
Palmer, R. (2000) *Herschell Gordon Lewis: Godfather of Gore: The Films* (North Carolina: McFarland).
Pearce, R.H. (1953, 1965) *The Savages of America: A Study of the Indian and the Idea of Civilisation* (Baltimore: The John Hopkins Press).
Podruchny, C. (2004) 'Werewolves and Windigos: Narratives of Cannibal Monsters in French-Canadian Voyageur Oral Tradition', *Ethnohistory*, Vol. 51, No. 4, Fall, 677–700.
Punter, D. (1981) *The Literature of Terror: Vol. 1* (London: Longman).
Quinn, D.B. (1998) *European Approaches to America 1450–1640* (London: Ashgate).
Rarick, E. (2008) *Desperate Passage: The Donner Party's Perilous Passage West* (New York: Oxford University Press).
Reed, S.C. (1979) 'A Short History of Human Genetics in the USA', *American Journal of Medical Genetics*, Vol. 3, No. 3, 282–295.
Reiterman, T. (1982, 2008) *Raven: The Untold Story of the Reverend Jim Jones and His People* (New York: Penguin).
Reynolds, D. (2011) *Beneath the American Renaissance: The Subversive Imagination in the Age of Emerson and Melville* (Oxford: Oxford University Press).
Ringel, F. (1995) *New England's Gothic Literature* (Lewiston, New York: Edward Mellen Press).
Rockman, M. and J. Steele (2003) *Colonisation of Unfamiliar Landscapes: The Archaeology of Adaptation* (London: Routledge).
Rosenthal, B. (1993) *Salem Story: Reading the Witch Trials of 1692* (Cambridge: Cambridge University Press).
Rowlandson, M. (1676) 'The Sovereignty and Goodness of God' in N. Philbrick and T. Philbrick (eds) *The Mayflower Papers: Selected Writing of Colonial New England* (New York: Penguin, 2007).
Ryskamp, C. (1959) 'The New England Sources of *The Scarlet Letter*', *American Literature*, Vol. 31, No. 3 (Nov.), 257–272.
Schulman, B.J. (2002) *The Seventies: The Great Shift in American Culture, Society and Politics* (New York: Da Capo Press).
Shirley, C.D. '"You Might Be a Redneck if...": Boundary Work among Rural, Southern Whites', *Social Forces*, Vol. 89, No. 1, 35–62.
Shover, J.L. (1976) *First Majority – Last Minority: The Transforming of Rural Life in America* (Dekalb: Northern Illinois University Press).

Simpson, C. (2010) 'Australian Eco-horror and Gaia's Revenge: Animals, Eco-nationalism and the "New Nature"', *Studies in Australasian Cinema*, Vol. 4, No. 1, 43–54.
Slotkin, R. (1973) *Regeneration through Violence: The Mythology of the American Frontier, 1600–1860* (Normal: University of Oklahoma Press).
Smith, D. (1987) '"Cultural Studies' Misfit": White Trash Studies', *Mississippi Quarterly* Vol. 57, 369–388.
Sontag, S. (1962, 1976) *Against Interpretation and Other Essays* (London: Octopus).
Stewart, G.R. (1949, 1999) *Earth Abides* (London: Millennium).
Stewart, G.R. (1936, 1988) *Ordeal by Hunger: The Story of the Donner Party* (New York: Houghton Mifflin).
Stockwell, J. (1998) *The Encyclopaedia of American Communes, 1663–1963* (North Carolina: McFarland).
Stojanova, C. (2012) 'A Gaze from Hell: Eastern European Horror Cinema Revisited' in P. Allmer, E. Brick, and D. Huxley (eds) *European Nightmares: Horror Cinema in Europe since 1945* (London: Wallflower Press).
Sydenstricker, V.P. (1948) 'The History of Pellagra, Its Recognition as a Disorder of Nutrition and Its Conquest', *The American Journal of Clinical Nutrition*, July–August, 409–414.
Taylor, A. (2001) *American Colonies: The Penguin History of the United States* (New York: Penguin).
Taylor, A. (2002) *American Colonies: The Settling of North America* (New York: Penguin).
Thompson, P.K. 'A Puritan in the Wilderness': Natty Bumppo's Language and America's Nature Today' *James Fenimore Cooper: His Country and His Art (No. 11)*, Papers from the 1997 Cooper Seminar (No. 11), The State University of New York College at Oneonta. Oneonta, New York. (pp. 60–63)
Thomsen, B.M.S. (2009) '*Antichrist* – Chaos Reigns: The Event of Violence and the Haptic Image in Lars von Trier's Film', *Journal of Aesthetics & Culture*, Vol. 1.
Thoreau, H.D. (1854, 1995) *Walden: Or, Life in the Woods* (London: Wordsworth).
Toles, G. (1981) 'Charting the Hidden Landscape: *Edgar Huntly*', *Early American Literature*, Vol. XVI, 133–53.
Tompkins, J. (1986) *Sensational Designs: The Cultural Work of American Fiction, 1790–1860* (Oxford: Oxford University Press).
Tuan, Y. (1979) *Landscapes of Fear* (Oxford: Basil Blackwell).
Turner, F. (1980) *Beyond Geography: The Western Spirit against the Wilderness* (New York: Viking Press).
Turner, F.J. (1920, 2008) *The Significance of the Frontier in American History* (London: Penguin).
Varma, D. (1985) *The Gothic Flame* (London and New Jersey: Scarecrow Press).
Vatnsdal, C. (2008) *They Came from within: A History of Canadian Horror Cinema* (Winnipeg: Arbeiter Ring Publishing).
Warnes, A. (2008) *Savage Barbecue: Race, Culture, and America's First Fast Food* (Athens: University of Georgia Press).
Wehmeyer, M.L. (2003) 'Eugenics and Sterilization in the Heartland', *Mental Retardation*, Vol. 41, No. 1: 57–67.
Wetmore, K.J. (2012) *Post 9/11 Horror in American Cinema* (New York: Continuum).

Williams, N. (2008) 'The Population Bomb', *Current Biology*, Vol. 18, No. 13, 535–536.

Williams, W.C. (1925) *In the American Grain* (New York: New Directions).

Williamson, J.W. (1995) *Hillbillyland: What the Movies Did to the Mountains and What the Mountains Did to the Movies* (Chapel Hill: University of North Carolina Press).

Wilson, J.Z. (2002) 'Invisible Racism: The Language and Ontology of "White Trash"', *Critique of Anthropology*, Vol. 22, 387–401.

Wiseman, A. (2007) *The World without Us* (Virgin: London).

Zuckerman, M. (1977) 'Pilgrims in the Wilderness: Community, Modernity and "The Maypole at Merry Mount"', *The New England Quarterly*, Vol. 50, No. 2, 255–277.

Filmography

Albino Farm (Joe Anderson, Sean McEwen, 2009)
Antichrist (Lars von Trier, 2009)
The Bay (Barry Levinson, 2012)
The Birds (Alfred Hitchcock, 1963)
The Book of Eli (Albert Hughes; Allen Hughes, 2010)
Bug (Jeannot Szwarc, 1975)
Cabin Fever (Eli Roth, 2002)
The Cabin in the Woods (Drew Goddard, 2011)
Carriers (Alec Pastor; David Pastor, 2009)
Day of the Animals (William Girdler, 1977)
Deliverance (John Boorman, 1972)
The Descent (Neil Marshall, 2005)
Eaten Alive (Tobe Hooper, 1977)
Empire of the Ants (Bert I. Gordon, 1977)
The Evil Dead (Sam Raimi, 1981)
Eye of the Devil (J. Lee Thompson, 1966)
Frogs (George McCowan, 1972)
The Happening (M. Night Shyamalan, 2008)
The Hellstrom Chronicle (Walon Green; Ed Spiegel, 1971)
The Hills Have Eyes (Wes Craven, 1977)
Hostel (Eli Roth, 2005)
Hot Fuzz (Edgar Wright, 2007)
House of 1000 Corpses (Rob Zombie, 2003)
The Hunger Games (Gary Ross, 2012)
I Spit on Your Grave (Stephen R. Monroe, 2010)
Jaws (Stephen Spielberg, 1975)
Jug Face (Chad Crawford Kinkle, 2013)
Kingdom of the Spiders (John Cardos, 1977)
The Last Winter (Larry Fessenden, 2006)
Meek's Cutoff (Kelly Reichardt, 2010)
Motel Hell (Kevin O'Connor, 1980)
Night of the Lepus (William F. Claxton, 1972)
Phase IV (Saul Bass, 1974)
Population 436 (Michelle MacLaren, 2006)
Prophecy (John Frankenheimer, 1979)
Ravenous (Antonia Bird, 1999)
The Road (John Hillcoat, 2009)
The Shining (Stanley Kubrick, 1980)
Shoot (Harvey Hart, 1976)
Skeletons (David DeCoteau, 2007)
Southern Comfort (Walter Hill, 1981)
Squirm (Jeff Lieberman, 1976)

Straw Dogs (Rod Lurie, 2011)
Take Shelter (Jeff Nichols, 2011)
The Tall Man (Pascale Laugier, 2012)
Texas Chainsaw 3D (Jonathan Luessenhop, 2013)
The Texas Chain Saw Massacre (Tobe Hooper, 1974)
The Texas Chainsaw Massacre 2 (Tobe Hooper, 1986)
The Texas Chainsaw Massacre: The Beginning (Jonathan Liebesman, 2006)
Timber Falls (Tony Giglio, 2007)
Trigger Man (Ti West, 2007)
Tucker and Dale vs Evil (Eli Craig, 2010)
Two Thousand Maniacs! (Herschell Gordon Lewis, 1964)
The Village (M. Night Shyamalan, 2004)
Wendigo (Larry Fessenden, 2001)
The Wicker Man (Robin Hardy, 1973)
Winter's Bone (Debra Granik, 2010)
The Woman (Luck McKee, 2011)
Wrong Turn (Rob Schmidt, 2003)
YellowBrickRoad (Andy Mitton, 2011)
Zombieland (Rueben Flesicher, 2009)

Index

Printed by Printforce, United Kingdom